LEGAL REALISM REGAINED

Jurists: Profiles in Legal Theory

William Twining, editor

Legal Realism Regained

SAVING REALISM FROM CRITICAL ACCLAIM

Wouter de Been

STANFORD LAW BOOKS

An imprint of Stanford University Press

Stanford, California 2008

Stanford University Press
Stanford, California
© 2008 by the Board of Trustees of the
Leland Stanford Junior University
All rights reserved

Library of Congress Cataloging-in-Publication Data

de Been, Wouter.
   Legal realism regained : saving realism from critical acclaim / Wouter
de Been.
      p.   cm.
   Includes bibliographical references and index.
   ISBN 978-0-8047-5659-4 (cloth : alk. paper)
      1. Law—Philosophy.   I. Title.

K341.D43   2008

340'.1—dc21   2007018590

Printed in the United States of America
on acid-free, archival-quality paper

Typeset at Stanford University Press in 10/13 Galliard

Contents

Preface

"There are some books that refuse to be written," Mark Twain once commented. "They stand their ground year after year and will not be persuaded. It isn't because the book is not there and worth being written—it is only because the right form of the story does not present itself." This is one of those books. It resisted being written for many years. Eventually the recalcitrant material fit into a coherent narrative. Whether it is also the "right form" will be for the readers to judge.

One of the reasons I kept going all this time is my affection for its topic: Legal Realism and Pragmatism. These two movements are emblematic of the kind of America that got me interested in the field of American studies when I first became a student. They express an iconic American can-do optimism that is still infectious and that still speaks to us from the beginning of the last century. This sprightly optimism should by no means be equated with simplemindedness or naïveté. On the contrary, Pragmatism and Legal Realism are some of the most sophisticated intellectual currents of American Modernism. Nor should we be deterred by the ripe old age of these movements. In a way it is a boon that these theories no longer relate directly to the issues of today; that they are no longer partisan positions in ongoing struggles. As the poet Thomas Gunn once wrote about his examples, his "sad captains":

> True, they are not at rest yet,
> but now that they are indeed
> apart, winnowed from failures,
> they withdraw to an orbit
> and turn with disinterested
> hard energy, like the stars.

Pragmatism and Legal Realism still shine with this "disinterested hard energy." They offer no advice on how to deal with Al Qaeda, on whether to adopt the flat tax, on what to do about immigration, or on how to reform the welfare state. Yet they do express a sensibility, a way of looking at problems that is still important. It is this sensibility that I have tried to recapture in this book.

I was lucky to receive support from a great many people in writing this book. First of all, I would like to mention the motley crew of the *Pioneer Group*. I was part of that diverse group of academics for most of its existence. Wibren van der Burg, Margreth de Bonth, Timon Oudenaarden, Caroline Raat, Peter Blok, Bert-Jan Wolthuis, Marc Hertogh, Anton Vedder, Roland Pierik, Maarten van Dijck, Bert van den Brink, Sanne Taekema, and Willem Witteveen have all contributed to my research with their comments and discussions. I would also like to thank William Twining for his stern and fair remarks, as well as the two reviewers Hanoch Dagan and John Henry Schlegel, who have greatly improved the book with their thoughtful comments. Finally, I would like to thank my wife, Catherine, and my children, Max and Anna, simply for being there.

LEGAL REALISM REGAINED

A Tale of Two Movements

Much that is natural, to the will must yield.
Men manufacture both machine and soul,
And use what they imperfectly control
To dare a future from the taken routes.
—Thom Gunn[1]

American pragmatism was not some naive form of scientism and it did not hinge on some blindly optimistic faith in the spread of democracy. It only appears as
such to those who rule out there being postmetaphysi-
cal justifications for democracy and science.
—Hans Joas[2]

This book is a study of two twentieth-century schools of American legal
theory and their relationship—Legal Realism and Critical Legal Studies
(CLS). According to received opinion, these two schools of legal theory
are kindred approaches. This study will challenge that notion. It will argue that there is little basis for the claim that these approaches are marked
out by a close intellectual kinship. Hence, the following pages are not so
much a genealogy of close family relations as an account of mistaken iden-
tities provoked by misleading similarities. It is a story about how the CLS
movement adopted Legal Realism as an intellectual parent and attributed a
family resemblance to it that it never possessed. It is also a tragic tale about
how many valuable aspects of the Realist movement have become obscured
by the genuine attempts of CLS scholars to revive and reinterpret Legal
Realism for the present age.

Many readers will be acquainted with the protagonists in this story. For
those who are new to this topic, however, this first chapter will start with
a general introduction to the leading characters in the tale. This will lay all
the necessary groundwork for the central theme to be defined more clearly.
This central theme, in turn, will be divided into three subtopics around

which the book will be organized. Finally, this chapter will be rounded off with a number of remarks on the method employed and the approach taken.

A TWICE-TOLD TALE

The story of the short-lived Legal Realist movement—how it rose to prominence in the 1920s and 1930s, how it influenced American legal understanding, and how it formed the inspiration for the Critical Legal Studies movement from the 1970s onward—has been told many times. In its rough outline this story is largely uncontroversial. In the interbellum period the American legal field was stirred up by a loose group of legal scholars known as the Legal Realists. These liberal reformers with modernist sensibilities were impatient with the conservatism and formalism of American law. They were intent on putting law and legal scholarship on a new footing. Freely borrowing insights from the emerging social sciences, contemporary linguistic theory, psychoanalysis, cultural anthropology, and above all American Pragmatism, they tried to fashion a new approach to the study of law and gain a fresh understanding of the legal system. Hallmarks of this new Realistic ferment were a skeptical view of the power of legal rules to decide outcomes; a Pragmatic, social-engineering outlook on law as a tool for social development; a commitment to the empirical methodology of the social sciences as an alternative to traditional legal scholarship; and a conception of law as organically interwoven with society and bound up with the unique historical conditions of its developmental stage. These ideas were often expounded in a brash and racy style. With Legal Realism, in the words of one commentator, the jazz age had produced a "jazz jurisprudence."[3]

For all its ambition to change things, however, the Realist movement would prove to have only a short life span. After its emergence as a distinct movement, Legal Realism enjoyed a period of brisk activity. Yet the Realist movement was soon beset by a backlash in American academia against skeptical theory of the Realist variety. As international tensions heightened, the Realist critique came to be seen as a subversive influence, sapping the very foundations of free and democratic government with its alleged relativism and its skepticism about the fundamental principles of the American republic. With the totalitarian threat looming large in Germany, Italy, and Russia, casting doubt on the time-honored fundamentals of the American political and legal system seemed like an act of gratuitous irresponsibility. In the anxious atmosphere of the late 1930s Legal Realism went into retreat. By the beginning of the 1940s Legal Realism had lost most of its momentum and had largely petered out. To be sure, some Realist scholars continued to write books and articles during and after the Second World War. Yet World War II marks a sea change in the American intellectual climate. These later writings are no longer in the same spirit.

Realism flared up and died out in a relatively short period of time. Realist ideas never settled into an authoritative statement. Hence, there is a sense of bemusement about Realism which persists to the present day. For many it is still not quite clear what to make of the Realist movement. In a recent history of American jurisprudence, English legal scholar Neil Duxbury describes Legal Realism as "one of the great paradoxes of modern jurisprudence. No other jurisprudential tendency of the twentieth century has exerted such a powerful influence on legal thinking while remaining so ambiguous, unsettled and undefined."[4] This remark reflects the dominant opinion on American Legal Realism today, namely, that it had a "powerful influence on legal thinking" in the United States, even though it is unclear what that "powerful influence" amounts to.

The Realism of Legal Realism

For the definition of Legal Realism, the term *realism* should not be taken as a reference to some systematic theory. Nevertheless, the term does provide some general clues as to what the Realist movement was about. For the Realists, *realism* primarily seems to have signified an approach that cut through the institutional pieties of law and focused on the way law operated in the real world. This declared devotion to *realism* was not unique to the Realist movement. It was a mind-set they shared with many of their contemporaries. Realism was part of a broader current in late nineteenth- and early twentieth-century academic culture, which intellectual historian Morton White has characterized as a "revolt against formalism." This revolt entailed a "reaction from the formal, the deductive, the mathematical, the mechanical, in favor of the historical, cultural aspects of human behavior."[5] Scholars involved in this revolt, White maintained, were united in their rejection of formal and abstract models of social behavior and shared a preference for more richly textured explanations of social phenomena, explanations that took into account the unique cultural and historical conditions that shaped them. Closer attention to the processes of *real* social life, they believed, should replace such disembodied concepts as the economic man in economics or the immutable principles of justice in law. Legal Realism was an integral part of this trend in academic thought.

Beyond the world of academia, Legal Realism also had an affinity with the popular muckraking and debunking spirit of the early twentieth-century United States. As the eminent historian Richard Hofstadter observed in his classic study of the period, the muckraking journalists and realistic writers of the Progressive Era, exposing political corruption and social injustice in their articles and novels, pioneered "a fresh mode of criticism" in which the dominant feature was "realism."[6] Realism for these journalists and writers meant the unembellished description of the harsh, hidden realities of American life, which often contrasted sharply with the edifying myths of American society. This "fresh mode of criticism" carried over to other realms of thought including law, Hofstadter noted, and "as scholars reached out for their own 'realistic' categories, the formalistic thought of an earlier and more conservative generation fell under close and often damaging scrutiny."[7] Hence, much in the style of the muckraking journalists and the realistic novelists, Hofstadter believed, the Realists were intent on tearing down the solemn facade of the law to expose what went on behind it.[8]

Langdellian Orthodoxy *principles or doctrines*

The facade that the Realists were aiming to demolish had been erected only half a century before under the auspices of Christopher Columbus Langdell, dean of the Harvard Law School from 1870 to 1895. The view of law he inspired in the late nineteenth century was still widely accepted among legal scholars in the interwar period. It is important to sketch the broad outlines of this Langdellian, or Classical, view of law because so much Realist work was written in opposition to it. In a way, Langdell set the agenda for many of the Realist concerns. The innovation Langdell is most famous for is his case method, still the standard method of teaching in American law schools today. For present purposes, however, what is important is not so much the case method as the rationale Langdell provided for introducing it. In the introduction to his first casebook on the law of contracts, Langdell claimed that law, "considered as a science, consists of certain principles or doctrines." These principles and doctrines had been expressed in long series of Common Law cases dating back centuries. The best way to get at them was to retrace the cases in which they were embodied. This involved only a limited number of the reported cases. In the ma-

limited no. of cases

jority of cases the judge simply got it wrong, and these, Langdell claimed, were "useless, and worse than useless, for any purpose of systematic study." A casebook could thus be limited to a moderate number of select cases. Also the number of fundamental doctrines on which the Common Law was based was much smaller than one might suspect from the great diversity of reported cases. The same doctrine or principle was "constantly making its appearance" in "many different guises," Langdell contended, and this had led to "much misapprehension" about the number of doctrines and principles embodied in the Common Law.[9]

The rough outlines of Langdell's view of law and legal scholarship can be gleaned from these introductory remarks to his first casebook. Law understood as a science involved an exercise in taxonomy. The legal scholar's job was to bring order to the chaotic mass of reported cases. The truly significant cases had to be separated from the inconsequential ones and subsumed under the rubric of one or another fundamental Common Law doctrine. Implicit in this understanding of legal scholarship was the assumption that there was a set of timeless, immutable, and fundamental principles of law, which found only imperfect expression in the welter of Common Law cases. Legal inquiry was a search for these true and fundamental principles in the messy particulars of Common Law adjudication. This is why Langdell believed he could attach the label of science to legal scholarship—legal scholars unearthed the fundamental legal principles underlying the multifarious judicial decisions handed down from the past, much like the scientist uncovered the general laws shaping diverse natural phenomena. Thus, Langdell advocated in a famous speech that "the library is the proper workshop of professors and students alike; . . . it is to us all what the laboratories of the university are to the chemists and physicists, the museum of natural history to the zoologists, the botanical garden to the botanists."[10]

Langdell's approach clearly bore the credentials of nineteenth-century laissez-faire liberalism. His science of law provided a realm of fundamental legal principle that existed separately from the political process. In the courts this autonomous realm of legal principle was vigorously defended against legislative incursions, as it was believed to provide a private sphere in which individual American citizens could shape their own lives free from any government intrusion. Judges thought of themselves as applying eternal and true principles of justice. Ill-considered legislation that did not fit with these true and unchanging principles had to be strictly construed or declared unconstitutional. The true in law did not admit compromise by the unwise and fickle preferences of democratic majorities. In practice this meant enforcement of a formal, legal equality between citizens that was blind to existing social and economic inequalities, as well as judicial resistance to legislative attempts to counteract these inequalities. Regulation of the economy by the legislature was believed to impinge on the basic rights of free citizens to work out their own arrangements.

The Langdellian view of law was highly influential. Langdell's case method was rapidly adopted as a teaching method by most American law schools, and the conception of law inherent in it gained wide acceptance among legal scholars. It was still the dominant view in the 1920s when the Realist movement started to take shape. In fact, the Langdellian science of law seemed to reach a new high point in the big Restatement projects orchestrated by the American Law Institute—especially created for the purpose—in the early 1920s. These Restatement projects were aimed at reducing the increasing complexity of American law. With the growing divergence of decided cases in the burgeoning American republic and the explosive growth in the number of case reports, the body of case law had become too heterogeneous and unwieldy for American lawyers to work with.[11] The Restatement projects were attempts to provide authoritative and accessible restatements of the law in the respective legal fields to afford lawyers with an easy reference to existing law. The leading authorities in the different legal fields were brought together in the American Law Institute to furnish these codelike summaries of case law, which were based on old-time Langdellian legal science. As the legal historian Edward White observed, the Restatements were meant to be "a perfected version of Langdellian geometric and taxonomic logic."[12] In other words, the Restatements tended to reaffirm the immutable Common Law principles and doctrines that had been the focus of the Langdellian science of law for half a century. The Restatements were conservative efforts, aimed at recapturing the old unity and coherence that American law no longer had.

The Realist Critique

Realism was a reaction against everything the Classical, Langdellian view of law stood for. The Realists disliked the formalism of the Langdellian approach: its Platonic search for pure and static principle behind the disorderliness of everyday adjudication; its library-oriented conception of legal science; its bias against legislation; its inherent conservatism; and its affinity with laissez-faire economics. The Realists provided a profound critique of these aspects of the Classical view and offered radical alternatives to its basic tenets. Where the Classical view centered on the importance of legal rules in the judicial decision-making process, the Realists were skeptical about the efficacy of these legal rules in the real world of adjudication. Where the Classical view reassured legal scholars that they could practice their science within the confines of the library walls, the Realists wanted to turn law into an empirical social science and chase legal scholars out of the library to study legal practice firsthand. Where the Classical view assumed the given-ness of a set of fundamental and unchanging principles of law, the Realists saw the legal system as a function of the ever-changing social and cultural context. Where the Classical view had led to a principled obstruction of social reform and economic regulation in the courts, the Realists proposed a more instrumental view of law that would foster, and not hinder, social change.

Of the elements listed above, the renowned rule skepticism is probably most commonly identified as a defining characteristic of Legal Realism. The Realists were highly skeptical of the Langdellian systematization of case law in a limited set of fundamental principles and doctrines, such as the American Law Institute was undertaking with its Restatement projects. These rules did not accurately reflect what went on in the courts, the Realists maintained, nor were they as important in the judicial decision-making process as was commonly believed. This rule skepticism was informed by a sophisticated understanding of language which took meaning to be socially constructed rather than given. The law, in other words, did not reflect some preexisting, rational, or natural social order. Rather, it imposed an order on the messy social world with flawed and imperfect concepts and categories fabricated and developed by the legal community and the wider society.

Rule skepticism often went hand in hand with another famous Realist notion, namely, "predictivism." Since the law in the books was of only limited help in predicting what judges would decide, the Realists started wondering whether the new social sciences would not do better. Following the lead of Oliver Wendell Holmes and his "bad man theory" of law, the Realists suggested that maybe Holmes's view that "prophecies of what the courts will do in fact and nothing more pretentious" should be adopted as the focus of legal study. This led to the notion of predictivism, that is, the idea that not ratiocination but accurate scientific knowledge about judicial behavior patterns should be the information with which lawyers assisted their clients. Many Realists believed that the scientific study of the law would disclose common factors that conditioned judicial decisions and would suggest more accurate predictive rules. More than any other Realist idea, predictivism came to symbolize the new approach and was taken to sum up its contribution to legal theory. It also became a focal point for critique. Indeed, it was the argument that H. L. A. Hart criticized in his famous discussion of Realism, a critique which many have thought was so devastating that it sealed the fate of Realism.[13] Hart's influential critique has recently received harsh criticism itself, however. Brian Leiter has argued that the type of rule skepticism that Hart managed to invalidate so convincingly was not in fact endorsed by any Legal Realists and that the rule skepticism they did endorse is not affected by his arguments.[14]

A second Realist idea was the suggestion to use social science as a method to chart the policy alternatives available for the case involved. Law was not an end in itself, the Realist claimed time and again. It was an instrument to promote the welfare of society. To foster the welfare of society, empirical knowledge about social and economic conditions was called for, and that knowledge could be gained from the social sciences. The Legal Realists here followed the lead of Roscoe Pound and his sociological jurisprudence. Long before the Realists formulated their critique of legal formalism, Pound had warned lawyers not to become "legal monks" in their sanctimonious reverence for the law as a self-sufficient system of rules.[15] As an alternative, Pound had recommended his "sociological jurisprudence," which entailed "the movement for Pragmatism as a philosophy of law, the movement for the adjustment of principles and doctrines to the human conditions they are to govern rather than to assumed first principles, the movement for putting the human factor in the central place and relegating logic to its true position as an instrument."[16] The Realists took many of these ideas on board. Yet, even though they were indebted to Pound, they also believed he had not succeeded in executing his program. The "brilliant buddings" in Pound's work, as Realist Karl Llewellyn contended, had "in the main not come to fruition." Pound's sociological jurisprudence had remained "bare of most that is significant in sociology," he remarked, and his idea of law-in-action had been "left as a suggestion."[17] Legal Realism was going to change this. Realism was going to bring Pound's "brilliant buddings," which had never flowered, to fruition at last. Or so Llewellyn hoped.

The Legacy of Legal Realism

The Realist movement is often seen as a kind of adolescent phase in American law. Through the turbulent Realist experience, the narrative goes, American law finally came of age. The Classical late nineteenth-century notion of law that preceded Legal Realism had been premised on the idea that law was autonomous, determinate, neutral, and based on a small set of timeless and unchanging principles of justice. The rebellious and iconoclastic Realist movement was needed to dislodge these nineteenth-century illusions and to pave the way for a more mature view of law that openly acknowledged the unavoidable policy choices made in the judicial process. Pubescent foolhardiness accompanied this ascent to full maturity, and Legal Realism was characterized by an exaggerated skepticism about the determinacy of legal rules, a concomitant and undue belief in the omnipresence of judicial discretion, and a naive faith in the promise of social science to offer solutions to these problems. Rid of these adolescent excesses, however, Realist insights about the limits of legal formalism and about the need to include considerations of social policy in the analysis of law became common currency in postwar legal scholarship. While the more immoderate views of the Realists have been outgrown, the story goes, the valuable lessons of Realism have been learned and adopted into mainstream legal scholarship—an assessment succinctly expressed in the adage "Realism is dead. We are all Realists, now."

This complacent view of postwar legal scholars has been challenged in recent decades by the left wing of American jurisprudence—Critical Legal Studies. CLS grew out of the radical New Left of the 1960s. Its central claim is that the liberal legal system is not a neutral body of rules but a devious form of politics. Law is seen as a structure of dominance, as a system degenerated beyond reconstruction. As Critical Legal scholar Alan Hutchinson puts it, liberalism "has become a dangerous political anachronism" and the adherents of CLS "do not wish to embroider still further the patchwork quilt of liberal politics, but strive to cast it aside and reveal the vested interests that thrive under its snug cover."[18] CLS is not a movement for piecemeal reform but for radical, comprehensive critique of the legal system. CLS adherents believe that Legal Realism preceded them in some of their core insights—notably that law is not certain but indeterminate, not neutral but political, not natural and necessary but arbitrary and contingent. Critical Legal scholars assert that their mainstream brethren have mainly tried to deflect these elements in the Realist legacy. Hence, they argue that the lessons of American Legal Realism have not been learned at all. On the contrary, they believe that postwar American legal scholarship is best understood as a set of evasive maneuvers aimed at circumventing the unsettling problems posed by the Legal Realists. These evasive maneuvers, however, have led academic lawyers nowhere. The Realist insight that law is indeterminate, political, and contingent, CLS adherents claim, cannot be skirted around so easily. In contrast, Critical Legal scholars claim not to elude but to face squarely the implications of Realist thought. They see themselves as picking up where the Realist project was cut off.[19]

The Critical Legal Studies Movement: Realism Meets Radicalism

The CLS movement seems to have taken an interest in the Legal Realists right from the start in the mid-1970s. Mark Tushnet, one of the founding members of the CLS movement, has attested to this early fascination with the Realists in an autobiographical account of the genesis of the movement. According to Tushnet, in 1976 he, Duncan Kennedy, and David Trubek decided to create a "location" for a number of legal scholars on the left who were scattered over the United States but who were writing academic legal work which displayed some common themes. Critical Legal Studies was created to provide these various legal scholars with a platform to explore their shared ideas. One of the mutual themes in the work of these left-wing scholars, Tushnet maintains, was "the identification, in numerous substantive areas of law, of paired oppositions and standard arguments deploying sets of claims from one side of those oppositions against sets drawn from the other side." Drawing from the work of the Realists, this insight led to the development of the "indeterminacy argument," according to Tushnet, which held that "within the standard resources of legal argument were the materials for reaching sharply contrasting results in particular instances." In other words, the legal system was made up of opposing principles that allowed for the development of contradictory legal arguments on almost any legal issue—a CLS version of rule skepticism, which, Tushnet claims, later developed "into philosophically more sophisticated deconstructionist techniques."[20]

The Realist legacy also presented a problem for CLS scholars, however. The indeterminacy argument, Tushnet maintains, "had led some of the realists to offer a relatively informal descriptive and normative sociology of law." The object of the descriptive sociology, Tushnet believes, was to show that "the existence of a community of lawyers, sharing what Llewellyn called a 'situation sense,' eliminated the possibility that the contradictory results, available as a matter of theory, would actually be realized in practice." While the normative aspect of the Realist sociology sought to establish that "the values of that community, or some other community into which it could be transformed, justified the choices among possible results at which the legal system arrived." The Legal Realists, in other words, claimed that legal rules by themselves did not decide outcomes but that constraints such as the ethos of the legal institution and the shared intuitions about what kind of solutions certain sets of practical problems required made sure that this legal indeterminacy did not translate into indeterminate judicial decisions. The postwar Law and Society movement, Tushnet believes, had tried "to provide a more systematic basis for the realists' informal sociology of law." Yet to Critical Legal scholars this was an approach that seemed to turn into apologetic support of the status quo. CLS was more skeptical about "the normative acceptability of the results found acceptable by the community of lawyers." Hence, a second theme in the CLS movement "was a critique of the sociology of law that was implicit in the way legal realism had been assimilated in the legal academy."[21]

In contrast to the traditional sociology of law, CLS stressed the autonomy of law as an ideological structure, rather than its foundation in the social context. CLS adherents saw the sociology of law as a mode of explanation that was too deterministic in its emphasis on the social setting as the primary factor shaping law. "The cultural-radical strand in cls," Tushnet notes, "contributed an . . . impetus to the forces emphasizing freedom of choice rather than determinism."[22] CLS wanted to show that the law was not the natural and necessary product of social circumstances but a contingent system that could very well be replaced with another. In "Classical social theory"—the tradition of Marx and Weber—fundamental legal terms and categories like "ownership of private property" played a large role. However, such legal terms preceded, rather than were explained by, these social theories. Hence, these fundamental categories of law were implicated in the social theory that tried to explain them. Because the indeterminacy argument had shown these legal categories to have shaky foundations, the social theory built on them also became suspect. Thus, Tushnet observes, "the indeterminacy thesis threatened the social theory that legal realists had relied on to resolve the normative and descriptive difficulties exposed by their analysis of law. Put in a different way, the indeterminacy thesis, developed in the specific context of legal doctrine, created an atmosphere in which the deterministic leanings of classical social theory were suspect."[23] Consequently, the CLS movement focused on the law as an autonomous, ideological artifact rather than as a product of social forces. And because in their perspective there was choice as to how law should be conceived, the existing system was not necessary but based on ideological preference. Law, in the way it arbitrarily classified and ordered society, was political through and through.

CLS built on neo-Marxist + critical theory

This view of law as an ideological artifact derives from the strands of neo-Marxist and Critical Theory that CLS builds on. The legal historian and CLS scholar Robert Gordon has provided some insight into these intellectual sources of the CLS movement. An important inspiration is the work of the Italian Marxist Antonio Gramsci and his concept of "hegemony." Gramsci's theory taught CLS scholars to search for forms of domination that both dominators and dominated do not perceive as domination but accept as the natural order of things. In other words, following Gramsci, CLS does not look for blatant forms of domination but for domination in the accepted and seemingly unobjectionable aspects of the social order that people believe are necessary and natural and therefore unchangeable. The law is of central importance here, Gordon argues, because it convinces "people that all the many hierarchical relations in which they live and work are natural and necessary."[24]

Another important source for CLS, according to Gordon, is Structuralism. CLS scholars claim "that legal ideas can be seen to be organized into structures, i.e., complex cultural codes." CLS scholars, Gordon contends, believe that the "way human beings experience the world is by collectively building and maintaining systems of shared meanings that make it possible for us to interpret one another's words and actions." This Structuralist view of reality is fundamentally at odds with the way social scientists would understand the world and explains, in part, why CLS scholars believe that their view of law as an ideological artifact is in conflict with the sociology of law. Since, from the Structuralist viewpoint, in the words of Gordon, "what we experience as social reality is something we ourselves are constantly constructing," it makes no sense to search for the empirical causes of social phenomena in social and economic conditions. Things like legal rules are not necessary consequences of the empirical circumstances in which they arose but part of the cultural "system of shared meanings" that people construct collectively.[25]

A final inspiration highlighted by Gordon is the notion of *reification*. This term is ubiquitous in CLS writing and originates from Critical Theory. Gordon describes the notion of reification as a way in which people erect a cage of social structures around themselves, in which they become their own prisoners. "It is a way people have of manufacturing necessity," Gordon explains; "they build structures, then act as if (and genuinely come to believe that) the structures they have built are determined by history, human nature, economic law."[26] Again, this concept of reification is at odds with the approach of empirical social science. What empirical social science tries to prove is exactly what the idea of reification denies, that is, that the way things are should be explained, at least in part, by social and economic conditions. Hence, the task Critical Legal scholars have set for themselves, according to Gordon, is diametrically opposed to that of empirical social scientists. The point of the critical exercise "is to unfreeze the world as it appears to common sense as a bunch of more or less objectively determined social relations and to make it appear as (we [CLS scholars] believe) it really is: people acting, imagining, rationalizing, justifying."[27]

THE PROBLEM

The CLS claim on the legacy of Legal Realism, on the whole, has been uncritically accepted. There is little contention among Critical Legal scholars that they are engaged in an extension of the Realist project, and most non-CLS legal scholars seem only too willing to accept that CLS is committed to the same excesses they believe the Realists were guilty of. Realism is widely equated with radical skepticism about the certainty of law. This seems to make the label appealing to CLS and non-CLS scholars alike, as either a badge of honor or a convenient stigma. Yet, are Critical Legal Studies scholars justified in claiming there is a close affinity between their critique of law and the Realist project? And are mainstream legal scholars right in relinquishing Legal Realism to them?

The central premise of this book is *that Legal Realism and Critical Legal Studies are not continuous bodies of legal thought and that the attribution of Realistic antecedents to CLS ideas is in fact highly problematic.* The Realists wanted to make law more responsive. They wanted to make sure that it did not lag behind social and economic developments. For this project of ongoing adjustment of law to changing conditions, they chose the Pragmatic course of piecemeal reform, that is, reform based on empirical research and developed within a democratic framework. CLS, on the other hand, is a movement in the tradition of the New Left and is engaged in a more radical, transformative project. CLS tends to emphasize the fundamental plasticity of social arrangements. This does not call for social science, but for the radical insights of Critical Theory and Postmodernism. These sources, however, represent an intellectual tradition that is quite distinct from Pragmatism and openly hostile to its melioristic aspects.

Key to understanding why Legal Realism is at odds with CLS, as well as why CLS is captivated by Realism, is Pragmatism. Pragmatism does the best job in providing Realism with a degree of coherence and in tying its disparate ideas together. It combined some of the same basic elements into a connected whole, that many commentators have found jarring in Legal Realism. To wit, Pragmatism linked a thoroughgoing skepticism about the constancy and objectivity of the prevailing categories of our knowledge with an unswerving faith in science and in the possibility of social progress. It is this counterintuitive combination of unalloyed epistemic relativism with unabated confidence in the merits of scientific method and the promise of intelligent reform, so characteristic of Pragmatist philosophy, which the Legal Realists translated into a new perspective on law. Counterintuitive insights are easily mistaken for contradictions, of course, which is what Critical Legal Studies seems to treat it as.

Yet the way Pragmatism joined science with relativism was not a mistake. The Pragmatists adopted a naturalistic perspective that embraced the fluidity and impermanence of the world and treated legal and political institutions as transitory arrangements in a constant process of adaptation. The marks of Darwin were all over this Pragmatic perspective. Indeed, Darwinian evolution was quite basic to many Pragmatic ideas, especially Dewey's. And with this "Darwinian logic," Dewey explained, interest "shifts from an intelligence that shaped things once for all to the particular intelligences which things are even now shaping; shifts from an ultimate goal of good to the direct increments of justice and happiness that intelligent administration of existent conditions may beget and that present carelessness or stupidity will destroy or forego."[28] Note that this "Darwinian logic" did not carry the implication of determinism. Quite the reverse, human institutions did not conform to some enduring idea of right or justice, nor to some notional functional optimum. They were simply the fleeting product of human intelligence trying to cope with changing circumstances as best it could. Instead of predetermined movement toward a fixed ideal or a deterministic process of adaptation, the creation and transformation of social institutions for the Pragmatists exemplified the freedom and creativity of action.

The same lack of permanence and fixity also characterized language for the Pragmatists. Antiessentialism was inherent in Darwin's theory of evolution. Darwin, after all, had shown that, far from being immutable, the natural species were merely temporary classifications of evolving organisms which lacked any true or permanent nature. By thus obliterating one of the cornerstones of traditional Western thought, that is, the givenness and permanence of the natural species, Darwin had undermined the belief in objective definitions for categories and concepts. This skepticism about words and categories having a true or objective meaning, however, did not lead the Pragmatists to doubt the possibility of meaningful dialogue. What was important to them was not that meaning was true or objective, but that it was shared, and the social character of language suggested that it was. This allowed for deliberation, for collaborative effort, and for the pursuit of science. With the use of scientific method, in turn, people could test whether their notions of the world were warranted, that is, whether they produced desired results or whether they needed to be revised. Hence, through observation and experiment people could bootstrap themselves up to a set of warranted notions about the world and, if necessary, adjust and fine-tune those notions if they no longer fit with the changing environment.

Thus, in a nutshell, Pragmatism reconciled freedom with evolutionary functionalism, the pursuit of science with antifoundationalism, and democratic deliberation with antiessentialism. The Legal Realists embraced this Pragmatic synthesis and made it the basis of their inquiry into law. CLS scholars, however, treat this combination of elements as something evidently contradictory and no longer tenable. They claim that there can be no freedom if an evolutionary-functionalist framework is adopted, no truth if antifoundationalism undermines any notion of objective knowledge; and no dialogue if antiessentialism makes all meaning unstable. In effect, Critical scholars truncate Legal Realism and discard most of its talk about scientific research and policy deliberation as a retreat from the disturbing consequences of its own critical analysis.

According to CLS scholars, contemporary historicism suggests that social and legal institutions are largely underdetermined by social and economic circumstances. These institutions are not functional adaptations but the erratic result of arbitrary power and contingent choice. Moreover, Thomas Kuhn has shown that scientific paradigms are incommensurable and that there is no Archimedean point from which they can be evaluated. Consequently, claims generated by one discourse cannot be objectively compared with those of another. Science should primarily be seen as a political and sociological phenomenon, a discourse propping up the status quo rather than a neutral procedure for the determination of "objective truth." Antiessentialism, finally, has much more disturbing consequences than the Realists were ready to admit. The Realists and Pragmatists were politically naive. They failed to see that if meaning is socially constructed, language becomes a profoundly political instrument. If there is no objective meaning, if meaning is up for grabs, it will end up reflecting the perspective of the dominant and powerful. As a result, language should be distrusted as an attribute of the existing power structure, as the imposition of a dominant perspective on people, which makes it difficult for them to even voice a dissenting point of view.

Yet, by on the one hand presenting the antifoundationalism and nominalism of Legal Realism as something that is continuous with their own project and akin to the Critical Theory they draw on, and on the other hand treating the Realist embrace of science and rational deliberation as outdated positivism, as a quaint leftover from the nineteenth century that can simply be amputated from the body of Realist theory without loss, CLS scholars misconstrue Legal Realism. When the Legal Realists combined these two elements, they were following in the footsteps of Pragmatism and applying its insights to the legal field. Indeed, this is one of its redeeming features. Pragmatism, as Hans Joas argued, "possesses an incredible modernity." Contrary to the CLS analysis, its proposal for a new understanding of the practices of science and deliberation is still very relevant today. It is an understanding that is not dependent on any foundational bedrock and is impervious to the antifoundational critique CLS builds on. Hence, in the words of Joas, Pragmatism's attempt to deal with "the end of metaphysical certainties" and to show that "neither science nor democracy had ceased to have validity simply because it no longer seemed possible to provide any final justifications for them" has lost little of its pertinence.[29]

The central premise of this study—that Legal Realism and CLS are not continuous bodies of thought—does a lot to narrow the discussion of these two movements to a manageable set of themes. Both Legal Realism and CLS are sprawling bodies of theory which would be difficult to describe and define as movements. The set of ideas that CLS scholars discuss when they relate their movement to Legal Realism, however, is much more limited. Notably, three themes come up time and again in CLS discussions of Legal Realism: (1) historicism, (2) social science, and (3) linguistic theory. These three issues will be the focus of later chapters, but a brief introduction here will help to further clarify the central thesis of this study.

HISTORICISM *(hc 2+3)*

One of the central claims of CLS with respect to the Legal Realists is that the latter were trailblazers with regard to the employment of historicism as a tool for legal critique. The Realists pioneered a skeptical use of historical analysis that sought to undermine the supposed necessity of existing legal arrangements by highlighting how different the law and the understanding of legal concepts had been in the past. This use of historical analysis to expose the contingency of the legal system has become a cherished method within CLS. Indeed, Critical Legal scholar Mark Kelman notes that "[m]uch of the Critical writing has been historical."[30] Most of the Critical scholars, Kelman maintains, "use a certain style of historicist inquiry to remind us how unlikely it is that things we may take for granted will always be so, because we can so readily see that things once taken for granted have hardly proven indispensable."[31] Critical scholars, in other words, revert to history, like the Legal Realists before them, to make the point that there is nothing natural and necessary about the rules we adopt to regulate social life.

Yet there are also elements in the Realist legacy that do not accord with the historicist sensibilities of CLS scholars. Notably, they distance themselves from what they see as adaptationism in the historical work of the Realists. Thus Robert Gordon claims that there "are apologetic aspects" in the Realist view of law "that the Critics feel compelled to resist." The problem with Realism is that it takes an evolutionary-functionalist view of law and legal history, Gordon contends. This evolutionary-functionalist view presents the world as something that is largely shaped by detached social forces and, therefore, hides the fact that these seemingly inescapable social forces are really created by people, indeed by the very people who at the same time believe and claim that they are only passively accommodating to those social forces.[32] For CLS, Gordon explains, there is no independent social reality that shapes the legal system, because our understanding of social reality is dependent on the concepts and categories provided by that very legal system. In practice, he argues, "it is just about impossible to describe any set of 'basic' social practices without describing the legal relations among the people involved—legal relations that don't simply condition how the people relate to each other, but to an important extent define the constitutive terms of the relationship."[33] Hence, Gordon claims, whereas "the program of the Realists was to lift the veil of legal Form to reveal living essences of power and need, the program of the Critics is to lift the veil of power and need to expose the legal elements in their composition."[34] The real power of the legal system is its capacity to predetermine how existing social and economic arrangements will be conceived. This is why historicist analysis is so central to CLS theory, because it shows how contingent these congeries of categories and concepts really are and exposes the extent to which they determine our understanding of social reality. This is also why CLS adherents reject the evolutionary-functionalist view of legal development as inadequate, because it suggests that we are stuck with the way things are, with only marginal opportunities for change and reform.[35]

This critique of Realist functionalism and adaptationism repeats the criticism that classical Critical Theory at one time leveled against American Pragmatism. For Max Horkheimer and Theodor Adorno, Pragmatism was primarily a philosophy of adaptation, which they understood as conformism and passive accommodation to the given socioeconomic structure.[36] This Horkheimer-Adorno critique was based on a mistaken understanding of Pragmatism, however. The whole point of Pragmatism was to escape from the deterministic implications that seemed to follow from science and Darwin's theory of evolution. Indeed, the bleak and predetermined world that appeared to ensue from Darwin caused one of the originators of Pragmatism, William James, to fall into a deep depression, from which he finally managed to emerge with his new Pragmatic philosophy. This Pragmatic philosophy was aimed at the intellectual roots of his crisis; that is, it was framed to reconcile science with free will and evolution with the open-ended nature of the future. Hence, the Pragmatic notion of adaptation is not at all passive or deterministic. On the contrary, determinism was a problem that Pragmatism was designed to be an answer to right from the beginning.

When CLS adherents discuss the functionalist and adaptationist underpinnings of the Legal Realist conception of history, however, they seem to hark back to Critical Theory's critique of American Pragmatism as a philosophy of acquiescence. Yet, much like Pragmatism, Legal Realism treated adaptation not as a form of reactive or passive accommodation that led to a predetermined outcome, but as a form of creative action that led to a contingent outcome. Likewise, the Realists did not acquiesce in the legal system as if it was some near-perfect functional optimum which merely needed a little pruning and trimming. Rather, the Realists approached law as a system that was rife with rules that were solutions to yesterday's problems and based on outdated notions and myths from the past. Their use of historical analysis was aimed precisely at the exposition of these "survivals," so that they could be cleared out of the way and replaced with something better.

This picture of law as an evolving institution should not be confused with a crude analysis of a cultural superstructure being determined by a material substructure. From the Pragmatic-Realist perspective, the social actor was both product and author of the social environment. In the struggle for survival, human beings had developed intelligence and had become reflexive agents vis-à-vis the (social) strategies to cope with their environment. The Realists never settled for an absolutist notion of truth. Hence, even though our most reliable knowledge was circumscribed by the facts, it could never be a mirror of reality. It was by definition an ingenious and imaginative conception of the changing social universe. Joas has coined the term *situated creativity* to express this notion, which he believes goes to the heart of Pragmatism.[37] Situated creativity comprises both the notion of situatedness, of being constrained by the social and natural conditions of the environment, and the notion of creativity, of being able to transcend circumstances and find new, inventive, and unsuspected solutions to life's problems. This idea of situated creativity rejects the dichotomy between adaptation and freedom and seeks to reconcile the two into an integrated position.

The insights the Pragmatists derived from evolutionary theory do not add up to a deterministic, mechanistic, or reductionist theory. The naturalism of the Realists seems much closer to Joas's notion of "situated creativity," that is, they proceeded from an appreciation that human beings are the product of their physical and social environment but that they remain, for all that, independent actors capable of autonomous and genuinely innovative creativity. For them the notion of evolution was not an enemy of freedom. This Realist approach to historical understanding with its adaptationist or functionalist underpinnings will be compared in greater detail with the type of idealist historicism advocated by CLS in Chapters 2 and 3.

SOCIAL SCIENCE

The second issue concerns the social scientific ambitions of the Realists. Although the Realists differed on how exactly to incorporate social science in law, there was scarcely anything they agreed on more than that the social sciences were the way forward in the legal field. Neil Duxbury even claims that "for most legal realists, social science was realism."[38] The purpose for which the Realists engaged in social science research was, on the one hand, to gain a more accurate, empirical account of the real considerations that determined legal decisions and, on the other hand, the aspiration to adjust law to the moving social and economic scene. Legal Realism started from the assumption that legal issues could be translated into problems of social policy and studied scientifically. This would both explain much better why judges decided cases the way they did and show what could be done to improve law. The Realists believed that the Classical legal doctrine was completely out of step with social and economic conditions and provided a misleading account of the actual considerations that informed the courts. American law was dangerously lagging behind the times. Social science, the Realists expected, would show this to be true and suggest new ways to regulate society.

All this suggests that social science was a crucial component of the Realist program. However, when CLS gauges the importance of Legal Realism, it tends to claim that social science was not central but peripheral to what was truly significant in Legal Realism. What is more, it tends to view the social-scientific element as a kind of Trojan horse, an element that the Realists wheeled in to their theoretical position believing that it held the promise of a more responsive, forward-looking legal system, but which turned out to be a treacherously conservative element that undermined the reformist enthusiasm of Realism and made it lose much of its critical edge. CLS clearly does not rate social science very highly. The Realist use of social science, CLS scholars claim, is reductionist, apologetic, deterministic, and intellectually regressive. The Realists' attempt to explain law as a function of society, Critical Legal scholars claim, did not take into account the autonomous ideological character of law and the importance of legal categories and concepts for social theory.

The CLS historian Morton Horwitz primarily blames Karl Llewellyn for the unfortunate turn to social science. Llewellyn was the first to describe the critical intellectual currents in prewar legal scholarship as a Realist movement, and he was the first to give a general description of that movement in his famous article. Yet, according to Horwitz, he misrepresented contemporary trends in legal scholarship by emphasizing a sterile, positivistic, social science approach, at the cost of the critical aspects of Realistic thought.[39] This understanding of Realism should be adjusted, Horwitz believes, to accommodate the fact that "some Realists were among the earliest American thinkers to understand the social and historical contingency of structures of thought." Such a reinterpretation would show CLS to be the true heir of Legal Realism, Horwitz maintains, because it is this central "strand of cognitive relativism that Critical Legal Studies revived and extended."[40]

The question is whether the Realist project is aptly described as a "sterile, positivistic, social science approach"? CLS is not alone in assuming that a positivistic science of law is what the Realists were aiming for. Brian Leiter, for instance, has put Legal Realism squarely in the tradition of positivist social science.[41] Yet, there are good reasons for rejecting this qualification of the Realist conception of social science. Realist pleas for social science did not betray a "positivistic" point of view but clearly expressed a Pragmatic perspective. This Pragmatic perspective was not at odds with an appreciation of the "social and historical contingency of structures of thought." On the contrary, open recognition of this social and historical contingency was an integral part of the Pragmatic conception of social science. The Pragmatists were always careful to distinguish their position from positivism. They diverged from positivism in a number of fundamental respects. The Pragmatists did not adopt a strict separation between fact and value, for instance, which was one of the hallmarks of positivism. Nor did they believe that social science could deliver objective truth in the way the positivists did. For the positivists, the social scientist was an outside observer standing apart from the social setting and recording in a disinterested and impartial way what was going on. Hence, the positivists believed the researcher could steer clear of any of the subjective values and notions people attached to their behavior and could remain completely disinterested and objective in the research. The Pragmatic view, however, rejected this notion as a view from nowhere. For the Pragmatists, the researcher was every bit as situated as the subjects being studied and was always, and unavoidably, working with the assumptions, prejudices, concerns, standards, and concepts current in the researcher's time and place. Hence, for the Pragmatists, the researcher was not a disinterested outsider simply observing and recording from a neutral position, but an engaged insider, trying to cope with the problems of the day with the time-tested methodology of science.

The type of knowledge this Pragmatic conception produced was not equivalent to positivism's lawlike generalizations that held for all time, but confined itself to warranted notions that worked for the present. Hence, the Pragmatist never conceived of science as a conversation-stopper but always recognized the transient nature of human knowledge. Science was an ongoing process aimed at extending the range of the possible for social policy. Dewey believed that in a constantly evolving world, eternal truths were not in the cards. The only way to cope intelligently with such a changing world was through experimental knowledge that was constantly tested against projected results. If hypotheses no longer delivered the outcomes expected, they had to be replaced with better ones. The focus, in other words, was on the practical consequences of hypotheses, not on their ultimate truth content. The pursuit of knowledge should start from practical problems, he believed. Knowledge derived from the scientific evaluation of our different actions to solve those problems. The knowledge produced by such an experimental method was always tentative. Conditions changed, and a hypothesis that worked today might no longer be relevant tomorrow.

Applied to law, these Pragmatic principles would have serious consequences for the logic of judicial argument, Dewey maintained. These principles showed, he argued, "that either logic must be abandoned or that it must be a logic *relative to consequences rather than to antecedents*, a logic of prediction of probabilities rather than one of deduction of certainties." The problem with traditional legal scholarship was that it adhered to a "doctrine of immutable and necessary antecedent rules." This doctrine, Dewey claimed, consecrated the old and led to a widening gap between "social conditions and the principles used by the courts."[42] In other words, the belief in true and certain principles of law led to the ossification of the legal system and, when social and economic conditions changed, to an ill-adapted and dysfunctional law. The wiser approach was to see legal rules as only temporary solutions that could be discarded if they no longer produced expected results. In the end, legal rules were tools of social policy, in Dewey's view, and they should be informed by scientific study of social and economic conditions, rather than by speculation about the true and eternal in law.

The Realists absorbed these Pragmatic insights into their approach to legal scholarship. As a result, their speculations about, and ventures into, social science were very different from those of positivist social scientists. Hence, the CLS critique of social science may be relevant to a positivist conception of social science—which is a relatively rare thing among social scientists—but is largely beside the point when it comes to Legal Realism. The many differences with respect to, and misunderstandings produced by, the issue of social science will be elaborated upon in Chapters 4 and 5.

LANGUAGE

The Legal Realists applied their brand of contextualism on the level of language as well. Not only the legal system but also language was a socially constructed tool shaped by circumstances and environment. Words were merely handy symbols that referred to sets of facts in the real world. Since that real world was continually evolving, words could have no definite meaning. Thus, Llewellyn warned that "although originally formulated on the model of at least some observed data, [categories] tend, once they have entered into the organization of thinking, both to suggest the presence of corresponding data even when these data are not in fact present, and to twist any fresh observation of data into conformity with the lines and shape of the category."[43] The concepts and categories, moreover, emanated from the social and cultural matrix. The cultural idiosyncrasies, ideals, and prejudices of a people crystallized around their use of words and settled themselves in the vocabulary with which they made sense of their world. As a result, language was too indeterminate to give legal rules a clear and objective meaning in the world of fact, and vice versa, the real world was too unsteady and chaotic to be divided up into neat categories.

CLS adherents rightly contend that the Legal Realists were far ahead of their time with such skepticism of legal concepts. The Realist critique pioneered a profound skepticism of concepts and categories, long before this became common with the "linguistic turn" in philosophy. The CLS movement, for its part, draws heavily on the work that issued from this "linguistic turn." Indeed, it is fair to say that linguistic philosophy is an indispensable component of their legal theory. Critical scholars, as a rule, claim that language mediates the observation of reality. What the social world looks like is largely determined by the conceptual vocabulary employed. This claim comes in several guises: sometimes it builds on Ludwig Wittgenstein, sometimes on Postmodern philosophers like Michel Foucault or Jacques Derrida, sometimes on neo-Pragmatists like Richard Rorty or Stanley Fish. Yet within CLS theory, by hook or by crook, these several perspectives eventually lead to the same general conclusion, that is, a hermetic view of language, a view in which language groups are believed to manufacture their own reality through their shared language and are no longer believed to have direct, unmediated access to the real world. As a result, CLS scholars do not think that there is any way to judge the relative value, or veracity, of conceptual frameworks or discourses or paradigms or language games, either rationally or empirically. We are basically cut loose from the world and should stop pretending that reality can be a touchstone for our concepts and theories. Evaluation always proceeds from within one or another paradigm, and there is no Archimedean point, no neutral position from which to judge competing paradigms.

This thoroughgoing social constructivism, in which the world is created in the image of our language, is not confined to CLS. It has achieved a surprising degree of academic respectability. Indeed, Susan Haack, defending the kind of chastened realism first proposed by the Classical Pragmatists (and emulated by the Legal Realists), contends that she now often finds herself a beleaguered moderate. To defend such a view, these days, she writes, "is to invite the criticism on the one hand that you have naively failed to grasp the conceptually or linguistically or textually constructed character of the world, or the relativity of truth or evidence to the community or paradigm; and on the other hand that you must be committed to indefensibly ambitious metaphysical or epistemological ideas." Like Haack's own variety of realism, this book will argue that the Realists' is "modest enough to escape the charge of indefensible ambition" and "subtle enough to accommodate the complexities that have tempted some to succumb to indefensibly ambitious forms of linguistic or conceptual idealism."[44]

At any rate, CLS theory seems a good deal more radical than Realist skepticism about legal concepts and categories ever was. Realists conceived of legal language as an artificial tool, to be sure. Yet, it was a tool constructed to do real work within a changing environment. They never understood language to be largely severed from reality. Indeed, it would have been inconceivable to them that legal language could be treated purely as a product of social and cultural conventions. Concepts and categories were shaped and molded by their facility in dealing with real-world problems. There was always a reality check when language was put to work. Legal discourse could never remain a mere flight of fancy; at some point the tires would have to hit the tarmac and concepts would have to prove their mettle on the ground. Language that no longer described what was going on and legal rules that no longer had expected results were bound to wither away. Hence, Legal Realism made allowance for social and economic circumstances as factors conditioning and shaping legal terminology. The performance of concepts and categories in dealing with real-world phenomena was the foremost criterion on which they were assessed. For Pragmatists and Realists alike, the emphasis was on the practical results that could be achieved with concepts, not on their ultimate truth or objectivity. The respective theories of language forwarded by the Legal Realists and CLS scholars will be discussed in Chapters 6 and 7.

METHOD

This book is a comparative study of two American schools of legal theory. Yet it is not a study of American law, as such. An affinity for, and a sense of engagement with, American legal and political thought does in-

Incorporate as Intro.

form these pages. Yet this is an affinity and an engagement aimed at mining the American legal and political tradition for its valuables, not at making an unsolicited contribution to its further growth or getting involved in its substantive issues.

Perhaps this study can be treated as an exercise in jurisprudence at a more general level, as a modest attempt to engage in what Jeremy Bentham once described as the work of the "censor." With respect to legal inquiry, Bentham made the distinction between the pursuits of the censor and the task of the expositor. The job of the latter was to explain what the law was, "to shew what the *Legislator* and his underworkman the *Judge* have done *already*." Hence, the expositor was "always the citizen of this or that country." The task of the censor, on the other hand, was "to *teach* that *science* which when by change of hands converted into an art, the LEGISLATOR *practises*."[45] The censor, therefore, was a "citizen of the world." In rather grandiloquent terms, this is what the present volume sets out to do; it seeks to discuss what can be learned from the Realist movement concerning the art and science of the legislator. In other words, it wants to recover the general background theories about language, interpretation, history, the legal tradition, society, and epistemology that the Realists applied to questions of law.

Unlike Bentham, the Legal Realists mainly focused on the judge, and not the legislator, of course. Yet, this difference between the two approaches is more apparent than real and does not invalidate the application of Bentham's notion of censorial jurisprudence. The seeming difference is primarily a consequence of the peculiar focus on the judge in American legal culture. The questions of law-government that the Legal Realists sought to address, centering on the judiciary, would fall squarely under the purview of the legislator in Bentham's approach. Indeed, the kinds of theories the Realists drew on to reform American law were remarkably akin to the ones that informed Bentham's general jurisprudence. In a recent discussion of Bentham, William Twining distinguishes five pillars on which his general jurisprudence was built. These included Bentham's Theory of Fictions, a precursor to the linguistic theory of the Realists; his Principle of Utility, a forerunner to Realist welfarism and their demand for more social science in law; his legal positivism, a predecessor to the Realist critique of natural rights; and his embrace of democratic theory, an antecedent to the democratic sentiments of the Realists and their goal to bring law in line with the preferences of the people.[46] It is these background theories of the Realists that are the main interest of this study. Their significance is not confined to American law. They have a much wider application.

The present study is, therefore, not purely written as a work of intel-

[handwritten margin notes: translation of Realism to the present]

lectual history. There is a lot of historical description, to be sure, and the standards of contemporary intellectual history have been heeded to avoid the pitfalls of ahistorical interpretation. The past is a foreign country, as the adage goes. Thus, in a way, an examination of Realism and CLS presents problems similar to those of cross-cultural comparison. As a result, the Realist works needed to be "translated" to the present, in a way, to make meaningful comparison possible. Yet, the following discussion of Legal Realism and CLS does not constitute a straightforward historical analysis.

[handwritten margin notes: historically informed work of legal theory]

It is a historically informed work of legal theory. The chief aim of this study is not to make the rather pedantic point that CLS got one of its sources wrong. Its main purpose, rather, is to disentangle Legal Realism from CLS, to clear away some of the misconceptions about Legal Realism that CLS has given rise to, and to recapture what is of enduring importance in the Realist movement. Legal Realism still offers promising points of departure for legal research, but these have become obscured by the dominance of the CLS interpretation of Realism.

[handwritten margin notes: L.R. Catholic in embrace of disciplines other than law]

Legal Realism was rather catholic in its embrace of academic disciplines other than law. As a result, a large number of disciplines embraced by the Realists have also crept into this work. Beside law and legal theory, this study has tread on the fields of history, psychology, philosophy, political science, sociology, anthropology, linguistics, and even evolutionary biology. Such disciplinary roaming might seem reckless and to demand a Faustian pact to get away with. Yet the complexity is not as serious as it might seem. There is a discernible theoretical core of Pragmatic origin in the work of the Legal Realists that informs their excursions into these different fields. Hence, there is method in their madness and coherence in their disciplinary eclecticism. This coherence is provided by their common theoretical outlook, however, rather than by the methodological constraints of their shared discipline.

[handwritten margin notes: Pragmatism core + legal realism]

E PLURIBUS UNUM

This last notion, that a common outlook can be formulated which defines Legal Realism as a movement, is also a disputed issue. Although the term *Legal Realism* seems to have settled firmly in the vocabulary of legal theory, the effort to define and describe Legal Realism as a movement, in general terms, has become quite uncommon. With recent exceptions like Brian Leiter, who believes the Legal Realists all shared in a common, positivist approach, or Hanoch Dagan, who argues that the Realists presented a coherent and novel theory of law as an institution accommodating a number of constitutive tensions, few people think the Realists can be grouped together without at least making some finer distinctions.[47] Most work on Legal Realism includes a section in which the term is debunked as a meaningless label. The individual theorists it describes are simply too diverse, and a general discussion would not do justice to their individual accomplishments. These admonitions reflect the current climate in intellectual history, which is deeply suspicious of generalization and tends to celebrate complexity, nuance, and difference. Legal historians working on Legal Realism tend to focus on distinctions between subgroups and individuals, rather than commonalities. In his book on Legal Realism, for instance, John Schlegel suggests that talking about intellectuals as representatives of one or another position is deeply misleading: "It is just as reductionist to turn the activities of intellectuals into either topics—republican theory, welfare economics, or social thought—or disciplines—economics, sociology, or law—with problems and coherent schools of thought, as it is (or was) to reduce the actions of individuals to their place in the drama of the ownership of the means of production."[48] Indeed, Schlegel believes we should simply give up the notion of a "history of ideas" and instead think in terms of a "history of intellectuals," that is, stories of three-dimensional people, with backgrounds and life experiences.

Schlegel expresses a sentiment that is more widespread. William Twining, the English biographer of Karl Llewellyn and chronicler of the Realist movement, was one of the first to object to a lumping together of all theorists that have become known as Legal Realists and treating them as if they belonged to a coherent school. Indeed, he claimed that "there is no alternative to the detailed study of the contributions of particular individuals."[49] In her work on Roscoe Pound and Karl Llewellyn, N. E. H. Hull also claims we should "stop looking for the core of realist thought or any other persuasion's thought and try to follow the human story."[50]

His reference to "the drama of the ownership of the means of production" makes it patently clear what Schlegel wants to stay away from. Yet the rigid, armor-plated analysis of orthodox Marxist historians should not be treated as a paradigmatic example of generalization in history and social theory. It is an example of what Daniel Dennett would call "greedy reductionism," that is, the sin of underestimating complexity and trying "to explain too much too fast."[51] The fact that there have been perpetrators of such greedy reductionism is not an argument against generalization in general. In itself there is nothing wrong with generalization. Indeed, one could argue that Schlegel's own classic example of excessive simplification, the "drama of the ownership of the means of production," when Marx first described it, was quite a useful and faithful general description of the socioeconomic developments that were taking place in western Europe and in the United States in the nineteenth century. Subsequent ideologues, still toeing the party line when developments had clearly taken another turn, might have given Marxism a bad name, but there was nothing wrong with Marx's original efforts to formulate a grand theory. If anything, we need more of that kind of theory today.

Hence, this study will try to describe Legal Realism as a movement, rather than a collection of individual legal theorists. This is not to deny that there are important differences between members of the Realist movement. There are. Yet, it *is* to deny that these differences are in any way more remarkable than, for instance, the differences between all the diverse theorists we normally refer to as Marxists, or between all the members of the heterogeneous group of thinkers we commonly refer to as liberals. The reason why Marxists and liberals are commonly lumped together into a single group is not that their thought is in any way more regimented than that of the Realists. They have not somehow all been forced into line, where the Realists have not. Rather, the point is that they have some important ideas in common, ideas that are characteristic and distinguishing—ideas, in short, that justify assembling them together under a single label.

With respect to the label of Legal Realism, these common ideas can largely be summed up with the term *Pragmatism*. It is important to keep this central concern in mind when discussing the Legal Realists, because a good number of the supposed divisions within Legal Realism simply derive from different aspects of their shared Pragmatic stance. The most important of these is undoubtedly the issue of social science. In the later reception of Realist theory, the embrace of social science is often presented as a dividing issue within the Realist movement. One group of Realists wanted to engage in pure social science research, according to this view, while another remained committed to the professional character of legal scholarship. Twining named these two groups of Realists the "Scientists" and the "Prudents," respectively.[52] The Scientists were devoted to the study of law as a social phenomenon and distanced themselves from the traditional discipline of law with its focus on the development of legal doctrine. The Prudents among the Realists were less prone to getting out of their studies to collect data on the judicial process. They did not translate their commit-

ment to social science into a fact-gathering exercise but mainly confined it
to the incorporation of social theory in their understanding of law.

To be sure, there is nothing inherently wrong with making this distinction between Scientists and Prudents. It captures a real difference among
the Legal Realists. The question is, however, what this distinction signifies
and why it should be important. Does it show a fundamental rift within the
Realist movement, or mainly a differentiation in the way shared assumptions informed inquiry and research projects? Does it prove there was a fundamental antithesis within Realist thought, or primarily that the Pragmatic
core of Realism lent itself to the development of various approaches? The
position defended in this study is that the things the Scientists and the
Prudents have in common—a Pragmatic recognition of their situatedness
as scholars combined with an unshaken confidence in scientific research and
rational deliberation—are much more salient than the things that separate
them. What is more, this work will defend the argument that Scientists and
Prudents are only properly understood when their respective approaches
are seen as continuous rather than contradictory. In other words, to interpret the pursuits of the one as incompatible with the work of the other
is to misconstrue them both. The two groups started out from a shared
Pragmatic position, however different the flavor of the work they subsequently produced. With the attention primarily fixed on the distinctions
between Realists, students of Legal Realism have lost sight of the continu-
ities in Realist jurisprudence.

This shared Pragmatic position is still of topical interest. It has a relevance that goes beyond the inception of the administrative welfare state
in the Progressive and New Deal era. Pragmatism should be seen as an
approach, or technique, with an attendant set of values, rather then a full-
fledged conception of what society should be like. It simply would not
make sense for a theory that put the reality of change and evolution at center stage to formulate a static conception of the well-ordered society. To be
sure, the Pragmatists supported the welfare programs of the Progressive
era and the New Deal, but they were quite self-conscious about the limited applicability of these programs. A different time and a different set
of circumstances might call for a very different set of policies. For the
Pragmatists, in other words, "change was part of the plan," to borrow a
catchy slogan from an IBM commercial. Pragmatism only proposed a set
of procedures and practices that would allow society to deal with change in
an intelligent and broadly democratic manner. "The culminating achievement of Dewey's philosophy" Rorty claims, "was to treat evaluative terms

such as 'true' and 'right' not as signifying a relation to some antecedently existing thing—such as God's Will, or Moral Law, or the Intrinsic Nature of Objective Reality—but as expressions of having found a solution to a problem: a problem which may someday seem obsolete, and a satisfaction which may someday seem misplaced."[53] Pragmatism was about fostering such things as democratic deliberation, scientific research, and education. These mutually reinforcing practices could be marshaled to harness a participatory and inclusive conception of democratic government and would allow the democratic process to arrive at the kind of good and intelligent solutions that Rorty refers to. This remains as relevant today as it was in the 1930s, even though it would no longer translate into alphabet programs like the Tennessee Valley Authority (TVA), the Public Works Administration (PWA), or the Works Progress Administration (WPA).

CHAPTER TWO

The Seeds of Time:
Legal Realism and Legal History

> For what is the present after all but a growth out of the past?
>
> —Walt Whitman[1]

> Men make their own history, but they do not make it just as they please; they do not make it under circumstances chosen by themselves, but under circumstances directly encountered, given and transmitted from the past.
>
> —Karl Marx[2]

> While postmodernists have denied the possibility of historical understanding and historians have barely noticed, developments in the natural sciences have put an evolutionary history of humanity firmly back on the agenda.
>
> —Eric Hobsbawm[3]

A comparison between the respective views on history forwarded by Legal Realism and Critical Legal Studies (CLS) is a good place to start an appraisal of the relationship between the two movements. The issue of historical understanding brings to a focus some of the central differences between Legal Realism and CLS. Key to historical analysis is the question of what shapes and conditions law, what explains the historical genesis of a legal system. Legal history, in other words, is a topic in which the basic assumptions about the way law develops are brought to the fore. In traditional conceptions of legal history, the development of legal doctrine was usually treated as largely an internal legal affair, as something unfolding according to law's own native logic and to be explained in isolation from the wider social and historical context. Legal Realism departed from this type of historical analysis and tried to understand law as an embedded social practice; that is, it tried to relate the development of legal understanding to the relevant social, economic, and cultural environment. CLS, in turn, rejects this type of history, as we shall see in the next chapter, and opts for a Structuralist, Postmodernist approach in which the focus moves back to law as a self-moving ideological structure or paradigm.[4]

This chapter will deal with the Realist conception of historical analysis. Legal history was only of limited concern to the Legal Realists. With their embrace of Pragmatism, the Realists seemed to be more interested in the present and future of law than in its historical genesis. Nonetheless, the Realists did engage in historical research—mostly studies of the development of legal doctrine in their different fields of specialization. This work was quite accomplished and expressed a sophisticated view of the history of law. In their historical studies the Realists provided detailed descriptions of law's evolution. A broad range of factors were included to explain the development of legal doctrine. These factors ranged from social and economic conditions to the idiosyncratic influence of individual judges; from technical developments to the political backdrop; from the prevalent ideas and theories in a certain historical period to the kinds of cases that happened to come before the court. The development that resulted from this complex array of factors could be quite erratic and unpredictable. Yet it was only the result of historical happenstance to a point. The Realists saw the evolution of law as something that was broadly shaped by the functional demands of changing social and economic circumstances, with idiosyncratic historical factors such as the prevalent ideas and theories in a certain period twisting and molding the end result. One could describe this understanding of legal change as a chastened functionalism, a functionalism that made allowance for a certain degree of peculiarity and unpredictability in human affairs. However, ultimately, law remained an instrument to keep society going in a changing world, and the Realists stayed faithful to the hypothesis that basic changes in that world were bound to provoke adjustments in the legal system.

The Realist forays into the history of legal doctrine have been described by Laura Kalman as "presentist" history—history engaged in not for its own sake but for the light it throws on contemporary concerns.[5] And the concern that dominated the Realist project above all was the wish to reform Classical legal thought and its set of timeless and unchanging principles of justice. The Realists reverted to history, in other words, to discredit the alleged perpetuity and immutability of these fundamental principles in order to lay the necessary groundwork for their reform. Thus, their historical accounts of doctrinal development typically involved an argument aimed at proving that a certain rule had once been introduced to deal with a unique set of historical conditions, but that those conditions had changed and that the rule had become dysfunctional. For the Realists, historical analysis was a critical tool, first and foremost. It was not taken up for its own sake, or for the purpose of investing law with the dignity of an eminent historical lineage. Rather, it was engaged in with the aim of exposing the supposed fundamental principles central to classic nineteenth-century legal thought as outdated survivals from a bygone era.

The theoretical underpinnings of the Realist approach to history were fairly straightforward. In broad terms, two elements coexisted uneasily with one another in the Realist conception of history: (1) the element of historicism, and (2) the element of functionalism, or adaptationism. To begin with the first of these two, for the Realists change and flux were the inescapable reality of our existence. Legal understanding as well as language, culture, social and economic conditions, and the practice of politics were always changing, and each historical stage was irreducibly different from any other. This Realist historicism was not a teleological historicism in the Hegelian tradition. There was no millennial expectation, no ideal toward which the development was moving. The main purpose of Realist history was not to highlight some inexorable historical trend but to engage in legal critique. And historicist analysis was well suited to the task of showing that some venerable legal rule did not hold for all time but was an outdated leftover from a previous age formulated to deal with a contingent problem that no longer existed.

This did not mean that for the Realists legal history boiled down to sheer chance and contingency, however. The Realists believed in the distinctiveness and singularity of historical periods, to be sure, but they did not think a broader understanding of the way law adjusted to changing conditions and circumstances was therefore beyond the ken of legal scholarship. Legal doctrine did not simply develop according to the law of fashion. Under the strain of continuous change, the law had always been adjusted and accommodated to shifting social necessities and demands. These efforts had left a record of how earlier generations had assessed and evaluated the problems of their day and how they had sought to deal with them. The point the Realists were *not* trying to make with respect to this historical record, it is important to note, is how flawed and erroneous it was, because it looked so flawed and erroneous in hindsight. Rather, they took the concepts and rules handed down from the past quite seriously as solutions that would have once made good sense in their own context of application, even though times had changed and they might no longer be adequate for the present. Thus Llewellyn warned first-year law students against "chronocentric snobbery" and the notion that "*we* are the Greeks; all others are barbarians."[6]

There was a story to be told, in other words, about how the law—in however an idiosyncratic and historically contingent a manner—had taken shape against the backdrop of the social and economic environment. This brings us to the second element of the Realist conception of history, the analysis of legal development in a functionalist, or adaptationist, framework—a framework based on the assumption that the alternatives available for organizing society were not unlimited and that it was worthwhile to investigate how existing conditions had put bounds on what could be done with law. This framework derived from evolutionary theory and the way it had been co-opted into American social theory and Pragmatic philosophy in the late nineteenth and early twentieth century. It was a framework that extended the Darwinian notion of adaptive fitness to social institutions.

This adaptationist framework is deceptively simple and easily misunderstood. Indeed, it has invited the charge of Panglossianism against Realism.[7] This reproach refers to Dr. Pangloss, of course, the famous character in Voltaire's *Candide* who explained away every unfortunate disaster and every quirk of history with the adage "Everything is for the best in this, the best of all possible worlds." The term was picked by paleontologists Stephen Jay Gould and Richard Lewontin some years ago to criticize what they considered the exaggerations of adaptationism in evolutionary biology, that is, to denounce the position that every aspect of every organism should in principle be assumed to be a necessary adaptation to deal with some problem of survival.[8] Panglossianism led to all kinds of far-fetched and tortured arguments, according to Gould and Lewontin, that sought to explain any and all characteristics of an organism as prerequisites for its evolutionary success, without taking into consideration the possibility that a particular characteristic might not necessarily be there *for* something. Certain characteristics could simply be redundant or excess features, for instance, resulting from chance and serving no purpose at all. The charge of Panglossianism was also extended to functionalism and adaptationism in social theory. In a social context Panglossianism refers to the argument that social institutions like law must be well adapted, for otherwise society would have collapsed and disintegrated. For a Panglossian functionalist, therefore, all is largely for the best in the legal system, with only some minor shortcomings. If this were not so, the legal system would have fallen into crisis or even disintegrated.

This chapter will seek to dispel the charge of Panglossianism. There is no reason to accept that functionalism and adaptationism should necessarily lead to a conservative outcome. Indeed, Panglossianism provides a rather poor characterization of the Realist understanding of legal history. In their historical research the Realists were not typically interested in showing how *well adapted* the overall legal system was, but in exposing how *ill adapted* certain individual rules, concepts, and doctrines were and how they had managed to survive despite their inadequacy. The intention of their functionalist arguments, in other words, was overwhelmingly critical, not apologetic. The charge that the Legal Realists were somehow acquiescing in the given state of affairs with their functionalism seems wildly off the mark.

In the remainder of this chapter the themes introduced above will be elaborated upon. The discussion of Realist legal history will fall into three main sections. The first part will discuss the historical work of Oliver Wendell Holmes. Holmes was an important inspiration for the type of historical analysis undertaken by the Realists. A description of his conception of legal history will provide a good introduction to the general mind-set with which the Realists approached legal history. This will merge into the second part of this chapter, which will provide an overview of evolutionary theory. The notion of evolution was quite pervasive in the social theory and historical writing of the late nineteenth and early twentieth centuries. For a good understanding of Realist legal history, it is important to gain a better understanding of this body of theory from its social Darwinist beginnings, to its reformulation into scientific naturalism and Pragmatism, and up to contemporary insights into evolutionary theory. This second part will start with a comparison between Oliver Wendell Holmes and Herbert Spencer, to get a sense of the different varieties of nineteenth-century Social Darwinism. Then the "evolution" of this classic Darwinism into scientific naturalism and Pragmatism will be discussed. The middle section will conclude, finally, with a brief introduction of contemporary meme theory. Legal Realism presaged some central aspects of this theory, and it will provide a helpful framework to gain a better understanding of the Realist conception of history. Last but not least, in the third part of this chapter the historical work of the Realists will be described against the background of the preceding discussion. The chapter will be rounded off with a recap of the findings so far.

IN THE FOOTSTEPS OF OLIVER WENDELL HOLMES

In "A Realistic Jurisprudence—The Next Step," Karl Llewellyn acknowledged with regard to the new Realist jurisprudence that "Holmes' mind had traveled most of the road two generations back."[9] This certainly holds true for the Realist view on history, which found early expression in the work of Holmes. Holmes's historicism is succinctly conveyed in one of the most quoted passages from his magnum opus, *The Common Law*. On the first page of this work, Holmes described in protein form what most Legal Realists would come to believe about the development of law half a century later:

> The life of the law has not been logic: it has been experience. The felt necessities of the time, the prevalent moral and political theories, intuitions of public policy, avowed or unconscious, even the prejudices which judges share with their fellow-men, have had a good deal more to do than the syllogism in determining the rules by which men should be governed. The law embodies the story of a nation's development through many centuries, and it cannot be dealt with as if it contained only the axioms and corollaries of a book of mathematics.[10]

Unlike his contemporary Christopher Columbus Langdell, Holmes did not believe that the Common Law conformed to some a priori rational and logical design which was being progressively uncovered by legal science.[11] For Holmes the legal system resulted from the cumulative sedimentation of the concerns, ideas, and prejudices of earlier periods of legal development. The law, according to Holmes, embodied "the story of a nation's development through many centuries." Holmes did not conceive of this historical development as progress toward a fixed ideal, but as a contingent process shaped by the unique concerns of earlier generations. "The development of our law," Holmes observed, "has gone on for nearly a thousand years, like the development of a plant, each generation taking the inevitable next step, mind, like matter, simply obeying a law of spontaneous growth."[12] Hence, "instead of conceiving law as founded in science and its factual claims," intellectual historian John Diggins notes, "Holmes saw it as contextualist in that it embodied particular social practices and habits rather than reason, and thus that it signified not objective truth and morality but the adaptive processes of evolutionary growth."[13]

As a consequence, Holmes did not afford these deposits in the legal system from earlier time periods with any privileged status. The fact that a given legal rule or doctrine was of ancient origin was no cause for respect. "It is revolting to have no better reason for a rule of law," Holmes contended, "than that so it was laid down in the time of Henry IV. It is still more revolting if the grounds upon which it was laid down have vanished long since, and the rule simply persists from blind imitation of the past."[14] If the survivals from earlier periods no longer served a purpose, they should be discarded, a view he made more explicit in his speech "Learning and Science":

Holmes- learning + Science   Holmes (1913), 67-68

The law, so far as it depends on learning, is indeed, as it has been called, the government of the living by the dead. To a very considerable extent no doubt it is inevitable that the living should be so governed. The past gives us our vocabulary and fixes the limits of our imagination; we cannot get away from it. . . . But the present has a right to govern itself so far as it can; and it ought always to be remembered that historic continuity with the past is not a duty, it is only a necessity.[15]

Holmes thought of legal history as a discipline that could keep the legal profession from mindlessly enforcing rules from the past that were no longer adapted to the common interest. Legal history should uncover the original function of legal rules, and their later adaptations, in order to assess their continued value in current circumstances. If the past to a considerable extent ruled the present, then the study of history could liberate the present from the past. History, Holmes asserted, "sets us free and enables us to make up our minds dispassionately whether the survival which we are enforcing answers any new purpose when it has ceased to answer the old."[16]

This leaves the question of how, according to which criteria, Holmes believed people were to make up their minds about the future development of law. Holmes was ambiguous on this issue. In his optimistic moments Holmes showed faith in reason and science as final arbiters between different policy alternatives. Yet in his darker passages, Holmes seemed to opt for the view that "might is right," that the group which prevails in the Darwinian struggle for life will have the final say about the course of legal development. As to the first view, Holmes asserted in his famous essay "The Path of the Law" that "[f]or the rational study of the law the black-letter man may be the man of the present, but the man of the future is the man of statistics and the master of economics."[17] Holmes believed that the most rational way to decide between competing policy proposals was to ascertain, as far as possible, what the value of each proposal was, and at what cost they could be achieved. Thus, Holmes looked forward "to a time when the part played by history in the explanation of dogma shall be very small, and instead of ingenious research we shall spend our energy on a study of ends sought to be attained and the reasons for desiring them." This would involve legal scholarship in political economics in order "to consider and weigh the ends of legislation, the means of attaining them, and the cost."[18]

Hence, Holmes's historicist view that every generation understood and changed the law according to its own ideas and prejudices and that, consequently, there was no uniquely right answer to legal problems which transcended the historical and cultural context did not mean that it was folly to try to make law better. It was true, Holmes admitted, that "an evo-lutionist will hesitate to affirm universal validity for his social ideals, or for the principles which he thinks should be embodied in legislation." But that did not mean that "each of us may not try to set some corner of his world in the order of reason, or that all of us collectively should not aspire to carry reason as far as it will go throughout the whole domain." Even if an evolutionist knew "nothing about the absolute best in the cosmos" or "about a permanent best for men," then, according to Holmes, it would still be true that "a body of law is more rational and more civilized when every rule it contains is referred articulately and definitely to an end which it subserves, and when the grounds for desiring that end are stated or are ready to be stated in words."[19]

Yet, Holmes was not always so hopeful about the forces driving legal change. In his work the development of law was also regularly explained as the outcome of a bleak Darwinian struggle, a social battle red in tooth and claw in which the victors wrote their interests and preferences into law. Holmes did not believe that the interests of society coalesced in any-thing like a common interest, but that the nature of social life was strife and competition. "Th[e] tacit assumption of the solidarity of the interests of society is very common, but seems to us to be false," Holmes claimed. "The struggle for life, undoubtedly, is constantly putting the interests of men at variance with those of the lower animals," he explained, and that "strug-gle does not stop in the ascending scale with the monkeys, but is equally the law of human existence."[20] In Holmes's social Darwinist perspective, a detached analysis of the benefits and costs of alternative policy proposals did not decide which view would find expression in the legal system, but supreme power in the social struggle. Thus he could write to his friend Harold Laski: "I see no right in my neighbour to share my bread. I mean moral right of course—there is no pretense of any other, except so far as he in combination has power to take it. I always have said that the rights of a given crowd are what they will fight for."[21] Might truly was right from this point of view.

With his references to the "life struggle" Holmes did not engage in ec-centric social theorizing, but tapped in to a broad current of Darwinism in late nineteenth- and early twentieth-century American social thought. It is important to understand this Darwinist influence in social thought, because it provided the rough outlines of the Realist understanding of the evolution of the legal system. It is to this Darwinist current in American thought that we will turn to next.

THE EVOLUTION OF EVOLUTIONARY THEORY: FROM
SOCIAL DARWINISM TO SCIENTIFIC NATURALISM

Today, evolution is a loaded and suspect notion, especially when ap-plied to human affairs. Yet in the late nineteenth and early twentieth cen-tury, Charles Darwin's theory of evolution had an enormous influence in the United States, as had the Social Darwinism of Herbert Spencer—para-doxically conceived several years before Darwin first published his theory of evolution. Indeed, Holmes ranked the two Englishmen as the most influ-ential thinkers of his day when he wrote about Spencer that he doubted that "any writer of English except Darwin has done so much to affect our whole way of thinking about the universe."[22] This remark by Holmes was hardly an overstatement. The obsession with Darwin's theory of evolution is hard to exaggerate. As Stephen Jay Gould has noted, "The concept of evolution transformed human thought during the nineteenth century. Nearly every question in the life sciences was reformulated in its light. No idea was ever more widely used or misused."[23] In a similar vein, the English intellectual historian J. W. Burrow has described Darwin's theory of evolution as an "all-embracing intellectual fashion" in the nineteenth century, that "in a human context could be all things to all men."[24]

Exactly because Darwinism was so influential, however, the term does not explain very much about the thought of any individual thinker of the age. The pertinent question is always, what kind of Social Darwinism? Social Darwinism developed into a range of different varieties that started out from disparate assumptions and ended up with very dissimilar conclu-sions about social development. It is impossible to do justice to this com-plex history of Social Darwinism in the late nineteenth and early twentieth centuries within the context of this book. For the purpose of understanding the Realist approach to the history of law, however, it will suffice to high-light some key distinctions within classical Darwinist social theory and to show how they were developed by Pragmatist philosophers and Progressive social theorists into the notion of scientific naturalism. At the end of this section, finally, the overview of evolutionary theory will be extended to the present. More current insights into evolution may be helpful in showing how Legal Realism is different from the tired and superseded notions of functionalism in social theory it is usually associated with, and how Realism ties in with rather different strands of evolutionary theory that are still topi-cal today.

Oliver Wendell Holmes Versus Herbert Spencer

A crucial distinction in nineteenth-century evolutionary theory is the difference between what Burrow calls "individualist" and "collectivist" Social Darwinism. "[A]ll the disputes in Social Darwinism turn on what entities the competition is between," Burrow notes.[25] Did the life struggle mainly take place between the individuals of a given group, or was it primarily a struggle engaged in by groups or nations? The issue at stake in this dispute was whether the struggle for life should be conceived as an individualist struggle of all against all, or as a collective struggle between groups, which allowed for forms of social cooperation. A second distinction dealt with the relationship between human beings and their environment. At issue in this distinction was whether that environment was beyond human control or whether it was amenable to conscious alteration. This distinction essentially pertained to the place of the human intellect in the process of evolution. Was the struggle for life simply mindless adaptation to a given environment which was beyond the power of any organism to control? Or did human intelligence alter the evolutionary equation because it gave human beings the power to consciously change and manipulate their environment to suit their purposes? The implications of these distinctions can be illustrated by comparing the classical Social Darwinism of Herbert Spencer with the evolutionism of Oliver Wendell Holmes, who were opposed on these two key issues. Spencer advocated an individualist version of Social Darwinism within an environment impervious to human reconstruction, while Holmes—albeit halfheartedly—adopted a collectivist variety of Social Darwinism that allowed for the possibility that human beings consciously affect their environment through intelligent action.

Spencer's social theory started out from a Malthusian assumption of population pressure. According to Spencer, this pressure had created strain to procure subsistence for a greater number of people and had stimulated the development of skill, intelligence, and self-control. Moreover, it had forced people out of a solitary and primitive condition of predatory life into a civilized social state of interdependence. This setting was essentially given and unchangeable: "The social state is a necessity. The conditions to greatest happiness under that state are fixed. Our characters are the only things not fixed. They then must be moulded into fitness for the conditions. And all our moral teaching and discipline must have for its object to hasten this process."[26] The way to hasten the process of moral improvement involved doing very little. The best way to serve moral progress was noninterference and letting nature run its course. Interference with the harsh struggle for life would only impede the natural processes through which human nature was perfected. Left to their own devices, people would slowly but surely adapt to existing conditions and finally develop to reach moral perfection.

Morality, in this view, was nothing more than adaptation to existing conditions, while immorality was simply ill adjustment to the given circumstances. All evil resulted from the maladaptation of human beings to their new social state—a state to which they would be adjusting for a long time to come. This process was a necessity. "Instead of civilization being artificial," Spencer argued it was "a part of nature; all of a piece with the development of an embryo or the unfolding of a flower." The modification that humankind was undergoing, he maintained, was the "result of a law underlying the whole organic creation."[27] This modification was by no means a painless process. It literally involved the suffering and death of the ill-adjusted specimens of the human species:

> He on whom his own stupidity, or vice, or idleness, entails loss of life, must, in the generalizations of philosophy, be classed with the victims of weak viscera or malformed limbs. In his case, as in the others, there exists a fatal non-adaptation; and it matters not in the abstract whether it be a moral, an intellectual, or a corporeal one. Beings thus imperfect are Nature's failures, and are recalled by her when found to be such.[28]

Spencer
(1892)
203

Thus, morality was an integral part of the evolutionary process, according to Spencer. Indeed, he called it "Moral Physiology."[29] Government intervention to alleviate the pain and stress inherent in this process of adaptation would only retard the mechanism of moral improvement. If people were simply left to fend for themselves, then the harsh struggle for life would eventually mold them to existing conditions and society would reach a happy equilibrium without the need for contrived, government-imposed practices.

Oliver Wendell Holmes was often critical of the social theory of Spencer. Spencer's Social Darwinism had taken America by storm at the end of the nineteenth century and had made a marked impression on American judicial opinion. Although Holmes was not an ardent proponent of social reform, he argued strongly against Spencerian judicial arguments opposing social legislation. For instance, in his dissenting opinion to the landmark case *Lochner v. New York*, in which the U.S. Supreme Court struck down a New York law regulating the working hours of bakers on the grounds that it violated the bakers' "freedom of contract," a freedom believed to be implied in the due process clause of the Fourteenth Amendment. This "freedom of

Holmes

contract" was one of the principal legal doctrines through which the courts sought to impose the kind of laissez-faire regime on American society that Spencer's Social Darwinism had called for. Thus, in his dissenting opinion Holmes argued famously that the "Fourteenth Amendment does not enact Mr. Herbert Spencer's Social Statistics." It would be a mistake to see Holmes as a critic of Social Darwinist ideology on the basis of this famous dissent, however. Holmes was more accurately a critic of the Spencerian individualist conception of Social Darwinism.

Like Spencer, Holmes believed that society was characterized by the struggle for life, but he did not believe that that struggle was, or should be, confined to competition between individuals. While for Spencer and his followers collective action by majorities through the legislative process, or by labor unions in the economic realm, constituted an abridgment of the life struggle, for Holmes it was merely its natural extension. Holmes, in other words, was a collectivist Social Darwinist. Competition, he believed, was something that went on between groups of people as well as between individuals. Thus, in his dissenting opinion to *Plant v. Woods*, Holmes claimed that the strike was "a lawful instrument in the universal struggle for life." In a similar vein, he argued in his dissent to *Vegelahn v. Guntner* that the struggle for life was "not limited to struggles between persons of the same class competing for the same end" but involved "all conflicts of temporal interests." Hence, laborers trying to push their demands by unified action were not engaged in the disruption of the evolutionary process. They were as much engaged in a natural and legitimate form of conflict as two merchants competing in the marketplace. According to Holmes, it was plain "from the slightest consideration of practical affairs, or the most superficial reading of industrial history, that free competition means combination." This was true for capital and labor alike. Consequently, organized labor unions had the same freedom that combined capital had "to support their interests by argument, persuasion, and the bestowal or refusal of those advantages which they otherwise lawfully control." In the struggle for survival human beings had turned to organization and combination as a strategy to cope with the pressures of their circumstances. This was a tendency that Holmes thought not only beneficial but also inevitable, "unless the fundamental axioms of society, and even the fundamental conditions of life, are to be changed."

The other element that Holmes added to the evolutionary equation was human volition. Whereas Spencer thought of the evolutionary process as something that people had to endure passively until they were shaped and conditioned by nature to fit with existing circumstances, Holmes believed that conscious human effort, to a point, could change the very conditions that Spencer believed people were fated to adapt to. In short, Spencer was fatalistic about human progress, with the discipline of nature shaping human character, while Holmes was voluntaristic, with human beings shaping the conditions of life through intelligent effort. "All that any man contributes to the world," he argued, "is the intelligence which directs a change in the place of matter."[30] Holmes did not believe the Common Law was the result of some external evolutionary process, but that it was the accumulated residue of the intentional efforts of earlier generations. For Spencer the endeavor to improve the circumstances of life was futile, if not downright harmful. Holmes, however, held that social institutions were the product of conscious human drive. "The mode in which the inevitable comes to pass," he believed, "is through effort." Consequently, there was "every reason for doing all that we can to make a future such as we desire."[31]

At the same time, however, Holmes often expressed a distaste for sentimental humanitarianism, as well as a deep pessimism about the efficacy of social reform. Thus, Holmes wrote to his friend Harold Laski: "I look at men through Malthus's glasses—as like flies—here swept away by pestilence—there multiplying unduly and paying for it. I think your morals (I am struck by the delicacy of your feeling) are not the last word but only a check for varying intensity upon force, which seems so far to me likely to remain the ultimate as far as I can look ahead."[32] Holmes often interpreted reformist legislation as a product of such social force, rather than as a result of benign sentiment. For Holmes reformist legislation frequently boiled down to a mere rearrangement of the social burdens and benefits to the advantage of the most powerful group in society—the majority. "The fact is that legislation in this country, as well as elsewhere, is empirical," Holmes maintained. "It is necessarily made a means by which a body, having the power, put burdens which are disagreeable to them on the shoulders of somebody else."[33] According to Holmes, there was only a certain quantum of wealth to go around in society, and directing resources to improve one area of social life always implied extracting resources from another. "The social reformers of today seem to me so far to forget," Holmes remarked, "that we can no more get something for nothing by legislation than we can by mechanics as to be satisfied if the bill to be paid for their improvements is not presented in a lump sum. Interstitial detriments that may far outweigh the benefit promised are not bothered about."[34]

Scientific Naturalism

These differences in the Social Darwinism of Spencer and Holmes to a certain extent reflected the direction into which Darwinist social theory had been developing. If Spencer had articulated the classic version of Social Darwinism, Holmes's thought reflected the changes and revisions Darwinist social theory had undergone since the mid-nineteenth century. Lester Ward, one of the first American sociologists, already expounded an evolutionary social theory in 1883 which gained currency among American academics and diverted from Spencerian Social Darwinism roughly along the same lines as Holmes's evolutionary views.[35] More important, however, was the work of the Pragmatist philosophers, who showed that the theory of evolution had an alternative application in the social realm to Spencer's conservative suggestions. In the beginning of the twentieth century, as Edward Purcell has argued, Darwinism developed into the more benevolent approach of "scientific naturalism." Under the influence of Lester Ward, William James, and John Dewey, Purcell notes, American social thinkers began to define evolutionism as "broadly humanitarian and democratic."[36] In its collective struggle with the environment, humanity was progressively understood to be cooperative, sympathetic, and prone to intelligent control of its life circumstances, rather than competitive and mutually hostile. It is important to stress how very different this evolutionism is from the kind of social theory that is usually associated with Social Darwinism.

What the Pragmatists stressed above all was the importance of human intelligence for the process of evolution. For Spencer, evolution had been an impersonal, cosmic process slowly inching humanity toward a predetermined end of blissful adjustment to the fixed circumstances of life. The Pragmatists, however, did not believe that humanity evolved by this slow and mindless process of natural selection. In the struggle for life, humanity had developed intelligence, and this had radically changed the evolutionary process. Thus, William James observed that human beings were not merely passive witnesses of the natural order:

> The knower is an actor, and coefficient of the truth on one side, whilst on the other he registers the truth which he helps create. Mental interests, hypotheses, postulates, so far as they are bases for human action—action which to a great extent transforms the world—help to make the truth which they declare. In other words, there belongs to mind, from its birth upward, a spontaneity, a vote. It is in the game, and not a mere looker-on; and its judgments of the *should-be*, its ideals, cannot be peeled off from the body of the cogitandum as if they were excrescences, or meant, at most, survival.[37]

And thus, John Dewey criticized theories like Spencer's for locating reason and purpose in the natural process, rather than in the actions of humanity: "[I]ntelligence is not an outside power presiding supremely but statically over the desires and efforts of man, but is a method of adjustment of capacities and conditions within specific situations."[38] Consequently, Dewey derided Spencer's "philosophy of the fixed environment and the static goal" as an "animistic survival."[39]

This shift in the interpretation of the evolutionary process heralded in the new scientific naturalism that provided an analytical framework for many of the Realists. The concept of evolution was developed in directions, radically different from Spencerian Social Darwinism. If in the nineteenth century, as Purcell puts it, "many intellectuals still placed Darwinian terms in an essentially static conceptual framework, one that assumed a comprehensive religious or rationalistic ordering principle," then in the beginning of the twentieth century they began to understand Darwinism in a fully naturalistic perspective, which "saw change as given, order as accidental, process as nonteleological, behavior as adaptive, values as experiential, and absolutes of any kind as superstitions."[40] This was a different kind of Darwinism. As Louis Menand pointed out in a recent study, it was a kind of Darwinism "that was openly hostile to the two most prominent Darwinists of the time, Herbert Spencer and Thomas Huxley" and that "had nothing in common with the thought of people like William Graham Sumner, or with the eugenics movement."[41] For James and Dewey, Menand claims, there was no progress along a pre-given and immutable path. Progress depended on the caprice of creativity. A new idea was "a chance outgrowth, a lucky variant that catches on because it hooks people up with their circumstances in ways that they find useful."[42]

As an explanatory model for the development of law, this naturalistic approach merged an understanding of legal development as something broadly determined by the necessities of a given environment with an understanding of the cultural and historical contingency of the responses provided to cope with those necessities. Legal change was determined, in other words, by the interplay of the functional demands of a constantly changing world and the historically and culturally determined theoretical frameworks used to understand and deal with those demands. In their application of this naturalistic perspective, the Realists often treated legal rules and concepts as things that possessed a certain degree of autonomy, as things with a life of their own. The term that best captures this sense of independent agency is the notion of survival. Survivals were concepts or rules or principles that had once served a useful purpose, that were still valued as essential parts of the law, but that no longer fit with new circumstances and had become redundant and dysfunctional.

The Realists did not develop a theoretical framework to express this last idea in a more systematic and elegant manner. Yet they were groping toward something that today would be called meme theory. Daniel Dennett, one of the most ardent defenders of meme theory, recently described William James as a "memeticist ahead of his time," who applied quite similar ideas "long before anybody talked of memes and memetics."[43] The same could be said about Oliver Wendell Holmes. When Holmes's view of legal history was discussed earlier, we also came very close to modern-day meme theory. Holmes, remember, complained about the staying power of legal rules that no longer served a purpose and simply survived through blind imitation. With this insight Holmes stumbled on what a meme theorist would call the replicator power of ideas. One of the most important rules in meme theory, in the words of Dennett, is that "replication is not necessarily for the good of anything: replicators flourish that are good at . . . replicating—for whatever reason!"[44] Holmes almost expressed this insight. Note that in Holmes's argument the primary units of analysis, the things that are doing the surviving, are not political and legal systems, nor the citizens within those political and legal systems, but the individual doctrines, rules, and concepts themselves. Holmes also suggested a mechanism through which these ideas gained their remarkable longevity. The eminence of the tried and tested passed down from time immemorial, the prestige of the venerable rule, these were what ensured the continued replication of "survivals" and the rejection of alternatives. This is consonant with meme theory. As Dennett points out, memes often possess properties "that tend to make their own replication more likely by disabling or pre-empting the environmental forces that would tend to extinguish them."[45] Essentially, this is what Holmes's venerable legal rules and concepts were doing when they advertised their inescapable necessity, underpinned by their continued survival through the ages. They carried the implicit warning that it would be self-conceited to presume any modern alternative could improve on the prudent solutions from the past. You tampered with the tried and tested at your own peril. Holmes did not have the language of meme theory available to express these ideas, of course, but he did foreshadow some of the notions that would become central to meme theory.

This leads to very different conclusions with respect to law and society. Instead of producing fit poli*ties*, evolutionary pressures should rather be thought of as producing fit poli*cies*, that is, poli*cies* that are good at getting themselves adopted and replicated, regardless of whether they benefit the poli*ty*. This is all about determining the most appropriate level for analysis. Where do evolutionary pressures make themselves felt? The answer Pragmatists and Legal Realists first considered, but which subsequently lay dormant until meme theorists revived it, was that those pressures operated at the level of ideas and concepts. This analysis follows a logic very different from the evolutionary functionalism that is usually imputed to Pragmatist and Realist social theory.

REALIST LEGAL HISTORY

In this section some actual examples of Realist legal history will be discussed. To the Realists, scientific naturalism suggested an understanding of the development of law that was dependent on both social and economic conditions, which were ceaselessly changing, and the conceptualizations of those conditions, which were constantly being modified, reformed, and superseded in an erratic process of adaptation. There was reciprocal influence between these two realms, of course. Changes in social conditions effected changes in the intellectual frameworks developed to deal with those conditions, and efforts to manage the circumstances of life, in turn, altered these circumstances. As Legal Realist Max Lerner observed: "Instead of positing an antithesis between dynamic economic activity and a static law, it is truer to see the growth of each interwoven with the other and conditioning the other."[46] The evolutionary adaptationism of the Realists should not be mistaken for a mechanical historical determinism, in other words. People had elbow room in the way they coped with their changing environment. Moreover, extant legal rules and concepts could promote their continued survival for reasons other than their appropriateness and relevance to the given conditions. Neither did these attenuating insights lead the Realists to conclude that it was therefore unimportant or uninformative to research what possibilities and alternatives were available and what their respective consequences would be, however. It was still imperative to gauge the social and economic realities and understand how legal doctrine related to them.

The purpose of this functionalist aspect of Realism was primarily legal critique. Thus, the Realist Walter Nelles noted in a pair of articles on the development of legal understanding that law perennially experienced difficulties with changing circumstances. The law was prone to "lag" behind social developments and always contained survivals—or "usuals" as Nelles referred to them—that were no longer adapted to the social reality they were devised to regulate.

> When they learn facts which cannot be reconciled with established conceptions of the physical universe, scientists reject the conceptions, not the facts. . . . The plan of the constitution or nature of law gets revised less quickly. For jurists resist awareness that one-time true enough conceptions lose their truth when clear observers find that they no longer fit the facts. Yet that certitudes are always decaying and getting superseded is obvious almost anywhere in human experience, if looked for.[47]

This was one of the stock arguments in the Realist critique of nineteenth-century legal doctrine. In his set of articles Nelles tried to show that since the Middle Ages, with many pendulum swings from the strict to the lax and back, jurists in England and later America had slowly been moving away from the notion that law was something supernatural that had to be strictly observed and toward a more relaxed attitude with respect to the interpretation of rules and precedents. These contractions and extensions of the interpretive freedom of jurists resulted from the social conditions: "permission of departure from paramount legal-moral obligation is forced into the judicial mores, and its limits widened or narrowed, by pressures for interests moralized by other classes in conditions in which their power approaches dominance in society."[48]

The objective of this type of analysis was reform. Indeed, that was the main purpose of Nelles's argument. "With release from the fetters of tradition," he believed it was certain "that many legal ways of almost undisputed unreasonableness would cease to be followed, and probable that reasonableness would become an object of study instead of guess."[49] His overview of the waxing and waning of juristic freedom was more subversive for the idea that there was a timeless, transcendental body of justice that needed to be strictly adhered to than for the notion that legal rules were primarily generalizations of contemporary morality and public policy that could be diverged from. Judges had taken liberties with the law before without any disastrous consequences.

Historicist analysis did not only focus on changing real-world conditions but also pertained to the intellectual climate of the historical period. Early on, the proto-Realist Thomas Reed Powell expressed this notion eloquently in his field of constitutional law: "We often hear that the lawyers have governed America. But it is equally true that America has governed the lawyers. The ideas that lawyers have expressed in the legislature, at the bar and on the bench have not sprung from any mysterious source whose hiding place is revealed only to those who read books in sheep bindings."[50] The intellectual climate was reflected in legal doctrine. This notion also rings through in the way the Realist Max Lerner conceived of the working of the Supreme Court. "The Court works within a cultural and institutional framework which the justices share with their fellow citizens," he claimed. "They live in and are sworn to preserve a society which is the end-product of a historical growth but is also changing under their very fingers." The Supreme Court, Lerner believed, worked "in a world of ideas which justices share with their fellow-men." And these ideas, he asserted, "are social products and are affected by changes in the social and economic structure."[51]

The Realist Walton Hamilton wrote several articles on the history of legal thought which were aimed at criticizing some supposedly immutable doctrine handed down from the past. In "The Ancient Maxim of Caveat Emptor," Hamilton sought to show that the principle of caveat emptor, or "buyer beware," was not the unchanging and time-honored maxim it was generally believed to be but could boast only a recent historical lineage. Hamilton's historical investigation disclosed that the principle of caveat emptor was unknown in Roman law; that it was foreign to medieval customs of trade, which centered on strict quality standards for sellers and producers set by lords, towns, and guilds; and that it was absent in the sixteenth and seventeenth centuries, which saw medieval custom develop into a royal system of quality standards. Only in the course of the eighteenth century did the maxim gain respectability, Hamilton claimed, when a burgeoning commercial class became suspicious of government supervision of trade and manufacturing and when rational individualism spread to the detriment of central authority. The doctrine of caveat emptor had received scant mention in the legal literature up to that point and had found support in only a handful of ambiguous cases. Yet, Hamilton claimed, "the words were there, ready to bear the ideas of a later age; and interpretation, the great creator, was to prove equal to the occasion."[52] This happened in the nineteenth century, when it was invested with an individualist ethos and judges discovered "that *caveat emptor* sharpened wits, taught self-reliance, made a man—an economic man—out of the buyer, and served well its two masters, business and justice."[53]

Hence, the antiquity of the precept of caveat emptor was an invention. Yet it was an invention that had all the trappings of a successful meme. It donned a faux eminence with great effectiveness. Consider Hamilton's explanation of the success of the upstart maxim:

> An adage was never fitted more neatly to the part than *caveat emptor*; it is among many excellent examples, the ideal legal maxim. It is brief, concise, of meaning all compact. Its terms are too broad to be pent up within the narrow confines of rules of law; they are an easy focus for judicial thought, a principle to be invoked when the going is difficult, a guide to be followed amid the baffling uncertainties of litigation. The phrase seems to epitomise centuries of experience; it is written in the language of Rome, the great law-giver; it comes with the repute of the classics and with the prestige of authority.[54]

The deceit worked exceptionally well. When lawyers invoked caveat emptor and criticized the imposition of quality standards as a departure from that time-honored principle, Hamilton pointed out, they were probably attacking a legal approach to commerce which was much older and more eminent than caveat emptor. By exposing caveat emptor and showing that it was not a venerable and timeless principle, Hamilton sought to undermine a basic tenet of nineteenth-century Classical legal thought and pave the way for social reform.

Llewellyn, perhaps, produced the most sophisticated examples of Realist historical analysis. In some excellent doctrinal studies, he gave expression to the Realist conception of legal history. Two detailed sets of articles by Llewellyn on the genesis of warranty of quality and on the historical development of sales law are pregnant with insights into the factors determining legal change. Although they are largely outdated as works of legal analysis, they deserve attention here for the light they throw on the Realist understanding of legal history and as a reminder that the Realists were not purveyors of a sterile historical materialism. In the first of this quartet of articles, ironically, Llewellyn denied that he was engaging in history. He claimed that his study should be understood as "an appeal to history" instead. The reasons for this appeal are telling: "It is a sad commentary on our dogmatics that sales cases over a hundred and fifty years and more than fifty jurisdictions have been treated as if they floated free of time, place and person. Whereas it is time, place, person and circumstance which give them meaning."[55]

In the first of his two articles, "On Warranty of Quality, and Society," Llewellyn claims that he set out to test the hypotheses that "case law reflects society" and that "case-law affects society" with respect to the issue of warranty. The general trend in the development of warranty of quality, he conjectured, was from the placing of risk in the buyer when trade is occasional, face-to-face trade with the "wandering peddler and the horse-trader," to a shift of legal obligation on the seller and producer of goods in a modern capitalist society when trade becomes settled and future business becomes important. Llewellyn sought to investigate these hypotheses by looking at the way in which warranty evolved in the developed commercial setting of England around 1800, by how it was adopted in the then predominantly agricultural scene of the United States, and finally, by how it evolved in the United States during the period of industrial expansion after the Civil War. However, although there had been several historical studies to explore these issues, Llewellyn admitted he was unable to put them together into a single story. Sales law had developed in such widely divergent ways in the different contexts of the individual United States and England that it was impossible to synthesize the studies into a coherent picture. History, Llewellyn asserted, involved "time, place, background, present circumstance, and particular men." Since these varied so considerably in the respective jurisdictions in the period from 1800 to 1935, every one of them presented a separate historical problem, and no general story emerged.[56]

With Llewellyn's sketch of the American scene up to the Civil War, an important reason for this variety becomes apparent. In a variation on the famous "frontier thesis" of the Progressive historian Frederick Jackson Turner, Llewellyn described the United States as a country that covered the whole spectrum of socioeconomic development, ranging from trapping and subsistence farming at the western frontier to an urban, industrialized setting at the eastern seaboard[57]:

> At the westing American frontier, there is factorage trade: blankets, rifles, whiskey, gaudiness, tobacco; with furs, especially, coming East. Shortly behind the frontier, farms isolated and, save for river routes, hampered beyond present understanding in freight-transportation; and largely self-contained communities visited by occasional peddlers, wandering shoe-makers and the like. At occasional trade-centers or power-sites, some small-scale manufacturing, dealers who took and gave long credit, served by water or by proud privileged carters. Back of this again, the "settled" seaboard, with some importing, with export centers for such raws as reached them, growing manufacturing, and the still cobbled and slough-streeted metropolitan magnificence of Philadelphia, New York, Boston, Baltimore, and New Orleans. The basic picture did not greatly change even with the first canals, save that the discrepancy between extremes increased as the settled East settled further in the direction of more modern capitalism. But certainly before the close of the Civil War the combination of power-factory, technical advance, natural resources uncovering, expansion of railroad mileage and unity, the Republican party, the tariff, and the general incorporation laws, set the stage nationally for widening a seller's mercantile obligation.[58]

Because there was such disparity of conditions and such heterogeneity of commercial activity, sales law was bound to develop in different directions in different jurisdictions. The stage of development of commerce in a certain locality determined the kinds of fact-situations that showed up in court cases, and it would be surprising, Llewellyn observed, "if horses and stomachs do not show influence divergent from that of blankets in bales and cargoes of wheat or mahogany." Moreover, the differences in legal development were compounded by the idiosyncratic personal influence of the judges: "With judges raised now on the seaboard, now in the hills, with cases involving now a buggy, now 187 bales of hemp, with force of personality or political prestige behind now one type, now another, of man on the appellate bench, kaleidoscopic possibilities open—and are realized."[59] In the end, however, modernization became a unifying force in American society and drove toward a widening of the seller's obligation.

Even when the emergence of a developed industrial capitalism during and after the Civil War encouraged a shift in obligation from the buyer to the seller and producer of goods, the development of legal doctrine was by no means straightforward. The American state in which new economic circumstances first made themselves felt and which, consequently, functioned as a trailblazer in American commercial law was New York. With the growth of industrial manufacturing in New York, business relationships steadied, and contracts for the future delivery of goods became common practice in the business world. This situation called out for quality standards of raw and semi-raw materials and for the producer's and seller's legal obligation to live up to those standards. It was the sale of iron products that epitomized this new situation for Llewellyn and which, according to him, made "clay of the law of contract-to-sell." Yet, whereas iron trade pushed New York law in the direction of seller and producer obligation, the judges, according to Llewellyn, had difficulty perceiving this trend: "The courts undershoot here, overshoot there, go off the mark to right or left. The impulse seems, however, unmistakable. It lies in the facts. How quickly or surely the relevant judges react to the impulse, lies in their background, or in accidents of temperament."[60] Thus, for Llewellyn the influence of socioeconomic conditions on law was not simple and direct—with the law simply registering every social and economic change. The effect of social change on the law was mediated by the judiciary and by social groups trying to bring about legal change. Hence, he concluded that "whereas over the long haul, the march of conditions can and does make itself felt upon private commercial doctrine, the process of this incidence of underlying conditions may be muddy and confused, over a full century; it may differ widely from period to period, from place to place, from judge to judge."[61] This view on legal change was also expressed in Llewellyn's historical overview of American sales law. There again we find the supposition that "packed into this small sector of the law is the course of [American] history over a century and a half."[62] And there again we find the assumption that although conditions press sales law in a certain direction, judges do not always sense the push of the facts. In sales law, according to Llewellyn, this came out with more clarity than in other fields because the historical changes that commercial conditions had undergone were "so easy, so familiar, so open to the eye" that they provided a conspicuous baseline against which the adjustments of law were easy to gauge.[63] "[W]hen the facts run clearly and repetitively on a single pattern," Llewellyn maintained, "*their* pressures become so predictable that one can observe which judge is sensitive to them, and which not; one can then *observe* doctrine when it produces outlandish results attributable in reason to no other cause."[64] This highlighted the role of doctrine in the interplay between law and society. That the pressures of the facts could influence law meant that they were efficacious independently of legal doctrine. Yet that the "fact pressures, if they can be canalized and kept moderately repetitive, give us some fair quantum of wise results despite ourselves," according to Llewellyn, did not mean that doctrine was unimportant: "*Unless* the *stock* intellectual equipment is apt, it takes extra art or intuition to get proper results with it. Whereas *if* the stock intellectual equipment is apt, it takes extra ineptitude to get sad results with it."[65]

It is important here to note that for Llewellyn the historical facts remained independent from the "intellectual equipment" used to understand and deal with those facts. As a result, he also remained confident that it was possible to compare different legal doctrines on their ability to deal effectively with the facts in their field of application, that it was possible, in other words, to make an informed judgment about the relative success of competing legal doctrines to deal with a given set of historical conditions. This separation of fact and theory will become problematic in the CLS approach, as we shall see in the next chapter, and constitutes a major difference between Legal Realist and CLS history.

CONCLUSION

At the beginning of this chapter, the charge of Panglossianism was introduced as a common objection to the Realist conception of history with its functionalist and adaptationist overtones. Much of this chapter has been directed toward dispelling this critique. The employment of such considerations as "adaptation" and "functionality" in historical analysis did not lead the Realists to assume some near-perfect functional purity for the current legal system. For them the legal system was not at all perfect but replete with flaws and failings. There are several reasons for this disparity.

To begin with, it is simply a misconception that an evolutionary process, by definition, should lead to functional perfection. Consider, for instance, what Janet Radcliffe Richards has recently written with respect to Darwinian theory. Once people gave up the notion that the natural world was the work of an omniscient Creator, she observes, and realized that organisms might have developed through a mechanism of natural selection, "what increasingly impressed biologists was the extent to which organisms turned out—despite being miracles of coordination and functioning—to be riddled with absurdities that no self-respecting designer would have allowed as far as the drawing board." The reason for this is simple, according to Richards: "Darwinian evolution does not work by planning from scratch with some end in view."[66] On the contrary, in evolutionary biology, just as in law, you are where you are. Organisms come with the baggage of their historical genesis and contain many elements that have developed to meet challenges which have long since disappeared. In the first chapter we introduced Joas's conception of "situated creativity" to convey this same notion in the realm of human affairs, the notion of being constrained by the world as you find it, while at the same time possessing the power to transcend the social and natural conditions of your environment with acts of sheer creativity.

The idea that evolution never involves "planning from scratch" also ties in with the notion of "historical lag" and "survival." Indeed, these ideas are not some quirky Realist preoccupation, but a central aspect of contemporary evolutionary theory. Dennett has popularized a new phrase for this notion, the QWERTY phenomenon. QWERTY refers to the top row of alphabetic keys on a typewriter keyboard. This was once a rational and functional arrangement of the alphabet on the keyboard. The keys were arranged to avoid the jamming of old-fashioned mechanical typewriters. Yet, since the development of the computer, the purpose of the QWERTY keyboard has disappeared. The QWERTY organization of the keyboard now simply lingers on because it is what people have learned and are used to, even though other, more rational systems to organize a keyboard are available.[67] QWERTY functionality is an important concept in evolutionary theory and explains why functional perfection is an unlikely outcome of adaptation. For adaptation involves not only introducing new tools to solve new problems but also leaving behind old machinery that was developed to deal with problems that are no longer there.

Finally, the idea that the notion of adaptationism necessarily leads to an assumption of near perfection in the legal system does not take into account the possibility that it might be things other than the legal system that are getting "fit" in the struggle for survival. There is no reason why the legal system as a whole should be taken as the primary unit of analysis, as the entity doing the adapting. The aspect of Legal Realism that resembles meme theory suggests that individual rules and concepts, rather than the entire system, are the main focus of the evolutionary process. Indeed, from the perspective of meme theory, legal rules and concepts may spread regardless of their benefit to society and thrive despite their deleterious effects. This puts to rest any presupposition that functionalism assumes a high degree of functional perfection, as well as any notion that functionalism must therefore lead to a conservative acceptance of whatever already exists.

The notion of "survivals," or "usuals," was quite central to the Realist analysis of law. This idea gave a twist to the Realist understanding of functionalism and evolutionary adaptationism because it suggested that adaptation was something that applied to such elementary aspects of law as individual concepts, categories, and rules, rather than to law as an integrated social system. The consequences of this difference are far-reaching. The idea that concepts or procedures are adapted to survive in the legal tradition is a notion that leads to very different conclusions than a holistic view of law as a social system aimed at keeping society as a whole going. The first invites a type of legal scholarship that is skeptical of accepted doctrine and willing to scrutinize any aspect of the law. The second leads to an assumption that most aspects of the law must be adapted to the survival of society; otherwise society would not have survived. This view drives toward the acceptance of the status quo and critical examination of only minor aspects of the legal regime at most. The Realists were unrecognized pioneers of the first view but have been dismissed as representatives of the second view.

CHAPTER THREE

The Wealth of Historicism: Legal History in the Critical Mold

Our little systems have their day;
They have their day and cease to be
—Alfred Tennyson[1]

Darwin did not change the islands, but only people's opinion of them. That was how important mere opinions used to be in the era of great big brains.

Mere opinions, in fact, were as likely to govern people's actions as hard evidence, and were subject to sudden reversals as hard evidence could never be. So the Galápagos Islands could be hell in one moment and heaven in the next, and Julius Caesar could be a statesman in one moment and a butcher in the next, and Ecuadorian paper money could be traded for food, shelter and clothing in one moment and line the bottom of a birdcage in the next, and the universe could be created by God Almighty in one moment and by a big explosion in the next—and on and on.

—Kurt Vonnegut[2]

In his historiography *That Noble Dream: The "Objectivity Question" and the American Historical Profession,* the historian Peter Novick concludes that at present there is no longer a consensus among historians on the standards of historical research, nor is there any agreement on whether an authoritative answer can still be provided to the central "objectivity question." The state of the historical profession is as described in the last verse of the Book of Judges, Novick claims dramatically: "In those days there was no king in Israel; every man did that which was right in his own eyes."[3] One of the groups instrumental in chasing the king out of Israel and destabilizing history as a coherent discipline, according to Novick, is the Critical Legal Studies (CLS) movement. CLS has blazed a trail for antiobjectivist tendencies in American academic thought, and historical analysis has been "a key weapon in the CLS armory." Indeed, CLS itself is involved in a "project of relativizing and delegitimizing legal consciousness through historical analysis," Novick notes, a project which has gone "considerably farther than that of the Realists."[4]

This acknowledgment of the importance of CLS historical research beyond the confines of legal scholarship is quite remarkable, of course. Yet such an accolade by a historian of history is not so curious considering the extent of CLS efforts in the field of historical inquiry. Unlike Legal Realism, the CLS movement has produced a great deal of historical research, and Critical Legal scholars have been exceptionally self-conscious about the wider implications of their understanding of history. There are many discussions of history in the CLS literature, discussions that probe such questions as how legal history should be approached and what significance a more sophisticated historical understanding can have for law and legal scholarship.

The attraction of legal history for CLS, above anything else, is the aspect of historicism and its critical uses. Frank Ankersmit, one of the most prominent theoreticians of history, recently commented that historicism is "one of the most caustic intellectual acids that has ever been prepared by Western civilization. The historism of Nietzsche's *The Genealogy of Morals* and of Foucault's later writings offers striking illustrations. Religion, Metaphysics, tradition, truth—all of them proved to be soluble in the acid of historism."[5] In his encyclopedic study, Ankersmit notes that this is a recurrent notion and that there was already a "crisis of historism" at the end of the nineteenth and the beginning of the twentieth century, a crisis which found its way into the work of the Realists as we saw in the Chapter 2.[6] This historicist sentiment was then revived at the end of the twentieth century by Postmodernist theorists. Indeed, Postmodernism "did historism all over again," as Ankersmit puts it.[7] CLS, of course, fits squarely within this Postmodernist revival of historicism.

It should come as no surprise, then, that CLS scholars in their historical studies often claim to build on their Realist predecessors. Notably, Critical Legal scholars embrace two aspects of Realist legal history: (1) their recognition of the historicity of legal notions, concepts, and rules; and (2) their use of history as an instrument of critique. To begin with the first, Critical scholars have taken up the historicist understanding of law and have analyzed the legal system as an institution situated in a contingent historical context. Law, from this historicist perspective, is understood to be radically tied to time and place. The way law is conceived and applied is largely dependent on the shared conceptions, meanings, and ideas of a certain society in a certain time period. All this is more or less consistent with the Realist understanding of history. CLS, however, has rejected the functionalist underpinnings of the Realist brand of historicism. It has not adopted the Legal Realist claim that social and economic conditions shape and direct the legal system, that law is determined in part by existing social and economic realities. Indeed, CLS scholars have argued that influence runs in the opposite direction. They claim that the legal system and legal thought, by providing people with their basic conceptions and ideas about social and economic relations, help to create the very social and economic realities that the Realists thought were shaping law.

With this focus on the primacy of ideas and the centrality of conceptual paradigms, CLS ties in with the contemporary trend in intellectual history exemplified by such historians as Bernard Bailyn, Gordon Wood, and John Pocock.[8] John Diggins has remarked that this strand in intellectual history is an approach in which "the historian no longer takes reality for his object but instead its varying representations, for reality owes its existence to those who conceive it, rightly or wrongly."[9] In fact, some Critical scholars would even fret about Diggins's talk of things being represented "rightly or wrongly," because such qualifications have become suspect in a thorough-going historicist conception. As a result, CLS has been highly critical of the adaptationist view of the Legal Realists. The emphasis of historical research should be on the conceptual paradigms that mediated reality, not on the elusive "real" social and economic conditions that supposedly informed those paradigms. At any rate, Critical scholars claim, historical scholarship has shown no clear relationship between socioeconomic and legal developments. Therefore, Realist adaptationism is not a tenable position anyway.

Second, CLS has adopted the Realist notion that history can be used as an instrument of critique. CLS takes the implications of historicism much further than Legal Realism did, however. Where the Legal Realists mainly sought to undermine the idea that legal rules could be timeless and unchanging, Critical Legal scholars claim that historicism undermines the rationalizing enterprise of mainstream legal scholarship altogether. The main attraction of history for Critical Legal scholars, in other words, is its ability to expose the vacillating and inconstant nature of legal arrangements. History provides CLS with an antidote against attempts to provide law with durable foundations, with timeless supports. Thus, Mark Kelman observes that "Critical scholars often use a certain style of historicist inquiry to remind us how unlikely it is that things we may take for granted will always be so, because we can so readily see that things once taken for granted have hardly proven indispensable."[10] In a similar vein, Morton Horwitz notes that "one of the most discouraging spectacles for the historian of legal thought is the unselfconscious process by which one generation's legal theories, developed out of the exigencies of particular political and moral struggles, quickly come to be portrayed as universal truths good for all time."[11] And Robert Gordon has concluded that "recognition of the historical and cultural contingency of law is a perpetual threat to the aims of our legal scholarship as conventionally practiced."[12]

A central issue within the CLS understanding of the Realist view on history, as we shall see, is its rejection of the naturalistic, or Darwinist, framework within which the Realists thought about historical developments as a mistaken and expendable remnant from a nineteenth-century intellectual rage. This aspect of Realist legal history cannot simply be repudiated as an intellectual mistake. It is a respectable view which derived from the Realists' Pragmatic stance and which throws a different light on their understanding of historical analysis—that is, it suggests that their thoroughly relativistic approach was a notion that could be combined with a view that legal change should be understood as causally related to developments in the larger social context. This idea, which is central to Pragmatism, is still very much alive among contemporary Pragmatists. Thus, in a recent book Richard Rorty describes Pragmatism as a current of "post-Darwinian intellectual life" and rehearses its Darwinian facets:

> For notions like "Reality" or "Nature," Nietzsche and James substituted the biologistic notion of the environment. The environment in which we human beings live poses problems to us but, unlike a capitalized Reason or a capitalized Nature, we owe it neither respect nor obedience. Our task is to master it, or to adapt ourselves to it, rather than to represent it or correspond to it.[13]

From this Pragmatic perspective, legal history is an account of the way former generations "mastered" or "adapted to" the circumstances they were faced with, an account of their assessment of their own situation and the technology they developed to deal with it. Such a view of history acknowledges that there is no transhistorical insight into the nature of reality to be gained from the historical record. It shows that we owe no respect to the true nature of reality, that we need not reveal the timeless fundamentals that drive history, and that we can content ourselves with an understanding of what worked and what was expedient for earlier generations. (Conversely, it also shows that reality need not demonstrate any respect for our notions about it—an adjunct that Rorty chooses not to stress in his reflections.)

This chapter will describe the CLS use of history in greater detail. The discussion of CLS historicism will fall into two sections. The first section will describe the critical use of the historicist perspective and the corrosive application of historical analysis in CLS research. This mode of historicist understanding is partly consonant with, albeit much more radical than, the Realist approach to legal history. The second section will deal with the part of the Realist legacy that CLS scholars explicitly reject—its embrace of a functionalist or evolutionary-adaptationist framework.

CLIO UNLEASHED

Historical analysis abounds in the CLS movement. There is no point in trying in vain to summarize this work within the context of this book. Instead, the discussion below will focus on the methodological and theoretical discussions of legal history provided by some of the protagonists in the CLS movement. The aim is to provide a rough outline of the way in which CLS scholars conduct historical research and to sketch the general purpose of their unusual concern with the past, that is, as an instrument of total critique.

One of the early examples of the critical use of history in CLS scholarship is a review by Horwitz of two biographies on Joseph Story. In this article Horwitz attacks what he calls "lawyer's legal history." Horwitz claims that historians have shied away from detailed legal analysis and that much of the legal history that does engage law on the level of technical legal doctrine has been written by lawyers and "has been stamped by lawyer-like concerns."[14] Horwitz provides a long list of things that he believes are wrong with this lawyer's legal history: it has been consistently conservative; it has been largely celebratory and self-congratulatory; it has been obsessively preoccupied with continuity and finding the origins of doctrines; and last but not least, it has "assumed that the basics of legal thought—with its canons of relevance, its criteria of good and bad arguments and its rules of authority, construction and interpretation—are equivalent to reason itself" and are therefore "governed by historically unchanging criteria." Consequently, Horwitz argues, "in most American legal history the received legal tradition is treated not as itself a contingent and changing product of specific historical struggles, but rather as a kind of meta-historical set of values within which social conflict has always taken place."[15]

The reason why lawyers' legal history should be so ahistorical is that an

emphasis on the historicity of legal understanding undermines the professional identity of lawyers as specialists skilled in a distinct and lasting body
of knowledge. Thus, Horwitz notes:

> Once legal history attempts to penetrate the distinction between law and poli-
> tics by seeing legal and jurisprudential change as a product of changing social
> forces, it begins to undermine the indispensable ideological premise of the legal
> profession—indeed of any profession—that its characteristic modes of reason-
> ing and its underlying substantive doctrines may not be universal or necessary,
> but rather particular and contingent.[16]

History, in other words, saps the status of the legal profession as a group
of specialists with privileged knowledge of an apolitical and autonomous
body of doctrine dictated by reason itself. If history shows law to be no
more than the "product of changing social forces," then what exactly does
this special expertise of lawyers consist of? In order to keep such questions
at bay in the legal field, Horwitz believes, "history must be ransacked in order to sing hosannas to all of the existing pieties of professionalization."[17]

With his rejection of lawyers' legal history, however, Horwitz does not
embrace the kind of Progressive history the Realists emulated and practiced
in their historical studies. The idea of historical development that Horwitz
seems to be driving at is what John Diggins, following Isaiah Berlin, has
called "parthenogenesis," that is, intellectual history based on the assumption "that ideas breed other ideas."[18] This notion of parthenogenesis suggests that intellectual frameworks can self-propagate independently from
raw human interests. It is intellectual history's version of the notion of im-
maculate conception. Thus, Horwitz seeks to explain law not primarily as
a product of the social context but as something undergoing independent
development. For instance, in his most famous book, *The Transformation
of American Law, 1780–1860*, he claims that the historian cannot "ignore the
ways in which the internal technical life of a field generates autonomous
forces that determine its history."[19] "Law is autonomous to the extent that
ideas are autonomous," according to Horwitz, "at least in the short run."[20]
In the sequel, *The Transformation of American Law, 1870–1960*, written a de-
cade and a half later, he associates his view of history with "the brilliant
book by Peter Novick" quoted at the start of this chapter. This is not to say
that he is a methodological purist in his own historical research. Indeed, he
is rather catholic in his embrace of different modes of understanding and
admits to a "tendency . . . toward multiple (and perhaps sometimes contradictory) explanations."[21]

In his article "Toward an Historical Understanding of Legal Consciousness: The Case of Classical Legal Thought in America, 1850–1940," Duncan Kennedy also goes down the parthenogenetic road. For an explanation of the development of legal thought, Kennedy argues it is essential "to recognize and confront the existence of legal consciousness as an entity with a measure of autonomy." Legal consciousness, he claims, "is a set of concepts and intellectual operations that evolves according to a pattern of its own, and exercises an influence on results distinguishable from those of economic power and economic interest."[22] Indeed, he contends, "We can identify, and follow through time, clusters of ideas that are *entities*. They develop, evolve, transform themselves, but are nonetheless somehow 'the same thing,' as opposed to other entities, that they were at the beginning."[23] Kennedy still subscribes to this view some two decades later in *A Critique of Adjudication*, in which he argues that "the body of ideas, the textual tradition, once constituted has a 'life of its own' in the sense that people using it experience it as capable of going against the interests, and even reshaping them."[24]

This Structuralist understanding of legal consciousness ties in with a recognition of the historicity of legal concepts and categories and forms a central component of the CLS critique of contemporary law. In his discussion of historicism in legal scholarship, Robert Gordon claims that "the fact that law exists in and must always be understood by reference to particular contexts of space and time" is a perennial threat to conventional legal scholarship. The first and most important aim of mainstream scholarship, Gordon claims, is that of "rationalizing the real, of showing that the law-making and law-applying activities that go on in society make sense and may be rationally related to some coherent conceptual ordering scheme." The second aim is legitimization, the furnishing of a plausible justification for the rationalizations provided. The third and final aim is to show that these attempts at rationalization and justification are in some way of practical use to lawyers and policy makers.[25] By emphasizing the impermanence of social and economic conditions and by stressing the transient nature and unique historical character of the shared conceptions with which people make sense of their world, historicism forms a constant threat to this conventional aim of rationalizing and justifying existing legal arrangements. To eliminate the threat of historicism, Gordon maintains, mainstream legal scholarship has reverted to a range of responses and strategies aimed at deflection and evasion of the disruptive potential of historicist insights, which in turn has led to a severe limitation of "its intellectual options and imaginative range."[26]

A powerful motive for CLS to embrace historicism is the desire to expose the political and legal setup as unnecessary rather than predetermined, plastic rather than inflexible. This is certainly the case in the work of Roberto Unger, arguably the foremost visionary of the CLS movement. In *False Necessity*—the first volume of *Politics*, a three-part work explicating Unger's social theory—Unger spells out what he intends to accomplish with his antinecessitarian view of society. As a descriptive approach, Unger claims, his theory "seeks to free social explanation from its dependence upon the denial of our freedom to resist and to remake our forms of social life." As a constructive theory, it tries to show "how we may carry forward the radical project of freeing our practical and passionate dealings from the constraints imposed on them by entrenched social roles and hierarchies." Taken together, his social theory "takes the last and most surprising step in the itinerary of modern historicism," Unger maintains, because "it recognizes that the quality of our relation, as context-revising agents, to the institutional and imaginative contexts we establish and inhabit is itself up for grabs in history. We can construct not just new and different social worlds but social worlds that more fully embody and respect the creative power whose suppression or containment all societies and cultures seem to require."[27]

The vision Unger puts forward is one of far-reaching autonomy. The kind of society Unger wants to institute is one in which the creative potential of people will no longer be hemmed in by the inertia of established social arrangements and their acceptance as necessary and natural elements of society. Hence, the development of legal and social arrangements should not be understood as a necessary chain of evolution, Unger claims, but as the product of contingent political choices. Put differently, because Unger embraces the notion of a future rich in opportunities to creatively and radically remake society, he has to reject the idea that there is only a narrow range of possibility to transform our existing forms of life, and therefore he is also committed to defending the notion that the way things have turned out in the past has little to do with social or economic necessity and everything to do with a self-inflicted limitation of people's sense of the possible.

a Second Reality

Critical scholars have also applied their corrosive brand of historicism in specific fields of law. For instance, in his article "Following the Rules Laid Down: A Critique of Interpretivism and Neutral Principles," Mark Tushnet employs the historicist insights of CLS to criticize American constitutional law—his field of expertise. He asserts that modern, liberal constitutional theory is based on "two leading dogmas": "interpretivism" and "neutral principles." "Interpretivism," Tushnet claims, "attempts to implement the rule of law by assuming that the meanings of words and rules are stable over extended periods; neutral principles does the same by assuming that we all know, because we all participate in the same culture, what the words and rules used by judges mean."[28] The point of these two dogmas is to make plausible that legal rules have a meaning that is sufficiently stable over time and that is sufficiently clear to all in a certain community to claim that judges are constrained by them in the administration of justice. For if the meaning of legal rules changes over time and if rules mean different things to different people, then there is latitude in the interpretation of these legal rules and, subsequently, room for arbitrary judgment.

Tushnet argues, however, that the twin tenets of "interpretivism" and "neutral principles" are fundamentally at odds with the mainstream liberal view of law that they are usually employed to support.[29] "The ways in which people understand the world," Tushnet maintains, "give meaning to the words that they use."[30] Thus, if the meaning of words, and legal rules made up of these words, is to be unequivocal, then people should share a way of life and share an understanding of the world; only then could they be expected to truly agree on the meaning of their vocabulary. Moreover, if yesterday's law has to apply in a similar fashion today, this shared way of life should remain relatively fixed through time. As a result, the kind of society in which interpretivism and neutral principles would be unproblematic is a society of great homogeneity and cohesion, and a strong traditionalist outlook. It is at odds with liberal constitutionalism, which seeks to provide a framework for a society that is principally a loose association of individuals free to shape their own lives. Such a liberal society lacks a shared way of life, is without a communal understanding of the world, and is deficient when it comes to a dedication to the settled ways of the community, which according to Tushnet are all requisite ingredients for a stable community of meaning.

Interpretivism, moreover, confines the interpretation of legal rules to the intention of the original framers of those rules. What rules mean is primarily determined by the original intention of the democratic institution that adopted those rules, not by the judges applying those rules. Yet since we do not live in a tight and inert community, words change meaning, and it is not an easy matter to uncover the original intention behind the rules adopted by earlier generations. Hence, a lawyer trying to unearth the original scope and meaning of an old legal rule would need to employ the hermeneutic method of the intellectual historian and would need to be immersed in the worldview of the earlier generation that adopted the rule to give a plausible interpretation of that rule's original meaning. Yet how past generations understood their world is something about which historians differ, and the hermeneutic inquiry would probably not produce a definite answer to the lawyer's query. As Tushnet puts it: "In imaginatively entering the world of the past, we not only reconstruct it, but—more important for present purposes—we also creatively construct it. For such creativity is the only way to bridge the gaps between that world and ours."[31] Consequently, Tushnet argues, it is "impossible to claim that any one reconstruction is uniquely correct."[32] Hence, there is no way to tell with any precision what the original meaning of old rules was, and the effort to avoid judicial discretion by uncovering the original intention of these rules is, therefore, self-defeating.

THE PROBLEM WITH FUNCTIONALISM
AND ADAPTATIONISM

If CLS is more radical than Legal Realism with respect to its historicist critique of law, the two movements really part company and move in opposite directions when it comes to the Realist understanding of historicism in a functionalist or adaptationist framework. For the Realists, legal concepts and categories changed meaning in part to keep up with changes in the world of fact to which they referred. The social and economic world changed, and this triggered the development of new and different modes of understanding to cope with these changes. For CLS, however, this whole notion is confused. Facts are never innocent. To an important degree, they are creatures of our conceptual frameworks. Hence, they can never be taken as independent variables that explain the development of our intellectual frameworks.

Gordon, for instance, praises the Realists for helping to pave the way for the historicist understanding of law. Yet he also believes they were implicated in creating the main defensive responses aimed at deflecting the disruptive potential of historicist analysis. Indeed, the two most important modes of response to historicism noted by Gordon are central features of the Realist approach. The first of these is "Cartesianism." With this Gordon primarily refers to the social scientific approach in legal scholarship. Cartesianism, he explains, embraces "formal modeling, the intellectual strategy of constructing highly simplified models of social reality for the sake of analytic rigor and elegance, in the manner of economic theory."[33] Thus, the Realist embrace of social science as a strategy to overcome the vagaries of legal doctrine is one of the examples of the Cartesian response provided by Gordon. The Cartesian response partly incorporates historical contingency, Gordon admits, because it embraces changing social variables in its models of reality. Yet because the social science models are so simple and include only variables that are "members of a highly exclusive club," the truncation of social complexity makes Cartesianism vulnerable to historicist critique.[34] The Realist embrace of social science and CLS is the topic of the next chapter, however, and this issue will be more appropriately confronted there.

That is not the case for the second of the two response strategies that Gordon confronts—adaptation theory. Adaptation theory, according to Gordon, embraces the belief that "there is an immanent rationality in social life, which it is the business of legal rationalization to incorporate."[35] Adaptationism encompasses different notions, Gordon asserts; sometimes adaptationist theorists claim that "the function of law is to learn to recognize, or imitate, regimes of spontaneous order already present in social life," and sometimes they argue that law is "a kind of problem-solving technology that responds, or adapts to 'needs' emerging from society."[36] In other words, some adaptationist legal scholars contend that law must shape itself into conformity with changing social customs and norms, and some claim that law should be adjusted to meet the exigencies of changing social conditions. Both of these elements are present in the Legal Realist version of adaptationism. As with Cartesianism, Gordon notes that adaptationism partially incorporates historicism into its framework. Conditions and ideas change, the adaptationist believes, and law adjusts itself to these changes. The problem with adaptationism is, however, that at one point or another it must find criteria to distinguish functional from dysfunctional law, adapted from ill-adjusted legal arrangements. This, according to Gordon, necessarily involves adaptationist theorists in a "theory of social change, or historical direction, that truly adaptive law must follow," which will invariably include some hidden notions about what law should promote and foster and what it should avoid.[37] Generally this results in a theory of sociolegal development that "simultaneously licenses most existing law as adaptive and permits historicist criticism of some of it as maladaptively 'lagging' behind the course of history."[38]

These theories and their hidden notions of legal propriety, in turn, are vulnerable to historicist critique. The most significant historicist criticism with regard to the Legal Realists is that they employ a "dualism between a 'society' that has 'needs' and a 'legal system' that responds to them."[39] This dualism is untenable, Gordon believes. Legal texts, he notes, "participate in the construction of the social world, populating it with creatures of law's own devising, abstract self-determining individuals and artificial corporate persons, ascribing 'interests' to them and deciding when their sufferings are recognizable 'harms.'" Thus, the social facts and needs to which the law is supposed to respond are "also in part artifacts of the legal system."[40] When legal understanding and the social facts are thus entangled, it becomes very difficult to regard the facts as an independent realm of data against which the adaptiveness of legal arrangements can be judged. In a historicist perspective the facts are theory-laden, to put it differently, and can no longer function as independent touchstones of the functionality of law.

In the article "Critical Legal Histories," a more extensive treatment of what is now called the dominant "evolutionary-functionalist" view of law, Gordon again explains why CLS is critical of the Realist view of history. He maintains that the basic assumptions underlying the evolutionary-functionalist view of the Realists "misleadingly objectify history, making highly contingent developments appear to have been necessary." By explaining the world "as largely determined by impersonal social forces, evolutionary-functionalists obscure the ways in which these seemingly inevitable processes are actually manufactured by people who claim (and believe themselves) to be passively adapting to such processes."[41] If there are such things as evolutionary processes in social life, Gordon states, "they are processes whose logic is one of multiplicity, not uniformity of forms." What characterizes human beings is not their ability to forge predetermined responses to their environment, but their ability to produce "an astonishing diversity of cultural responses" and their "repeatedly demonstrated capacity to re-imagine their situations." Stephen Jay Gould has shown, Gordon contends in the accompanying footnote, that "what is biologically determined is a brain capable of creative variation in its cultural environment."[42] There is not one single way to cope with our life conditions, in other words, but a whole range of possible cultural responses. Hence, evolutionary functionalism provides us with an artificial picture of history when it presents legal and social development as a necessary chain of events, when it suppresses the fact that at every point of the causal chain many legal responses that were not pursued, or even imagined, would have worked just as well.

The purpose of the CLS critique of the evolutionary-functionalist history, Gordon states, is to set us free from the assumption that the way law has developed has been determined in large part by the functional necessities of our condition. CLS wants to propose a different way of thinking about history that does not "trap us into supposing we're permanently stuck with what we happen to be used to, with only the tiniest margins for maneuvering."[43] Once we realize that historical development is not a fixed trajectory but the coincidental result of a hodgepodge of contingent factors, then we can set our minds free to explore alternative social visions.

This effort to disentangle legal thought from the social and economic conditions that are mistakenly believed to mold it leads CLS history to focus on the critical analysis of the conceptual vocabularies of law, on the structure of legal consciousness. Not social needs and interests but the way the law conceptualizes these social needs and interests in legal doctrine is of primary importance. This return by CLS historians to the idea of law as a "brooding omnipresence in the sky," Gordon believes, is not a return to the pure doctrinal studies of the nineteenth century, although the resemblance of what nineteenth-century American legal scholars did, studying law as an autonomous, self-contained body of doctrine, and what CLS historians do, studying law as an autonomous, self-contained body of doctrine, does seem to worry him.[44] Structures of legal thought, however, simply do not relate in any predictable way to social needs and interests. As a result, Gordon believes, a historian "couldn't put the history of structures in the context of political events in any way that would make a coherent narrative."[45] This does not mean that legal thought is severed from the larger society, that the study of legal doctrine only tells us something about the consciousness of a specialized legal elite. On the contrary, Gordon asserts: "Specialized elites may exercise a disproportionate influence on the manufacture of the forms that go into the constitution of legal relations, but the forms are manufactured, reproduced, and modified for special purposes by everyone, at every level, all the time."[46]

Roberto Unger emphasizes roughly the same themes as Gordon does in his social theory, albeit in much denser prose. Unger is a firm supporter of an antinecessitarian view of social development, as we saw earlier. This advocacy of the fundamental open-ended nature of our future leads Unger to reject naturalism and to call for an antinaturalistic social theory. The "naturalistic" view of society that Unger seeks to dismiss is defined in rather opaque terms:

> The canonical form of society is natural in the sense that the distinction between what it prescribes and what force and fraud conspire to establish is given: given in the truth about personality and society rather than merely chosen or brought about by fighting; changeless and only partly intelligible, like the great natural world around us. The reconstructive will and imagination can make only a modest dent on this natural order, when indeed they can exercise any influence at all.[47]

Unger is not very precise about whose theory he refers to with his particular understanding of naturalism. We can safely assume his naturalism includes Pragmatic and Legal Realist social theory, however, because he claims that the "naturalistic premise has been the central element in most of the forms of social thought throughout history."[48]

We might get a better grip on what Unger is driving at with his rejection of naturalism by focusing on what he wants to supersede it with. His descriptions of what antinaturalistic theory involves provide some indications about what it is in naturalism that he finds so objectionable:

> A relentlessly antinaturalistic social theory takes modern historicism to the final step: understanding that the relation between freedom and structure is itself up for grabs in history. Such a theory explores the interplay between the attractions of empowerment through the invention of less imprisoning social contexts and the countervailing forces that prod us into the prison.[49]

Where traditional naturalist theory would assume that our lives were largely controlled and determined by "the formative institutional and imaginative contexts of social life," in antinaturalist social theory the "central place that such an automatism might have occupied is filled up instead by the living, suffering, aspiring individual and by the open-ended experiences of practical collaboration or passionate attachment."[50]

Naturalist social theory, in other words, principally involves an overly deterministic view of social life in which the given social and cultural environment largely determines social behavior and in which there is little room for a view of human beings as autonomous agents making their own future. Yet Unger's conception of naturalism seems extraordinarily rectilinear, even with respect to traditional evolutionary theory. For instance, in his discussion of Darwin's "rather weak" theory of evolution, Unger suggests the following problem with evolution that Darwin failed to explain: "Why did diverse species flourish in an absolutely homogeneous environment?"[51] This question seems to have been suggested by the common objection against functionalism in the realm of social theory, that is, that it must necessarily lead to a uniform, single best social order. Translated into the world of biology, this insight suggests that if one species is well adapted to a certain environment, it will outperform any of its close relatives and there will only be one species, no branching into a family of species. The problem with this view is that "the environment" always consists of a number of other organisms and always offers different ways of making a living. There is always a choice of evolutionary niches to fill. Whenever the population of a species splits and lives apart without any interbreeding, the two populations will naturally drift apart. Chance mutations will then ensure that they will develop in different directions even within an homogeneous environment. Indeed, it would be surprising if these mutations led to similar results. There is nothing mysterious about any of these processes. Unger's conception of naturalism seems rather mechanical, even for the relatively straightforward world of biological evolution. He does not seem to realize that chance and drift are central concepts within evolutionary theory and that diverging results of the process of evolution are not an embarrassment to that theory.

Unger's views on naturalism do not seem to have changed much since the mid-1980s, when he wrote the sections above. In a recent book he still chides the "conceit" that "experience over time reveals what works better and worse, winnowing out the less effective through a relentless quasi-Darwinian process of selection."[52] According to Unger this misconception leads to the false conclusion that social practices and institutions must be converging on a single best way of doing things, that they must be reducing into an ever narrower range of viable arrangements. Whatever this view refers to, it is deeply un-Darwinian and completely at odds with Pragmatism. It seems to proceed from the assumption that the living environment is fixed and unchanging, so that an optimal accommodation to the unvarying circumstances is a possibility, while the point of Darwinism is that everything is always in flux and that adaptation is a never-ending process, an endless struggle.

Mark Tushnet also offers a view of history that is largely consonant with Gordon's, although he does not eliminate the importance of social and economic conditions as radically as Gordon does and is more skeptical about the influence of legal doctrine on the mind-set of the populace. Thus Tushnet stresses the autonomy of legal doctrine, but he does not deny that from a "magisterial perspective" the "legal system responds to gross, long-term trends in the society."[53] Social and economic conditions offer only limited help, however, in explaining law in its everyday operation. Hence, the ideology of the legal order is an essential component in the explanation of legal arrangements. And legal thought follows a logic of its own and to a substantial degree develops independently from social concerns.

For Tushnet the purpose of the ideology of law is largely the same as for Gordon. It is aimed at convincing people that the way things are is natural and necessary. Thus, the legal order helps "to reconcile the oppressed with the system that oppresses them," and it helps "the oppressors understand their actions as those of humane and reasonable people."[54] Yet, unlike Gordon, Tushnet seems to accord much more importance to legal ideology as a legitimating function for the elites than for the people at large. In fact, Tushnet is skeptical about the assumption that the ideology of the legal order penetrates deeply in the wider society. He believes that "the general public has only a vague conception of the role of law in society, and a weak belief that acts justified by the norms of the legal system are automatically just." Most people have only sporadic contact with the legal system, and these contacts often lead to alienation from the legal system. Moreover, social institutions like school, church, and family have a much firmer grip on people's lives than does law. Thus, to say that the legal order legitimates the status quo to ordinary people is to exaggerate the importance of the legal system.[55]

CONCLUSION

Debra Livingston has noted that CLS historicism is the maturation of Realist historical critique. She claims that "the critical legal scholar's historical analysis posits the malleability of fundamental legal ideas and simultaneously suggests that legal thought both directs legal change and legitimates the legal order in much more subtle and pervasive ways than the Realists would have recognized."[56] CLS historicism, although maybe not the maturation of Realist historical critique, is undeniably a radicalization of Realist historical insight. There are three main differences between these respective approaches to legal history. The first concerns the CLS critique of the idea that the development of law is shaped by functional constraints of social and economic conditions, a central notion of Legal Realism. The second difference pertains to the distinction between law and society, which was a necessary assumption in the evolutionary-functionalist history of the Realists but which is collapsed in the historicism of Critical scholars. The third distinction deals with the scope of the historicist critique. Where the Realists employed their historicism as a method to criticize outdated legal rules and doctrines, Critical scholars apply it to the overall ideology of the legal order.

The CLS case against functionalist history has been most forcefully voiced by Robert Gordon. Gordon seems to suggest that functionalism necessarily entails a deterministic understanding of history. If in the functionalist view law is a response to the necessities of the social order, then a functionalist must believe that there is only one optimal legal solution to those necessities. If there were more than one possible functional response to a given set of social exigencies, then functionalism would not provide us with any definite answers and would become empty. If there is only one, then the shape of the legal system is already predetermined by the factual conditions it responds to, which in turn means historical determinism. Such determinism, moreover, is not warranted by an evolutionary perspective on social development. According to Gordon, what characterizes the evolutionary process for human beings is their creative ability to develop a wide range of cultural responses to cope with the necessities of social life.

Gordon's argument against the Realists' evolutionary-functionalist view of history thus becomes strangely reminiscent of the arguments that the Pragmatists leveled against the classic Social Darwinism of Spencer. Gordon's own approach mirrors the Pragmatic emphasis on human intelligence and its creative possibility; while the version of evolutionary functionalism that Gordon ascribes to Realism mirrors Spencer's view of evolution, which saw people as passive subjects, powerless against the impersonal forces of history. The problem is, of course, that Gordon places the Realists on the wrong side of this dichotomy. Realist views were very much in line with the Pragmatist faith that human beings could shape their own destiny. Like the Pragmatists, the Realists saw people as efficacious agents shaping their own life conditions. Indeed, the whole point of Legal Realism seems to be that intelligent human effort can make a difference in this world. Thus, it seems odd to charge Realism with a fatalistic view of history. To the Realists, functionalism did mean that there were social and economic constraints on what could be done with law, that it paid to research those constraints, even that knowledge of those constraints could help decide between policy alternatives, but not that those restraints formed a straitjacket that precluded all movement.

This brings us to the second distinction between Realism and CLS. Whereas the Realists chose to treat law and society as separate realms, CLS scholars consider them to be thoroughly intertwined and tend to collapse the distinction between the two. For the Realists, the social realm was something apart from law; it was an autonomous sphere in which conditions changed, needs were felt, and interests were pursued. Indeed, Realists believed that the law responded and adapted to these events in the social realm. The way these conditions, needs, and interests were conceived and dealt with in a certain period was tainted by the historically contingent conceptual framework that was current, of course, but for the Realists the social facts nevertheless remained separate from the conceptual glasses through which they were perceived. CLS scholars, on the other hand, claim that this separation is artificial. The conditions, needs, and interests that we perceive are not separate from, but in large measure creatures of, our conceptual framework. If the way we understand the world around us is determined by our conceptual framework, then the conditions, needs, and interests we distinguish are also constructed out of the categories and concepts we apply. Consequently, those needs and interests are not the things that determine our conceptual frameworks, but our conceptual framework is what determines our needs and interests. This divergence from Realism is conveyed succinctly in Gordon's remark that "the program of the Realists was to lift the veil of legal Form to reveal living essences of power and need, the program of the Critics is to lift the veil of power and need to expose the legal elements in their composition."[57]

This move by CLS toward an idealist historicism creates a serious problem, however. If changing conditions, needs, and interests no longer determine legal ideology, as they did for the Realists, but legal ideology, instead, determines what we see as our conditions, needs, and interests, then what causes legal ideology to change? If social reality is constructed out of our conceptual paradigm, as Critical scholars seem to suggest, it can no longer be thought of as a separate realm that effects changes in our ideas and conceptions. As a result, CLS scholars seem to have made it very difficult to provide an account of human agency, an account of the causes and motivations for change in legal thought. They seem condemned to present the conceptual paradigm of law as something that somehow grows and develops by itself, independent of people's needs and interests. Gordon admits, in fact, that Critical Legal history sometimes appears to treat intellectual structures as if they "had a life of their own and human beings were enslaved to the needs of that life-cycle, building or demolishing as the World-Spirit might dictate." Yet he claims that this problem is more apparent than real. CLS scholars still believe, he claims, that behind the evolution of legal thought are real people trying "to satisfy their needs for cooperation with, while protecting against their terror of, one another."[58] This is not a very persuasive argument, however. For one thing, it smuggles in the conception of a human "need" that exists independent of our intellectual structures, to support an approach to history which seeks to deny that such independent needs exist. For another, it is hard to see how such a vague and basic dialectic as the one between social cooperation and mutual fear can explain the wide variety of historical changes that every tradition of legal thought has gone through.

The last distinction between CLS and Legal Realism pertains to the scope of their historicist critique. Here, the Realists seemed to heed Holmes's insight that the "past gives us our vocabulary and fixes the limits of our imagination," that "we cannot get away from it," and "that historic continuity with the past is not a duty, it is only a necessity."[59] Thus, their historicist critique was aimed at piecemeal reform of outdated elements of the legal system, not wholesale reform of the overall system. CLS scholars, however, seem to adopt the idea that continuity with the past is not only not a duty, but that it is not a necessity either. The whole purpose of their historicist critique is to make us realize that the way law understands the world is not necessary, that we can radically reimagine our overall legal perspective. But as a practical matter, it seems hard to imagine how that could be done. The historically contingent way we understand the world, CLS scholars argue, is embedded in our words and concepts, in the very language we use. But how could such a thing as our vocabulary be amended other than by way of slow and incremental change? How could we scrap the way we talk all at once and replace it with a new way of talking? How could we rid ourselves of our shared understandings and replace them with a completely new set of shared understandings? The Realists seemed to be more realistic, in this regard, and only sought to change outdated legal conceptions one at a time.

CHAPTER FOUR

Everything Flows and Nothing Abides: The Realist Turn to Social Science

> So far as reality means experienceable reality, both it
> and the truths men gain about it are everlastingly in
> a process of mutation—mutation towards a definite
> goal, it may be—but still mutation.
>
> —William James[1]

> The men of experiment are like the ant; they only
> collect and use: the reasoners resemble spiders, who
> make cobwebs out of their own substance. But the bee
> takes a middle course; it gathers its material from the
> flowers of the garden and of the field, but transforms
> and digests it by a power of its own.
>
> —Francis Bacon[2]

One of the most distinctive traits of Legal Realism was its enthusiasm for social science. This enthusiasm is evident in almost every piece of Realist writing. As a result, most students of Legal Realism equate Realism with a social scientific approach to law. Early critics, like Lon Fuller and H. L. A. Hart, for instance, presented Legal Realism as a theory that primarily claimed that not legal rules but the regular behavior patterns of judges should be the basis for the prediction of legal decisions.[3] Wilfrid E. Rumble Jr., Glendon Schubert, and David Ingersoll considered Legal Realism to be a precursor to Legal Behavioralism.[4] William Twining described Legal Realism as a movement split over the issue of social science in legal research— with a group of "scientists" who wanted to develop law into a full-blown social science and a group of "prudents" who merely sought to enrich traditional legal scholarship with insights drawn from the social sciences.[5] Edward Purcell saw Legal Realism as a facet of the broad movement for "scientific naturalism" in early twentieth-century academics, which meant a dedication to social science in Realist legal scholarship.[6] Laura Kalman believed that Realism would be "most aptly titled 'functionalism'"; Neil Duxbury claimed that "for most legal realists, social science was realism"; and

John Schlegel, finally, stressed that empirical social science was the most salient aspect of Legal Realism.[7]

According to Critical Legal Studies (CLS) historian Morton Horwitz, however, all these scholars are mistaken. They have all been misled by the first accounts of Legal Realism provided by Karl Llewellyn in his famous polemic with Roscoe Pound. In these first programmatic outlines of Legal Realism, Llewellyn embraced the social sciences, presented the Realist approach as a method of inquiry without any substantive commitments, and notoriously argued for the "*temporary* divorce of Is and Ought for purposes of study."[8] These admonitions for a neutral and value-free approach to legal research, Horwitz believes, provide a poor sketch of what was truly significant about the new trends in American legal scholarship in the 1920s and 1930s. Horwitz suggests that Llewellyn—going through a divorce when he wrote his famous programmatic statements of Legal Realism—embraced an "excessively systematic orientation" to offset the chaos in his personal life. Consequently, he exaggerated "the 'scientific' as well as the methodological aspects of realism." This, according to Horwitz, has resulted "in a substantial over-emphasis on a now largely discredited strand of positivist and behavioralistic social science that has deprived us of the true richness of the intellectual and political heritage of Realism."[9] Llewellyn's distorted view of Legal Realism has stuck, Horwitz claims, and has resulted in the virtual neglect of "a central element of the realist legacy—its interpretive or hermeneutic understanding of reality."[10]

Yet the question is whether Horwitz is not guilty of some distortions of his own. At the basis of Horwitz's claim is the notion that Legal Realism consists of two separable aspects; one is its interpretivism, which is worthwhile and important, and the other is its appeal to social science, which is flawed and insignificant. This chapter will seek to challenge that view. It will try to establish that the most accurate as well as the most fruitful way to understand Legal Realism is not as a purely qualitative theory but as a synthesis of an interpretivist and a scientific approach inspired by Pragmatism. To argue this point, the Pragmatic understanding of social science, which the Legal Realists sought to apply to legal research, will be described in more detail.

The thrust of the argument will be that as far as the Realists embraced social science, they should not be identified with the positivist and behaviorist vogue of the 1950s. This fashion only really took off after the demise of Legal Realism. Indeed, the downfall of the Pragmatic conception of social science, which informed Legal Realism in the interwar years, and the rise of the behaviorist approach, which reigned supreme for much of the 1950s and 1960s, are related developments. Both resulted from the fierce political debates within the academic world over the events of the Second World War. The Realists worked securely within the Progressive-Pragmatic consensus of the prewar years in which the values of science and liberal democracy were believed to be continuous and to follow from a fundamental recognition of the irreducible plurality of perspectives within the Pragmatic conception of truth. The burgeoning American republic seemed to establish as self-evident that free scientific inquiry and an open democratic society were tantamount to progress and prosperity. This secure and unassailable liberal-scientific framework allowed scholars to embrace a thoroughgoing relativism with respect to different substantive views without experiencing any anxiety or disquiet about the ultimate underpinnings of liberal democracy. However, this secure Progressive-Pragmatic consensus came under attack in the late 1930s with the rise of totalitarianism. The absence of a foundational argument supporting liberal democracy became a problem. Relativist theories such as Legal Realism and Pragmatism began to be accused, especially by natural law theorists, of sapping the moral strength of liberal democracy and leaving it vulnerable to the totalitarian challenge.[11]

Moreover, a wave of émigré scholars arrived from Germany—Leo Strauss, Hannah Arendt, Theodor Adorno, Max Horkheimer, Herbert Marcuse, Eric Voegelin, and Franz Neumann, to name the most important—who challenged the core beliefs of the Progressive-Pragmatic consensus. To them the ideals of science and liberal democracy did not form a bulwark against totalitarianism. On the contrary, as John Gunnell has argued, these émigré scholars came to the United States with the notion that totalitarianism was basically a problem *of* science and liberalism.[12] To them there was a clear link between the debasing and dehumanizing logic of utility and rationality that emerged from the Enlightenment and the subsequent rise of the totalitarian state in which everything was subordinated to the needs of the collective. The intellectual baggage of these German émigré scholars was existentialism, and many had bruising personal experiences with the Weimar Republic. They took a rather bleak view of democracy and generally had a poor understanding of Pragmatism, which they tended to equate with positivism and crass utilitarianism.[13] All this led to fierce debate and polarization within American academia. Many of the social scientists deeply resented being accused of furthering the cause of totalitarianism. By the end of the 1940s, this controversy came to a head in the behavioral revolution and led to a fundamental realignment within American social science. The social scientists had had their fill with the accusations hurled at them from within natural law theory and émigré scholarship and simply organized substantive and normative theory out of their discipline altogether. By embracing behaviorism as the central method of the social sciences, only questions of fact remained valid for social research. Questions of value no longer fit within the remodeled version of social science. Political theory as a distinct subdiscipline emerged as a home for the natural law and émigré scholarship, ignored by and separated from its mother discipline. Like the Pragmatists before them, the behaviorists still believed their science served to support democracy and democratic policy making. Yet the new social science lacked the ecumenical nature of Pragmatism and rejected the way Pragmatism had embraced political and substantive concerns.

CLS scholars are among the New Left heirs to the German émigré scholarship, of course. They have mimicked the condescending posture that the German émigrés once adopted toward Pragmatism and its embrace of social science. They uncritically copied its misinterpretation of Pragmatic social science as positivism and behaviorism. Moreover, they tend to accept the split between qualitative and quantitative research brought about by the behavioral revolution as an inevitability and see empirical social science and interpretivism as fundamentally incompatible and mutually hostile approaches. With regard to Legal Realism, this translates into an emphasis on its interpretivist aspect, which is presented as contradictory to, and exclusive of, its social scientific element. In other words, the later split between interpretivism and positivism is projected retroactively on the Realist movement. In this, CLS scholars fail to see that the Realists are not simply early positivists, or behaviorists, but that they adopted a Pragmatic approach to the study of law.

This Pragmatic approach was different in many important respects from the one adopted in the social sciences after the behavioral revolution of the 1950s. Notably, the Realists did not conceive of themselves as engaged in uncovering universal laws of social behavior, like die-hard positivists or behaviorists. Indeed, the Realists believed that the social world evolved too swiftly to allow for any permanent knowledge about it. Hence, their Pragmatic view of social science was not wedded to a conception of objective scientific knowledge, in the sense of knowledge that was valid independent of the contingencies of time and place. On the contrary, as Dewey had taught them, the Realists believed that the historical and social context not only provided the framework within which their experimental, scientific approach would proceed, but also fixed the limits of the applicability of the knowledge it would render. If the Realists are seen for the Pragmatic scholars they were, then the seeming contradiction between their social scientific and their interpretivist stance will no longer be so puzzling. More important, the Realists will no longer seem to be unenlightened predecessors, simpletons from an earlier age that failed to understand that they were mixing two incompatible modes of inquiry. Instead, they can be appreciated as innovative scholars who fashioned an interesting synthesis of empirical social science and interpretivism within the field of law.

The discussion of the Realist adoption of social science will fall into six sections. The first section will deal with the famous programmatic outline of Legal Realism by Llewellyn. Horwitz holds Llewellyn's first formulations of the new Legal Realist approach responsible for the subsequent misrepresentation of Legal Realism as a movement wedded to positivist and behaviorist conceptions of social science. The argument will seek to prove that a careful reading of Llewellyn's famous articles does not support Horwitz's view and that *positivism* and *behaviorism* are misleading labels for the approach Llewellyn proposed. In the second section, Llewellyn's description of the Realist approach will be related to the work of other Realists in order to show that his description of the epistemological and methodological framework of Legal Realism was not at all idiosyncratic but quite representative of the ideas of other Realists. His basic outline of Realism, when properly understood, was consonant with the arguments other Realists forwarded in support of their move toward social science. The third section will deal with the idea of functionalism, a central concern in the Realist discussions of social science. The discussion will seek to show that functionalism, at least in the way the Realists conceived of it, cannot fairly be equated with reductionism or determinism. In the fourth section, the most contested use of social science by the Realists will be dealt with, namely their employment of empirical research as an alternative to the traditional rule-oriented approach to legal study. Many Legal Realists believed that social science could provide empirically based predictions of judicial decisions. Not legal rules and principles, they believed, but the regular behavior patterns of judges should be the basis for predicting the outcomes of legal cases. There are serious problems with the idea of predicting legal decisions on the basis of the statistical probabilities of judicial behavior, however, and this approach has elicited broad and fierce critique, although some legal scholars have recently defended this aspect of the Realist turn to social science. Section five will discuss the use of social science as part of an instrumentalist conception of law. The Legal Realists understood law as a means to achieve social ends. In this instrumentalist understanding of law, the social sciences were awarded a central role. If the purpose of law was to pursue social ends, then it was important to ascertain what these social ends should be, as well as the most sensible way to achieve them. This meant gathering scientific knowledge about law as a social institution and about the effectiveness of different legal instruments to bring about desired outcomes. It is mainly within the framework of this instrumentalist conception of law that the Realist turn to social science still deserves our attention. Finally, in the sixth section, the Uniform Commercial Code will be discussed as an example of Realist instrumentalism.

THE LLEWELLYN-POUND EXCHANGE

To understand the Realist recourse to social science—and the way the Realist adoption of that new science has since been understood—it is important to take a close look at Llewellyn's first definition of Legal Realism as a movement for the social scientific study of law in his two famous programmatic articles, "A Realistic Jurisprudence—The Next Step" and "Some Realism About Realism—Responding to Dean Pound."[14] We already saw that, according to Horwitz, these two seminal articles have caused subsequent generations of legal scholars to misunderstand Legal Realism fundamentally. According to him, the articles completely misrepresent Realism as a movement and portray it as aimed primarily at the integration of a sterile, positivistic strand of social science into legal scholarship. Hence, it is imperative to see what Llewellyn actually wrote on the subject of social science in these two articles.

The first of the two articles "A Realistic Jurisprudence—The Next Step" is mainly famous for coining the phrase "Legal Realism," but as William Twining put it, "it is not to be recommended to someone who seeks a coherent introduction to realism."[15] Nonetheless, the article contains many of Llewellyn's later ideas in embryonic form. In this early paper Llewellyn presented Realism as an approach that focused on facts and behavior, in contrast to the dogmatic orientation of traditional legal scholarship. Traditional scholarship, he argued, remained fully preoccupied with its own concepts and categories.

> The traditional approach is in terms of words; it centers on words; it has the utmost difficulty in getting beyond words. If nothing be said about behavior, the *tacit* assumption is that the words do reflect behavior, and if they be words

of rules of law, do influence behavior, even influence behavior effectively and precisely to conform completely to those words. Here lies the key to the muddle.[16]

The Realistic approach sought to move beyond words. It questioned the accuracy of legal rules as descriptions of what courts actually did and the efficacy of legal rules as determinants of judicial behavior.

With this, Llewellyn did not mean to say that "the 'accepted rules,' the rules the judges say that they apply, are without influence upon their actual behavior."[17] Rather, his argument was that this convergence of paper rules and legal behavior could never be assumed as a matter of course. Hence, Llewellyn did not support the idea that legal rules were unimportant and that they had to be replaced by empirical rules that described the actual regularities of judicial behavior. On the contrary, his default position was that legal rules did inform judicial decisions:

> The approach here argued for admits, . . . out of hand, *some* relation between *any* accepted rule and judicial behavior; and then proceeds to deny that that admission involves anything but a problem for investigation in the case in hand; and to argue that the significance of the particular rule will appear only *after* the investigation of the vital, focal, phenomenon: the behavior. And if an empirical *science* of law is to have any realistic basis, any responsibility to the facts, I see no escape from moving to this position.[18]

Llewellyn, to put it differently, did not deny a close relationship between "law in the books" and "law in action," but he wanted to make the routine testing of this relationship the focus of an empirical approach to the study of law.

Llewellyn expected that the empirical method of Realism could greatly improve the efficiency of legal rules to achieve their declared purpose. The empirical method would not be confined to the behavior of judges but would extend to the behavior of other legal and government officials, lawyers, and laypersons. This would provide insights into the environment into which legal rules were introduced—that is, the prevailing practices that existed among the different groups that were to be influenced by the legal rules. Thus, Llewellyn contended:

> It seems patent that only a gain in realism and effectiveness of thinking can come from consistently (not occasionally) regarding the official formulation as a tool, not as a thing of value in itself; as a means without meaning save in terms of its workings, and of meaning in its workings only when these last are compared with the results desired. In the terms used above: as *prima facie* pure paper until the contrary is demonstrated; and as best a new piece of an established but

moving environment, one single element in a complex of practices, ideas and institutions without whose study the one element means nothing. Hence, what the proposed approach means is not the elimination of rules, but such a setting of paper in perspective as can hugely step up their power and effect.[19]

Such a broad understanding of the social context in which rules gained practical meaning, Llewellyn believed, would benefit the lawyer in advising clients, it would aid the legal theorist by grounding thought in actual life, it would help the judge with settling the inevitable policy issues in legal disputes, and it would assist the legislator in fashioning more effective legislation.[20] Llewellyn's call for such broad understanding of the social environment also underscored that he was not intent on limiting his research to observable behavior patterns. As a legal scholar he was interested not only in what people were doing but also in what they thought they were doing. "It is obvious," Llewellyn claimed, "that the set or attitude of those affected or sought to be affected by any piece of 'law' is at the heart of control; it should be equally obvious that the style of organization of those persons, their group ways of action—whether among themselves or with regard to society at large—is equally vital."[21]

Moreover, Llewellyn connected Realism with Pragmatism and the methodology of the emerging social sciences. He claimed that the Realistic method he recommended for legal scholarship was not new but merely followed contemporary trends. It was "of a piece with the work of the modern ethnographer" and "the development of objective method in psychology." It fitted with "the Pragmatic and instrumental developments in logic." And it sought to capitalize on "the methodological worries" that had been "working through . . . to new approaches in sociology, economics, political science."[22]

In "Some Realism About Realism—Responding to Dean Pound," Llewellyn returned to these themes. This famous article was written together with Jerome Frank in reaction to Roscoe Pound's somewhat uncharitable presentation of the new Realist movement in "The Call for a Realist Jurisprudence."[23] The article starts with a systematic refutation of all the characteristics that Pound had attributed to the new Realist movement and then proceeds with a description of the commonalities that Realist legal scholars did share, according to Llewellyn and Frank. The rebuttal, often neglected in discussions of the article, is as informative as the subsequent description of Legal Realism. It lists a number of conceptions about Realism that Llewellyn and Frank believed could not fairly be assigned to the Legal Realists. One of these misconceptions was that a sizable group of Realists expected "rigidly exact and workable formulas about law to be developed in ways analogous to mathematical physics" and that they expected these formulas "to be workable without more as rules of what to do." Adherence to such a conception of Legal scholarship would have been an indication of a positivist scientific outlook, with its stress on the unity of scientific method and its focus on physics as the exemplary model for other academic disciplines. Yet in the literature of the twenty Realists they canvassed, Llewellyn and Frank claimed they could find no support for this contention.[24] A second characteristic that Pound had attributed to the Legal Realists was that in their description of judicial practice they disregarded "the effects of the judges' own ideal pictures of what they ought to do." This would have been a sign of behaviorism, of an exclusive focus on observable behavior without attention to people's values and ideals. Again, Llewellyn and Frank claimed they could not find support for this among the twenty Realists examined.[25] Finally, Pound had charged the Realists with being "unmindful of the relativity of significance, of the way in which preconceptions necessarily condition observation." This would have been evidence for the belief that Realism was a neutral, value-free method that could uncover untainted, objective facts about law. Once again, Llewellyn and Frank claimed they could not find any Legal Realist among the twenty inspected that supported this view.[26]

In the enumeration of qualities that the Realists *did* share there was much overlap with Llewellyn's earlier programmatic outline of Legal Realism in "A Realistic Jurisprudence—The Next Step." Again there was the stress on the importance of studying the real effects and consequences of legal rules, and on the necessity to check these against their declared purpose. Again there was skepticism about legal rules being "*the* heavily operative factor in producing court decisions," which, Llewellyn and Frank were careful to point out, did not imply a denial of the importance of legal rules.[27] Yet there were several new elements too. Two of these need to be elaborated: (1) the "conception of society in flux, and in flux typically faster than the law," which made it a constant likelihood "that any portion of law needs reëxamination to determine how far it fits the society it purports to serve"; and (2) the call for the "*temporary* divorce of Is and Ought for purposes of study," which Morton Horwitz, as we saw, considered such an unfortunate characterization of what Legal Realism was about.[28]

The "conception of society in flux, and in flux typically faster than the law," to begin with, made it imperative, according to Llewellyn and Frank, to constantly back-check law on its fit with changing circumstances. There was a time lag between the point social or economic developments occurred and the point these were registered and legally dealt with. Implicit in this conception of constant flux in society and law was functionalism. The background picture was one of a perpetually evolving world and a legal system that was constantly readjusted to fit with new conditions. Such a conception of continual flux in the social and legal world is difficult to square, of course, with the positivist view that permanent patterns of judicial behavior could be fashioned on the model of the laws of physics. The constant-flux view fits uncomfortably with a Newtonian framework. It is deeply Darwinian in that it recognizes that something can only be functional relative to a certain setting, that today's wise ruling can be tomorrow's counterproductive folly. Hence, in a functionalist framework empirical knowledge of the social world is contingent, not cumulative. "Economic, political and social problems are ever-shifting," Frank maintained, consequently our "approximation" of them needed to be "revised frequently" and could "never be accepted as final."[29] Indeed, Dewey himself had warned against the ossification of legal arrangements suited only to the localized conditions of a given age, conditions that were bound to change.[30]

The second element I want to draw attention to is "*temporary* divorce of Is and Ought for purposes of study." For Llewellyn and Frank, this was a qualified appeal to separate the investigation of facts from normative and ethical commitments, not an effort to change legal scholarship into a pure empirical science in which there was no place for questions of value. It is important to point out that *temporary* was italicized in the original. This stress on the temporary character of the separation of Is and Ought is significant. The Ought, Llewellyn and Frank believed, should not and could not be permanently severed from the Is. The Ought, to begin with, was important for shaping research goals. "Value judgments," Llewellyn and Frank claimed, "must always be appealed to in order to set objectives for inquiry." The Is, or the research findings, in turn, were important for shaping the Ought. "No judgment of what Ought to be done in the future with respect to any part of law," they claimed, "can be intelligently made without knowing objectively, as far as possible, what that part of law is now doing."[31] In other words, in the initial phase of an inquiry value judgments shaped the research agenda, and in the final phase the research data formed the basis for value judgments about what ought to be done. Yet in between these phases, during the research, Llewellyn and Frank contended, "the observation, the description, and the establishment of relations between the things described are to remain *as largely as possible* uncontaminated by the desires of the observer."[32] Again, the italicization of "as largely as possible" in the original is important. With the italics Llewellyn and Frank seem to emphasize that during an inquiry objectivity is not an achievable goal, only an ideal to aspire to.

Llewellyn and Frank did not elaborate this point, however, and it is not entirely clear what they meant with their call for a separation of Is and Ought during research. Yet in relation to their other writing of the same period, some further remarks can be ventured. In the same year as "Some Realism About Realism," Llewellyn also wrote a paper entitled "Legal Tradition and Social Science Method." In this article Llewellyn provided a fuller account of the problem of objectivity in research. Here he contended that objectivity was impossible even during research, because values necessarily entered into the way research projects were conceived. The framing of the problem, the perspective chosen, and especially the research concepts employed determined how the facts took on meaning for the observer. Hence, if the research framework was necessarily biased, so was the observation of the facts. Yet according to Llewellyn, this did not mean that the researcher could not try to be as unbiased as possible:

> In the posing of problems, subjectivity remains. On the other hand, something the investigator can do to counter-act the inevitable. He can be aware of it. He can *try* to be awake for data which make initial categories look silly, make his hypothesis look non-significant, make his observations to date call for the junkpile. For concepts do not *wholly* condition observation—else we could never add to what we know. And he who knows their power holds a key which may bring him escape.[33]

Llewellyn, in other words, was fully aware that facts were mediated through theory, through a conceptual vocabulary that carved up reality in arbitrary ways. Nonetheless, this insight did not lead him to conclude that beliefs and theories could not be tested against the empirical facts or that "bias" and "objectivity" had become meaningless concepts. What he seemed to propose was not so much a scientific technique but a scientific ethic: a willingness to question one's assumptions, an openness to counterarguments and evidence that did not fit into one's framework. However, this attitude, which was thoroughly Pragmatic, made sense only if one assumed that the facts observed were not completely shaped by the conceptual paradigm of the observer—an assumption that explains a great deal about what sets Legal Realism apart from CLS.

Frank also believed that it was mainly a scientific attitude that Legal Scholars should take from the sciences. Frank was too nominalistic in his approach to put too much faith in scientific certainty and objectivity. Indeed, in a separate appendix entitled "Science and Certainty" in *Law and the Modern Mind,* he warned against the danger that for many science could become "a new source of illusion, a new escape from change and chance, a new road to the absolute."[34] This certainty-through-science idea was an illusion, Frank maintained, because of "the inescapable limitations of human observation and human intellection."[35] The illusion of certainty, in fact, expressed an unscientific conception of science. True science embraced the chanciness of reality and the "unavoidable imperfection of its technique."[36] It was this posture that Frank found most appealing in science:

> While lawyers would do well, to be sure, to learn scientific logic from the expositors of scientific method, it is far more important that they catch *the spirit of the creative scientist*, which yearns not for safety but risk, not for certainty but adventure, which thrives on experimentation, invention and novelty and not on nostalgia for the absolute, which devotes itself to new ways of manipulating protean particulars and not to the quest of undeviating universals.[37]

This stress on science as an ethic, rather than a procedure, again is much closer to Pragmatic notions of science than to positivist ones. What defined science for the Pragmatists, in the end, was not a body of precepts and rules—which represented only a temporary consensus—but an openness to rival notions and a willingness to accept alternative and better ways of approaching the "protean particulars."

REALISM IN THE AGE OF RELATIVITY

The recognition and acceptance of the relativity of scientific knowledge was quite widespread among Realist legal scholars, whether the more traditional or the more scientifically inclined. Because of their focus on—if not obsession with—social evolution and change, the Realists did not apply such universalizing concepts as rationality or self-interest to extend the applicability of their research beyond the limits of time and place. Their commitment to empirical research was always wedded to a view of behavior as culturally and historically contingent. Hence, it precluded anything as grandiose as general theories of judicial behavior.

William Douglas, for instance, believed that adaptability was one of the most important benefits of his functional method. With functionalism, he claimed, "[f]lexibility necessary for adaptation to a changing order is present." Contrary to the fundamental abstractions of classical legal thought, the postulates constructed in a functionalist approach, he believed, were "fashioned so entirely out of the phenomena with which they deal that they are not so apt to persist when new phenomena replace them."[38] One of the most scientifically oriented Realists, Underhill Moore, agreed wholeheartedly. Moore did not believe his research findings had any bearing outside of the region and the time period researched. Behavior was culturally conditioned, he maintained, and if cultural norms changed, so would behavior.[39]

This relativity of scientific knowledge was also an important element in the fusion of law and social science that Walter Wheeler Cook constructed. Cook belonged to the group of scientists among the Realists, and he was a tireless advocate for the use of scientific method in legal scholarship. Cook believed that developments in mathematics, biology, and physics were all converging on a rejection of the absolute and the certain. In mathematics, Euclidean geometry, long believed to have been the only possible geometry, had been supplemented with a number of non-Euclidean geometries, and one of these had been proved to be of practical utility in describing physical phenomena. Hence, the idea that Euclidean geometry was inherent in the order of physical space lost its appeal, and it became just a mathematical system that might prove more or less useful in describing reality. Darwin had undermined the idea that the natural world consisted of a collection of fixed and unchanging species. In a Darwinian framework, species became only a temporary classification of specimens observed in a certain phase of their development. And in physics, Einstein had inaugurated the era of relativity, in which even the fixity of time and space had to be given up. In these developments, according to Cook, "we find a frank and clear recognition of the extent to which all our thinking is based upon underlying postulates of which we frequently are entirely unaware but which color all our mental processes and in particular often give those generalizations which we are in the habit of calling 'natural laws' the form which they assume." Upon inspection these postulates, moreover, often did not "accord with anything in our experience."[40] This insight had not yet had its effect on law, Cook claimed. Legal thinking was still caught in the old framework in which "the ascertainment of all-embracing laws of nature, holding for all cognizable occasions," was sought.[41] In a scientific approach, laws should be treated as only tools for attaining social ends and evaluated on their success in achieving them. Thus he argued for the "non-professional study of law, in order that the function of law may be more clearly understood, its limitations appreciated, its results evaluated, and its future development kept more nearly in touch with the complexities of modern life."[42]

The intellectual historian Edward Purcell has noted that "non-Euclidean" thinking of the type that Cook promulgated was quite commonplace among early twentieth-century American intellectuals. The belief that the development and use of non-Euclidean geometries had profound consequences for disciplines other than mathematics and physics was a cliché of the period. Purcell maintains that non-Euclidean geometry helped to create a widespread faith in the non-Euclidean possibilities of reasoning of any kind. What was true for geometry was believed to be true for any form of deductive thought, according to Purcell. Hence, the assumption became that new and uncommon theories could be generated in law, economics, and politics, which could prove to be both useful and as logically valid as any traditional theory.[43] Thus, it is not surprising that Jerome Frank drew on the non-Euclidean revolution in physics and mathematics in very much the same way Cook did. "Axioms have been secularized," Frank contended about the impact of non-Euclideanism: "They are now regarded merely as assumptions, and no assumptions are considered sacrosanct. In any system of thinking, concealed assumptions can be brought to light and interrogated as to their usefulness."[44] The value of assumptions, in the end, was determined by their fit with existing, or potentially existent, conditions. "The legal thinker should never let himself believe that he is dealing with pure mathematics," Frank argued. "Logical deductions from legal postulates must square with observable phenomena—else the postulates are wrong."[45]

What is notable about Cook's advocacy of scientific method is its embrace of exactly the type of cognitive relativism that Realists like Frank expounded and that Horwitz believes was obscured by the Realist turn to social science. All thinking, Cook believed, was colored by underlying postulates of which people were generally unaware. Even scientific generalizations and laws were molded by these underlying postulates, he maintained, and should therefore not be confused with something inherent in reality. Scientific theories were merely tools, which were not more or less true but more or less valuable for the purpose they were designed to serve. This view of science was pure Dewey, who had had a profound influence on Cook.[46] With his Pragmatic stress on the practical value rather than the objective truth content of scientific theory, Cook departed from logical positivism, the proponents of which would have shuddered at the thought of renouncing the idea that science was anything less than a search for pure and objective knowledge. Indeed, Cook's Pragmatic view of science was Kuhnian rather than positivistic in its recognition of the way research was shaped irreducibly by the conceptual framework within which it proceeded, and in the concurrent insight that this precluded any ultimate standard of truth for scientific research. Like Dewey, however, Cook combined this cognitive relativism with an unremitting faith in the benevolence of science. Even though people were necessarily caught in a frame of reference that necessarily mediated and slanted their observation of the facts, scientific method and a scientific attitude still held the best promise for the intelligent pursuit of social ends.

FUNCTIONALISM

The way many Realists put this Pragmatic understanding of social science into practice was within a functionalist framework. What the Realists understood by the term *functionalism* should not be confused with contemporary notions of functionalism, however. Within the fields of law and social science, the term *functionalism* today comes with a set of powerful connotations. Functionalism stands for a highly abstract, holistic understanding of society, for esoteric theorizing in the style of Talcott Parsons, and for a reductionist perspective with a narrow focus on only those aspects of social institutions necessary for the continuity of society. One problem commonly attributed to this functionalist perspective is that it treats the status quo, by definition, as a social configuration necessary for the survival of the social whole. Another common charge against this type of functionalism is that it presents a circular argument in which what exists is explained in terms of qualities that promote survival and qualities that promote survival are defined in terms of what continues to exist. As a result, functionalism is widely denounced for presenting too hermetic an argument and for suffering from an inherent conservative bias, which invests existing circumstances with an air of necessity.

Most of the work of the realists, however, bears little relation to this timeworn notion of functionalism. Talcott Parsons is a far cry from what the Realists had in mind when they invoked the notion of functionalism. When the Realists used the term *functionalism,* it was rarely followed by an argument which showed that the legal order had withstood the test of time and should, therefore, be accepted as largely necessary for the survival of society. On the contrary, the use of functionalism was usually critical and oftentimes involved the claim that a particular aspect of the legal order had survived, even though it no longer served a purpose and had become dysfunctional. For the Realists, in other words, the shedding of dysfunctional elements was not an automatic and largely completed process, the result of which could be observed and admired in the present makeup of society. On the contrary, they viewed the weeding out of dysfunctional elements as a critical task to be fulfilled, as an ongoing project that needed constant attention.

This understanding of functionalism—which allows for the possibility that concepts and rules persist regardless of whether they benefit society—is closer to modern meme theory than to present-day notions of functionalism. In Realism, much as in meme theory, legal rules or concepts persevered not necessarily because of their success in promoting social welfare, but primarily because of their success in promoting themselves as valued rules and concepts. For memeticists, as we have seen, ideas or techniques can be treated as selfish replicators in their own right. They can thrive and propagate, even though they are deleterious to the fortunes of their carriers. We also saw that this idea is quite close to the Realist notion of "survivals," elements of the legal order that have outlasted their relevance but are cherished and perpetuated nonetheless. These survivals simply have a knack for surviving. They need to be actively exposed and criticized to be got rid of.

That was roughly William Douglas's take on functionalism when he applied it to the law of business associations. Douglas believed that the law in this field had traditionally been focused on form rather than function. This emphasis on form, Douglas claimed, had led to an essentialistic search for the true nature of the business unit:

> The focal point of study being the form of business unit it was not difficult to predict the emphasis of classroom discussion, lawyers' argument and courts' opinion. The kind of organization, its nature, its quality, its limitations, were analyzed. The analysis took the form of rules; the rules became the theology. The analysis, the rules, the theology emphasized the business unit. It was this. It was not that. It could do this. It could not do that. It was different from this but similar to that. It—and its qualities and characteristics—were the keystone of the law of business associations. The habit of thought crystallized. The theology obscured thinking. It instituted an endless process of refinement. It continued by its own momentum. The theology complete in itself left no room for growth. Postulates became firmly fixed. The flexibility required for adaptation to an ever-changing economic order was lacking.[47]

Douglas believed the law of business associations had become frozen in its legal concepts and had lost touch with the ongoing changes in the economic order. The analogy to meme theory is evident. Douglas's description of the concept of the business unit as a "theology complete in itself," that "obscured thinking" and that "continued by its own momentum," does not suggest an autonomous process of evolution toward a streamlined, well-adapted legal concept. Rather, it suggests the tenacity of a treasured set of abstractions firmly nested in the collective legal imagination, which managed to survive despite their inadequacy. As a result, Douglas recommended that the business unit be "visualized as a device adjustable to a changing order."[48] Such a functional approach to the law of business associations, he argued, would be "correlated to and coordinated with the facts of business practice" and would leave "room for growth and development in the direction in which the social and economic phenomena are moving."[49]

In a classic statement of the Realist approach, "Transcendental Nonsense and the Functional Approach," Felix Cohen suggested something similar. In this article Cohen maintained that Legal Realism, understood as a functional approach, should be aimed at debunking outdated and meaningless legal concepts. For Cohen, functionalism constituted a broad movement in a wide array of academic disciplines set on "eliminating supernatural terms and meaningless questions and redefining concepts and problems in terms of verifiable realities."[50] In law this meant, first and foremost, the elimination of supernatural legal concepts that could not be related to anything in empirical reality or their redefinition in terms of verifiable behavior or verifiable fact. Such an exercise, Cohen believed, would make many vexing legal questions disappear.

Thurman Arnold also forwarded a functionalist theory of law, of sorts. Arnold separated the creeds of social institutions from the practical work they did. To Arnold these institutional creeds—such as legal doctrine for the legal institution, or economic theory for the marketplace—bore little resemblance to the real work that went on in those social institutions. Economic and legal theory were for symbolic, not practical use; they should not be considered as accurate representations of what social institutions actually did, but as pep talks to boost the morale of the people working in those institutions. An institutional creed was something akin to Plato's "noble lie" in Arnold's theory; it was a fiction that made people feel good about the institution. The function institutional creeds performed, in other words, was not in terms of actual social regulation, but in terms of psychological comfort and peace of mind. Ideally, an institutional creed should instill warm feeling toward a social institution and simultaneously allow for the Pragmatic handling of problems by the practical technicians of that institution. People, however, grew attached to the institutional creeds of social organizations and often stuck to them even though they had become an obstacle to necessary change. Such "old myths," Arnold maintained, could lead to the malfunctioning of social institutions, because they encouraged "men to act in direct contradiction to observed facts."[51] People found it very difficult to give up cherished beliefs, however. The "process of building up new abstractions to justify filling new needs," he observed, "is always troublesome in any society."[52] Plainly, for Arnold, the survival of institutional creeds had little to do with their success or practical utility. People simply grew attached to certain beliefs and clung to them regardless of whether they contradicted experience.

In an article outlining his functionalist theory of law, Llewellyn also described the process in which social norms were formulated and selected in terms suggestive of present-day meme theory. Like memes from the meme pool, legal rules, according to Llewellyn, were drawn from an infinite and ever-changing set of "normative generalizations" all vying for acceptance by the relevant social group:

> The possibilities of normative generalization are limitless; the idiosyncratic actualities are almost so. The history of minority parties, freak sects, social and political dreamers, and paranoia, suggest the range. Some relatively few of these actual normative generalizations acquire peculiar social significance. They become accepted in a group and by it. They prevail. They control behavior. People who are found at odds with them have trouble with that group, be it a family or nation.

This process, for Llewellyn, was quite haphazard and unpredictable, and the social norms that ultimately prevailed by no means resulted from bare functional necessity. Norms could simply crystallize without any preconceived motive or plan. Patterns of "interlocking behavior" could just emerge, Llewellyn suggested, without "anyone wanting such patterns to develop, or planning them, or preaching them, though any or all these things may happen." Norms could also result from a high-profile "trouble-case" which absorbed public attention and stuck in people's minds. "The stress," Llewellyn observed, "the spectacular and memorable drama, the brain sweat, of a trouble-case, though it be an utterly unique one, drives by its whole quality toward generalization; and this doubly, if the trouble-case becomes, as many do, the *occasion* for awakening to, and voicing, normative drives which have been building unnoticed."[53] Attention-grabbing but "utterly unique" cases that could, nonetheless, drive irresistibly toward generalization are quite eccentric material to base a functionalist theory of law on, of course, at least as understood in terms of the stereotypical conception of functionalism. Yet Llewellyn's argument fits comfortably within a memetics perspective and its focus on the importance of the infectiousness and catchiness of ideas for long-term survival in the meme pool.

This is not to deny that Llewellyn's functionalist theory of law in many ways also resembles more commonplace notions of functionalism. His so-called law-job theory was formulated to form the basis for a research project into the legal culture of the Cheyenne Indians. For this project, undertaken together with the anthropologist E. Adamson Hoebel, Llewellyn needed a general, all-purpose functionalist theory of law, which could be used as a heuristic for the study of customary Native American law. This law-job theory started out from a set of fundamental functions of law, the so-called law jobs, defined as jobs necessary for group survival. These law jobs, Llewellyn claimed, were universal; they held "as basic functions for every human group, from a group of two persons on up." Indeed, they were "implicit in the concept of 'groupness.'"[54] Llewellyn distinguished five of these law jobs: (1) "the disposition of the trouble case"; (2) "the preventive channeling and reorientation of conduct and expectations"; (3) "the allocation of authority and the arrangement of procedures which legitimatize action as being authoritative"; (4) "the net organization of the group or society *as a whole* so as to provide cohesion, direction and incentive"; and (5) "the job of juristic method."[55] Each of these jobs needed doing to keep the group going.

All this seems to cover the familiar territory of functionalist social theory. Yet it is important to note that with his law-job theory, Llewellyn did not venture to derive a basic set of necessary legal rules which any society had to adopt in order to survive. For Llewellyn, the law-job theory primarily served as a heuristic to look at things legal. William Twining has noted with respect to Llewellyn's law-job theory that "unlike some functionalist theories, it makes no necessary normative or empirical assumption that conflict and dispute are inherently bad nor that there are uniform or universal ways of doing the law jobs." Indeed, Twining states that Llewellyn's theory "is almost devoid of empirical or normative content."[56] Hence, except perhaps for norms connected with the legal craft, with the technique of handling legal questions, he did not derive substantive norms from his functionalist framework. The law jobs, rather, were in large measure derivative of evolving social norms. These created the disputes and claims that law was called to settle authoritatively; these informed the "preventive channeling of conduct" and the "net organization of the group" that law was supposed to provide. And as we have seen, Llewellyn believed that the normative generalizations arising from the social and cultural setting were fundamentally idiosyncratic and evolved more or less autonomously through the processes of "drift"—the gradual and unpremeditated transformation of social conventions that forced change on the legal order—and "drive"—the conscious and unpredictable individual effort to change the legal order through the making of legal claims.

Thus, in Llewellyn's functionalist perspective, law was not built like a shark, sleek and perfectly adapted to its task. Indeed, he explicitly rejected the idea that a functional view of law presupposed that law had achieved, or should seek to achieve, some streamlined and highly efficient level of functional purity. His view was more accommodating to human idiosyncrasy. His understanding of what counted as functional was ornate and fully accepted that people's cultural and legal peculiarities formed a legitimate part of their legal system:

> With the idea of functional evaluation I have no desire to take over into legal esthetics the exaggerations, and to my mind absurdities, of those extreme "functionalists" in architecture and related arts who hold no form, no piece, no ornament to be esthetically legitimate which is not, with maximum economy and efficiency, a working portion of the thing designed. I hold another, and I hope a saner, view. I hold first that under such a bare "efficiency" conception of functional esthetics, purpose is yet an inherent part of any functioning structure; and so, that what expresses purpose expresses also an inherent part of function. Thus, to recur to the Gothic Cathedral, sculpture and glass-painting did not require to help hold up the edifice in order to be a right esthetic part of it. I hold, moreover, that man's love of play, and—yes—of loveliness, is as rightly satisfied as is his desire for work well done, or for economy, or for clean form. And objects of use are those which grow closest to the heart. Thus the only esthetic rule which I recognize about adornment in relation to function is that adornment is best when it can be made to serve function, and is bad when it interferes with function; beyond that, the quest for richness of beauty and meaning seems to me a right quest. You may call these prejudices; to me, they are considered values. But whether you like them or not, in general, you will have difficulty in dodging their applicability to things of law.[57]

If a functional view can accommodate the Gothic Cathedral, it might run the risk of becoming too broad and expansive, but it is unlikely to lapse into a reductionist and intellectually barren form of determinism. In Llewellyn's functionalist perspective, the development of law, clearly, was not reduced to movement along a necessary and given trajectory toward a predetermined end. For Llewellyn the development of law was more like "climbing Mount Improbable," to borrow a phrase from Richard Dawkins;[58] it was the slow buildup of a lavish, complex, and utterly unlikely system of rules through a haphazard process of picking up, testing, and selecting "normative generalizations."

PREDICTIVISM

One of the characteristics most commonly associated with Legal Realism, and a favorite among critics who want to make Legal Realism look silly, is its embrace of the notion of predictivism. It is what the mock Realist maxim "law is what the judge had for breakfast" seeks to poke fun at. A central reason the Realists offered for engaging in social science research was to improve the ability to predict the outcome of court cases. Following Holmes's famous adage "The prophecies of what the courts will do in fact, and nothing more pretentious, are what I mean by the law," many realists believed a central concern for a true legal science should be the scientific prediction of legal decisions. Social science knowledge about judicial behavior, they maintained, would enable lawyers to forecast much more accurately than the legal rules alone what a judge would decide in a given case. They hoped that, in the chaotic world of American law, knowledge about the behavior patterns of judges could bring the legal certainty that traditional legal doctrine had failed to offer. Much like the engineer or the doctor, Cook argued, the lawyer was engaged in forecasting future events: "What he wishes to know is, not how electrons, atoms, or bricks will behave in a given situation, but what a number of more or less elderly men who compose some court of last resort will do when confronted with the facts of his client's case."[59] Social science research could assist the modern lawyer in these predictions. Frank was of a similar mind. Since court opinions were "emasculated explanations of decisions," he claimed, they were of "limited assistance to the practicing lawyer." Thus, he noted: "Not only do they disclose merely a fractional part of how decisions come into being, but, if the lawyer takes them as adequate explanations of how decisions are reached, he will act with a treacherously false sense of certainty in advising clients, drafting instruments, writing briefs—or any other work he has to perform."[60] Felix Cohen believed that information about the socioeconomic backgrounds of judges could account for their behavior in court. Thus he regretted that there was "no publication showing the political, economic, and professional background and activities of our various judges," even though such a publication would be very valuable "to the practical lawyer who wants to bring a motion or try a case before a sympathetic court."[61]

This approach to law has earned the Realists much ridicule. By defining legal rules in terms of "what the courts will do in fact," in terms of the observable behavior patterns of the judiciary, Legal Realism seemed to have lost sight of the purposiveness of legal practice. This criticism was perhaps most forcefully voiced early on by H. L. A. Hart. Hart pointed out that concepts like "rights" and "duties" acquired their meaning within the framework of law as a rule-governed, social practice and that it would be a serious mistake to treat them as predictions of judicial behavior. Hart noted that when the Legal Realists were trying to resolve problems like "What is law?" or "What are rights?" they were asking the wrong questions. The assumption behind these kinds of questions was that language was always used to make statements about the world around us that were either true or false. Yet words could also be used to do something, to perform an action within an established social practice. Thus, Hart noted that if someone said "I have a right," this did not mean—as the Legal Realists would have it—that he was making a prediction that the courts would decide in his favor, but rather that he was appealing to a rule within an accepted moral or legal practice.[62] By adopting the idea that legal rules should be thought of as predictions of actual judicial behavior, Realist predictivism ignored the crucial and central aspect of law, namely, that it is a social practice in which lawyers sincerely engage in meaningful discourse about what legal rules and principles should mean in a given case. By treating legal rules as mere summaries of observed judicial behavior on which predictions of future judicial behavior could be based, Legal Realism misrepresented the character of what went on in the institution of law. When lawyers prepared a case, what they engaged in was not scientific prediction but interpretation and persuasion, not quantitative analysis but meaningful understanding of legal doctrine.

The idea of predictivism was undeniably popular among the Realists. However, the reception of the idea has not been kind. In the secondary literature on Realism, predictivism has been criticized as an indefensible notion many times. That is not to say that there have not also been defenses of the prediction theory of law. William Twining, for instance, has argued that Holmes and the Legal Realists have been misunderstood when they stressed the importance of prediction. With their embrace of predictivism, they were making statements aimed at a very specific audience, that is, practicing lawyers or students training to become professional lawyers. The prediction theory of law, in other words, was articulated for the workaday practice of providing legal assistance, not for the lofty perspective of the legal theorist or the appellate court judge. In the practical context of the working lawyer, accurate predictions of the likely outcome of a case were practical and useful.[63]

Another author who has called into question Hart's critique of Realist rule skepticism and predictivism is Hanoch Dagan. Dagan seems to disagree with Hart's critique on a more fundamental level, however. According to him, Hart primarily placed rule skepticism in the key of legal concepts having both a clear core reference and a penumbra of difficult-to-categorize references. Hart presented a good argument why *that* problem was not so serious and did not call for the replacement of legal reasoning with scientific prediction. Yet the Realists were concerned with a very different problem, according to Dagan: "The main reason for the realist claim that judges are never fully constrained by legal doctrine is not the indeterminacy of any given rule, an indeterminacy Hart domesticated, but, rather, the question whether the rule will contain a doubtful case." The law always provided a "multiplicity of doctrinal sources," a range of possible conceptualizations that could all be used to frame the facts of a case in a different way. Hence, the Realist point was mainly that: "In dealing with legal rules and legal concepts, the judicial task is never one of static application."[64]

This is pertinent criticism, but it only undermines part of Hart's argument. It does not invalidate the point stressed above that legal concepts often are not references to or predictions of observable behavior, but performative actions in an established social practice. They were more like moves in a game, than descriptions of some pattern of behavior. Dagan's analysis does not touch this problem with Realist predictivism.

Hence, even though the objections to Hart's critique are valid, they do not amount to a complete triumph over his arguments. There is still some bite to Hart's critique that law is a purposive practice in which lawyers and judges make meaningful moves and apply the rules in an established game. Such actions are distinct from making predictions on the basis of past behavior. Predictivism does not sum up what Realism amounted to, however. There are other aspects to Realism that still deserve our attention. One of those is Realist instrumentalism.

INSTRUMENTALISM

With respect to the instrumentalist conception of law the Realist turn to social science did not suffer from the drawbacks of predictivism. It is one thing to reduce the internal operations of a purposive legal practice to observable behavior patterns; it is quite another to study the effects and consequences of that legal practice in society at large and, vice versa, the influence of society at large on the legal practice. For the Realists, law was primarily a tool to further the welfare of society. Hence, they argued for a

broader view of law than Classical legal thought afforded. Instead of looking at law as an autonomous body of rules and principles, they proposed
to look at it as an instrument for social policy. This meant a focus on the
study of the social consequences of legal rules and doctrines, and this meant
an emphasis on the study of the existing social conditions, practices, and
norms that provided the context in which law developed and in which legal
rules eventually had to become effective.

As we have seen, in "Some Realism About Realism," Llewellyn and
Frank marked instrumentalism as one of the central characteristics of Legal Realism. According to them, Realists shared a "conception of law as a
means to social ends and not an end in itself," so that any part of law constantly needed "to be examined for its purpose, and for its effect, and to be
judged in the light of both and of their relation to each other."[65] Llewellyn
and Frank maintained that this focus on law as a means to social ends led
unavoidably to the consideration of topics that were outside the realm of
traditional legal scholarship. To them this meant a dedication to social science as an integral part of legal scholarship, because without research into
the people affected by law, it was impossible to gauge what the effects of
law were.[66]

Walter Wheeler Cook also made instrumentalism the aim of his scientific approach to law. Cook sought to combine in his vision of a Realistic
research program both an inquiry into existing social values and an examination of the success with which law managed to promote them:

> Underlying any scientific study of the law, it is submitted, will lie one funda-
> mental postulate, viz., that human laws are devices, tools which society uses as
> one of its methods to regulate human conduct and to promote those types of
> it which are regarded as desirable. If so, it follows that the worth or value of a
> given rule of law can be determined only by finding out how it works, that is,
> by ascertaining, so far as that can be done, whether it promotes or retards the
> attainment of desired ends. If this is to be done, quite clearly we must know
> what at any given period these ends are and also whether the means selected,
> the given rules of law, are indeed adapted to securing them.[67]

Cook asserted that his instrumental approach to law would involve "observation and study of the actual structure and functioning of modern social,
economic and political life, so that in dealing with what are in last analysis
problems of social and economic policy those working in their difficult field
will not rely upon hit-or-miss information which has been picked up acci-
dentally." Moreover, he argued that existing law would have to be studied
to determine just what it was. Before anything could be improved, accu-

rate knowledge about what needed to be improved was necessary. Finally, Cook contended that an instrumental approach would entail research into the actual operation of different legal devices in order to provide insights into the ways in which law could most effectively bring about changes and adjustments in the relevant community.[68]

In a similar vein, Leon Keyserling stressed the policy dimension in law and the need for social science knowledge. He observed that the "lawyer is the shock trooper in court, legislature and executive mansion, where many of the battles of peaceful societal reconstruction are finally resolved." As a result, he claimed, "the ramifications of the lawyer's function become increasingly manifest, the demand becomes more insistent that he be equipped to deal with the social and economic perplexities which are at the center of the congeries of problems known as 'legal.'"[69]

As we shall see in the next chapter, a common CLS critique of this Realist instrumentalism, of this policy-oriented social research, is that it could not avoid becoming one-sided and political. Because real societies do not usually consist of one single overarching interest, but of an excess of small conflicting ones, it is impossible to know, or to sort out, exactly which policy goals law should seek to realize instrumentally. Hence, according to CLS adherents, when the Realists tried to implement their policy approach, they were often unable to determine what the overarching interest of society was, which law was supposed to further. In practice, they claim, Realist policy research frequently ended up simply supporting some dominant social interest—which already found expression in the law—at the expense of the interests of the powerless. Thus, despite their zeal for social reform, the Realists inadvertently managed to develop a method which tended to invest hegemonic interests, the legal status quo, with an aura of necessity, fairness, and impartiality.

This criticism is unfair. The Realists were not oblivious to the pluralism and diversity of society. They were quite aware that modern societies were not monolithic bodies with a single interest. For instance, when Harold Laski, inspired by the legal thought of his friend Oliver Wendell Holmes, in Realist fashion admonished American lawyers "to set law to the rhythm of modern life," he proclaimed: "It is the harmonization of warring interests with which we are concerned. How to evolve from a seeming conflict the social gain it is the endeavor of law to promote—this is the problem by which we are confronted."[70] Laski clearly acknowledged the miscellany of conflicting interests that made up society and that needed to be mediated and harmonized through law. Hence, the task of the Realist legal scholar was not simply to register what the general interest was and translate it into law, but to synthesize and coordinate an array of conflicting wishes and claims in a way that would avail society as a whole.

Llewellyn also commented that the supposed unity of law was a fiction. Legal doctrine was always "instinct with diverse and warring premises of growth," he claimed. The notion of law as an ordered unity was only a "fictional frame of discourse within which particular partial reconciliations and hierarchical integrations [we]re constantly worked out." This unrealizable ideal of unity allowed for the absorption and digestion of all the diverse social trends and issues in "the pluralistic, vari-tendencied system" of law.[71] To be sure, in the end there was something Llewellyn referred to as the "Net Drive" of the legal system, "the net organization around something, toward something; the Whither of the net Totality."[72] Yet this use of the phrase "Net Drive" already suggests a balancing of different conflicting "drives." It is not "Dominant Drive" or "Requisite Drive." "Net Drive" conjures up a notion of disparate vectors pointing in different directions adding up to a resulting vector sum. It would also be a misrepresentation of Llewellyn's theory to associate his conception of an instrumentalist approach with the idea that technocratic policy research could somehow authoritatively and rationally determine where exactly the "Whither" of the "Net Drive" should be. Llewellyn indeed worked from the contrary assumption that "conscious production of Net Drive has been too big a job for man to handle with full success on a large scale." His conception of what produced "Net Drive" was rather more democratic. The "major effective device" for the creation of "Net Drive," he believed, was "the throwing of large—though vaguish—blocs of desired Net Drive into ideal pictures accompanied each by an emotionally stirring symbol." These "ideal pictures" were as elusive as they were important. "In two hands the same one may produce differences which startle," Llewellyn commented. Yet they were nonetheless influential and unmistakably mediated "their quantum of general coordination to our Legal System."[73]

THE UNIFORM COMMERCIAL CODE

An example of the Realist instrumental approach to law is the Uniform Commercial Code (UCC). The UCC was an effort to modernize and unify commercial law in the United States by providing a model code that individual states could enact into law. To a considerable extent, the UCC was a brainchild of Karl Llewellyn. He was engrossed in the drafting process of the UCC from the late 1930s to the early 1950s. Although the drafting of the UCC involved the teamwork and collaboration of a great many lawyers and business people, Llewellyn's influence on the UCC as the chief reporter for the National Conference of Commissioners on Uniform State Laws (NCC) and the American Law Institute (ALI)—the organizations framing the UCC—is generally believed to have been considerable. Llewellyn's influence is mainly evident in the correspondence of the UCC with commercial custom, reflecting the Realist notion that law should be in tune with existing social practices. Instead of the abstract concept of "title," which had been the central focus of the earlier 1906 Uniform Sales Act and had led to the intractable problem of when "title" had passed from one party to another in the complex commercial world of the twentieth century, Llewellyn sought to base the UCC on a functional understanding of modern trade practice. According to Horwitz, this is exactly what is wrong with the UCC and with the Realist turn to social science. "It has become a familiar criticism of Llewellyn that in drafting the Uniform Commercial Code to reflect mercantile custom," Horwitz observes, "he endowed economically dominant commercial practices with undeserved normativity."[74] The people that lost out in the UCC, because of Llewellyn's stress on mercantile custom, he argues, were the consumers. The Realist turn to social science simply made it imperative that social practices were presented as homogeneous. If society generated a heterogeneous multitude of normative expectations, then the Realist would simply not be able to ground law in reality without making a value choice for one, or another, social practice. Hence, Llewellyn chose to present mercantile custom as *the* relevant social practice and constructed the UCC around that, at the cost of conflicting consumer interests.

Yet if Horwitz's criticism might hold true for the finished product of the UCC, it does not for Llewellyn's original designs for the code. The UCC was a collaborative effort, the result of compromise and bargain, and many of Llewellyn's proposals for the UCC never found their way into the final version. Llewellyn's early drafts for the code provide a better picture of what Llewellyn wanted to achieve with his Realist approach. His early drafts were not as slanted toward existing mercantile custom as the final version of the UCC might suggest. Llewellyn wanted to build on commercial practice, to be sure, but he did not simply equate the interests of business with the public weal. Rather, he wanted to foster fair business practice, discourage unfair habits and customs, and supply normative restraints on the market to avoid excesses injurious to the public. Thus, for instance, Llewellyn formulated a number of merchant rules on the basis of commercial practice that imposed stricter standards on the business community than on individual consumers. Llewellyn believed that with an uneven distribution of information, skill, and knowledge, an extension of these merchant rules to nonmerchants would comprise an unfair application of merchant standards to the uninitiated. Many of the merchant rules Llewellyn proposed did not survive, however. Several were discarded or broadened into general rules.[75] One of these merchant rules even sought to increase protection for the consumer through a strict liability standard that placed responsibility for defective products on the manufacturer—decades before such a standard became part of American tort law. When Llewellyn proposed the idea of strict liability at the 1941 UCC conference, however, it evoked strong opposition. Indeed, Llewellyn later remarked that any proposal for strict liability "scared everybody that saw it pea green."[76] Consequently, strict liability never resurfaced as a recommendation in UCC deliberations after 1941, and it was never adopted in the final document. At any rate, if Llewellyn's original plans for the UCC are taken as the point of departure, then his approach can no longer be seen as endowing dominant social interests with normativity. This anecdotal evidence suggests that the problem with instrumentalism may not primarily be a problem of flawed methodology or the uncertainties of research, but rather a problem of gaining political support, that is, a problem of power and interests.

This leaves the question of how Llewellyn collected his information about existing commercial practice for the UCC. According to William Twining, the fact gathering that was engaged in within the framework of the UCC was not at all of a rigorous scientific nature. For knowledge about the relevant social context, experience and common sense rather than empirical research were usually thought to be sufficient to supply reliable and relevant information.[77] In other words, the UCC seems to have been based on exactly the kind of unreliable, impressionistic, hit-or-miss information that the Realists claimed they wanted to move away from in law. Consequently, the UCC is often seen as proof that the Realists did not practice what they preached. Despite all their rhetoric about turning law into a social science, they remained safely within the bounds of traditional legal scholarship and traditional conceptions of what legal work involved.

There is something to this criticism, but its bite should not be exaggerated. Llewellyn and the other Realists pioneered a new approach to law in a legal environment that was generally hostile to their ideas. Against this background, it seems a little unfair to criticize them for not being able to live up to their own ideal conception of legal research. They can hardly be faulted for not being able to forge the full-scale reorientation of legal scholarship and legal work they believed necessary. With reference to the UCC, for instance, Twining observes that a departure from the traditional practice of the sponsors, the NCC and the ALI, would have been highly unlikely: "the institutional context, reinforced by the predispositions of the Code personnel, the pressure of time and the relative modesty of the financing, made it virtually inevitable that empirical research on a large scale could not have been undertaken."[78] To be sure, neither did the lack of rigorously collected scientific data seem to worry Llewellyn too much. For the UCC, he reverted mainly to the modest fact-gathering missions of his assistants, to the practical expertise of lawyers and merchants involved in drafting the UCC, and last but not least, to his own knowledge of commercial practice—which interested him greatly in the minutest detail and about which he had built up extensive and detailed knowledge throughout his career. In spite of the lack of scientific rigor, Llewellyn's gaze was firmly focused on the practical realities of commerce.[79] That Llewellyn did not engage in rigorous scientific research because of institutional constraints and the infancy of the social sciences is hardly a conclusive repudiation of the main thrust of his approach, that is, that law reform and legislation should take existing social practice and existing norms and attitudes as their point of departure and that these social phenomena are amenable to empirical inquiry.

CONCLUSION

One conclusion to be drawn from the argument in this chapter is that Llewellyn did not make a freak observation when he claimed that the Realists tried to integrate social science into legal inquiry. The Realists were keenly interested in the possibilities of social science and widely accepted that it could make a valuable contribution to legal scholarship. A second conclusion suggested by the above is that it would be quite wrong to confuse this Realist embrace of social science with a belief in behaviorism or positivism. The Realists studied and quoted William James and John Dewey, not Carl Hempel and Rudolf Carnap. The latter's positivism might make an easy target for CLS critics—one they can simply marshal all the familiar arguments of German Critical Theory against—but it is not one that covers Realist theory. To frame the Realist argument for social science as a species of positivism is to set up a straw puppet with uninviting features that are widely disliked.

What the Realist approach should be understood as, instead, is Pragmatism. The odd Realist combination of cognitive relativism *and* faith in social science was not some flawed, hybrid form of Positivism, but a bold attempt to recast legal scholarship in a Pragmatic mold. What the Realists seem to have picked up on in the Pragmatism of James and Dewey is what Hilary Putnam has called "*the* basic insight of American Pragmatism," namely, that "one can be both fallibilistic *and* antisceptical," that one can both believe that no guarantees are to be had for even our most firmly held beliefs *and* that total doubt about all our knowledge of the world is misplaced. What the Pragmatists tried to explain, according to Putnam, is "that access to a common reality does not require access to something *preconceptual*. It requires, rather, that we be able to form *shared* concepts."[80] That there was no preconceptual world of facts untainted by our conceptual frameworks, that there were no facts unmediated by the theory that was tested on them, did not invalidate scientific inquiry for the Pragmatists. All that scientific inquiry required was a community of scholars with shared concepts, with a shared understanding of the world, engaged in a collaborative effort of debating, testing, and criticizing each other's work and trying to arrive at some measure of intersubjective agreement on what theory fit best with, and worked best in, the external world that was still believed to be out there and not to conform wholly to our conceptions of it. Hence, the elements of social science and cognitive relativism that Horwitz finds so jarring in the writing of the Realists were not incompatible to them; in Pragmatism they found a theoretical framework that showed how they could coexist.

The third conclusion to be drawn from the above is that the language of functionalism used by the Realists should not be equated unthinkingly with reductionism and determinism. The Realist understanding of functionalism was truly Darwinian in that it rejected any absolute notion of "functional adaptation." For the Realists, there was no teleology, no inexorable development toward the apex of well-adapted legal systems—contemporary American law. Their understanding of adaptation was much more relativistic and dynamic. Law could only be well adapted relative to a cultural and socioeconomic environment, and this environment was always changing. Moreover, law did not work itself clean of dysfunctional elements all by itself. Legal rules and concepts could survive, regardless of their inaptness, simply because people cherished and valued them. Hence, Legal Realism lacked any assumption of functionality when looking at contemporary law. That some legal rule had survived since the time of Henry IV, as Holmes had famously pointed out, did not automatically mean that it must therefore be performing some essential and necessary function. The rule might simply have persisted through blind imitation. This understanding of functionalism is much closer to present-day meme theory than to classic notions of functionalism within the social sciences. It is not some outdated perspective on social phenomena, in other words, which is only of interest to the legal historian, but one that is topical today.

Finally, we can draw the conclusion from this chapter that, although the idea of predictivism was fundamentally flawed, the Realist notion of instrumentalism and policy research was not as simplistic as many CLS adherents make it out to be. The Realists certainly did not harbor the foolish notion that society was monolithic and had a single, determinable interest which could form the basis for scientific policy analysis. The Realists knew full well that society consisted of an aggregate of conflicting interests that needed to be balanced in the legal system. Moreover, they never claimed that an instrumentalist approach would be easy and straightforward, or that the problem of social regulation could be reduced to a simple cost-benefit calculation resulting in some optimal and objective solution. Their new instrumental approach to law was always envisioned as something that had to take shape in the messy and unpredictable setting of a modern democratic society. As Pragmatists, the Realists were committed to both science and democracy. The point was not to replace democracy with disinterested policy research, but to enrich and elevate the democratic debate with pointed and cogent knowledge about legal matters.

CHAPTER FIVE

Oh, the Tangled Webs We Weave: The CLS Critique of Social Science

> This fine deceit, this perfect rift,
> Dissociating thought from sense
> —Yvor Winters[1]

> Yeah, well, you know, that's just, like, your opinion, man.
> —The Dude[2]

> Alice laughed. "There is no use trying," she said, "one can't believe impossible things."
> "I dare say you haven't had much practice," said the Queen. "When I was your age, I always did it for half-an-hour a day. Why, sometimes I've believed as many as six impossible things before breakfast."
> —Lewis Carroll[3]

Critical Legal Studies (CLS) scholars have been severely critical of the Realist turn to social science and policy research. Part of the explanation for this distaste can be found in the formative era of the majority of CLS adherents—that is, the politically turbulent 1960s. In an autobiographical account, Robert Gordon provides an insight into how the distrust of policy research took shape in that period. In the postwar years, Realist-inspired policy analysis had become prevalent in American law schools. Consequently, many Critical scholars were exposed to a "toned-down legal realism" when they became law students in the 1960s. This moderated variety of Realism, Gordon contends, was "a kind of quickie utilitarian method," which was supposed to enable lawyers "to argue for outcomes that could efficiently serve social policies somehow inhering in the legal system." If competing policies could be inferred that represented competing social interests, then the task of policy analysis was "to provide an on-the-spot rapid-fire 'balancing' of interests." The ideal aspired to was that of the lawyer who would be adroit at all the relevant social-engineering techniques and who "would be able to discover—by the use of legal reasoning alone—socially optimal solutions for virtually all legal problems." Thus, through the use of policy analysis, the lawyer would be able to uncover the functionally optimal lines along which the law was most likely—and most preferably—going to evolve.[4]

This law school vision of "neutrally benevolent technique," Gordon argues, became suspect amid the social and political upheaval of the 1960s. Rampant political strife undermined the idea that there was a consensus about basic social values on which policy analysis could be based. The appeal to a broad social consensus, Gordon notes, "was hardly a winner in a society apparently splintering every day between blacks and whites, hawks and doves, men and women, hippies and straights, parents and children." Such glaring social disharmony also made a mockery of the idea of "the underlying march of historical progress." If there was so little agreement on basic social values, then how could one assume that social developments naturally tended to move in a certain direction and that lawyers could somehow chart the way the law was going to develop?

Yet most damaging of all, according to Gordon, was the insight that policy science could apparently be used to rationalize some of the most odious and malign government policies. During the 1960s it was a group of liberal policy analysts in the Johnson administration who directed the war effort in Vietnam. To many law students this compromised the whole project of policy research. As Gordon puts it:

> The vision of law as a technocratic policy science administered by a disinterested elite was tarnished, to say the least, for anyone who watched the "best and the brightest" direct and justify the war in Vietnam. The fluent optimistic jargon of policy science in the middle of such unspeakable slaughter and suffering seemed not only absurdly remote from any world of experience but literally insane.

What policy science appears to conjure up for CLS adherents, in other words, is not the image of the New Deal contemporaries of the Legal Realists, who tried to relieve social deprivation through the benevolent welfare programs of the Roosevelt administration. Rather, the image Critical scholars associate with policy science is that of an emblematic number cruncher like Secretary of Defense Robert McNamara, applying the latest techniques in scientific management and statistical control to inflict suffering on the Vietnamese. Not the policy science of relief and public works, but the policy science of the "body count" is what primarily soured the young Critical scholars on policy analysis. Social science has been a major target of their critique ever since, especially in the shape of law and economics.[5]

This is not to say that CLS adherents have not also provided theoretical arguments for their rejection of social science. They have. Critical scholars have claimed, in broad terms, that empirical social science is deterministic, reductive, and ideologically conservative. Much of the remainder of this chapter will be concerned with a discussion of these points of criticism. Naturally, this has presented Critical scholars with an embarrassing problem. Many of their heroes in the Realist movement not only embraced social science wholeheartedly, but also committed their admiration for social science to paper. Hence, CLS scholars are at pains to explain how they can combine their radical rejection of social science with their simultaneous embrace of Legal Realism, a movement defined by its enthusiastic plea for the use of social science in the legal field. Three main responses to this quandary have been put forward in the CLS literature: (1) that Legal Realism should not be understood as a movement that embraced social science in the first place; (2) that Legal Realism should be understood as a movement that embraced social science, but that this is not really a problem for CLS theory; and (3) that Legal Realism should be understood as a movement that embraced social science, that this is a problem for CLS theory, and that, therefore, this social science aspect of Realist theory should be entirely rejected.

The first two of these responses are minority positions within the CLS movement and will be described only briefly below. The third response is the most broadly supported among CLS adherents and will be discussed in greater detail in the remainder of the chapter. The first response—the claim that social science was never really a central part of Legal Realism—is defended by CLS historian Morton Horwitz and was already introduced in the Chapter 4.[6] In his view, most legal scholars have simply been wrong about Legal Realism. By disproportionately focusing their attention on Llewellyn's first accounts of Legal Realism, they have come to believe that the entire Realist movement wholeheartedly embraced the social sciences and warmly recommended the divorce of Is and Ought. However, Llewellyn's admonitions that law should be shaped into an empirical, value-free discipline, Horwitz believes, provided a profoundly misleading sketch of the new developments in American legal scholarship. According to Horwitz, Llewellyn hugely exaggerated the scientific aspects of Realism and mistakenly connected the movement with now widely discredited strands of positivist and behavioralistic social science. This distorted view of Legal Realism has stuck, Horwitz claims, and has resulted in the neglect of the central, hermeneutic, and interpretivistic element in the Realist legacy.[7]

The second response—the claim that the Realists did embrace social science but that it is not really a problem for CLS—is primarily tied up with the name of David Trubek. Trubek is an odd character within CLS. He is a Critical scholar who has remained squarely within the Law and Society movement. Unlike his fellow Critical Scholars, he has not relinquished his sociological interests. Rather, he has sought to combine them with central aspects of CLS theory into something called "Critical Empiricism." Trubek has a sophisticated grasp of modern social science. Contrary to common CLS opinion, he does not equate social science with positivism and determinism but recognizes that most social scientists now work within a different epistemological framework. Thus, he emphasizes that full-blown positivists who seek to uncover the timeless laws of social behavior are extremely rare. Most of today's scholars who do social scientific research, he points out, "probably are aware of the limited, provisional, and pragmatic nature of the knowledge that it yields." Consequently, he criticizes the CLS community for jumping to the conclusion far too readily that "all people who interview, analyze statistics, conduct surveys, code records, and so on must be positivist determinists."[8]

The rejection of this facile critique of social science is necessary for Trubek to lay the groundwork for his positive program of redefining the CLS approach as an interpretive sociology of law. Trubek argues that CLS scholarship, rightly understood, is more akin to legal sociology than most CLS adherents care to admit. Trubek supports this claim by focusing on the discursive nature of social relations. Actions are shaped by ideas and concepts, he argues. There is, therefore, a clear causal link between legal discourse and social behavior. This perspective allows him to merge CLS inquiry into the sociology of law and to present the two approaches as complementary rather than conflicting.

> For those who engage in the critique of legal thought, ideas in some strong sense can be said to "constitute" society. That is, social order depends in a non-trivial way on society's shared "world views." Those world views are basic notions about human and social relations that give meaning to the lives of the society's members. Ideas about the law—what it is, what it does, and why it exists—are part of the world view of any complex society. These ideas form the legal consciousness of society. The critique of legal thought is the analysis of the world views embedded in modern legal consciousness.[9]

Because the "worlds of meaning that we construct in turn shape and channel what we do and do not do," Trubek claims, "social relations and world views become inseparable."[10] As a result, he would like CLS scholars to give up their polemics against social science and to admit that their views are continuous with, rather than hostile to, the law-and-society perspective.

The third response—the claim that the Realists did embrace social science, that this is a problem for CLS, and that it should therefore be rejected—finally is the one adopted by the overwhelming majority of Critical scholars. Most do not agree with Horwitz and his denial that social science was in any way central to the Realist approach. Rather than historical arguments that dismiss the importance of social science to the Realists, they believe CLS should provide theoretical arguments for rejecting the type of social science and policy research with which Legal Realism is commonly associated. Neither is the conciliatory stance chosen by Trubek at all typical for CLS. The majority of CLS scholars have no wish to reconcile their approach with any social scientific understanding of law. That way, they believe, lies reductionism, determinism, and the dehumanizing discourse of the liberal bureaucratic state.

This chapter will discuss these arguments in greater detail and compare them to the Realist vision of a social scientific approach to law described in the previous chapter. In that chapter we saw that the most accurate and worthwhile way to understand Legal Realism is as a Pragmatic synthesis of an interpretivistic approach and a scientific one. The argument suggested that as far as the Realists embraced social science, they should *not* be seen as predecessors of the kind of positivism and behaviorism that reigned supreme in American social science departments in the 1950s and 1960s, but as contemporaries of the Pragmatists, who were the vogue of the 1920s and 1930s. This chapter will seek to establish that the mainstream CLS critique of social science is directed largely at the later behaviorist fashion. It is this behaviorist fashion that CLS adherents like Robert Gordon grew disaffected with in the 1960s and that sparked the hermeneutic, or interpretivist, backlash that CLS is a facet of. Indeed, CLS theory seems so absorbed with the argument against behaviorism that it appears to have lost sight of the fact that behaviorism is not really the most salient aspect of Legal Realism. The *Methodenstreit* in the social sciences between, on the one hand, behaviorism and positivism, and on the other, hermeneutics and interpretivism that looms so large for Critical scholars is simply the wrong framework for interpreting Legal Realism. It postdates that movement by two decades and is largely irrelevant to its proper understanding.

Nevertheless, the CLS understanding of the Realist embrace of social science deserves to be discussed. Three broad themes will be highlighted in its description below. To begin with, CLS doubts about the ability of social science to provide determinate answers to legal questions will be discussed.

For the Realists, social science was the discipline of choice to replace the traditional doctrinal scholarship they were criticizing. CLS scholars, however, have cast doubt on the usefulness of social research and argue that social science is just as inconclusive and politically loaded as legal doctrine. Second, the CLS critique of science and reason will be sketched. Where the Legal Realists had high hopes for scientific inquiry and rational debate, CLS scholars question the very coherence of modern science and the privileging of scientific discourse over other modes of understanding. Third, the CLS critique of functionalism will be described. If for the Realists functionalism seemed to offer an exciting new framework to wed social science with law, for CLS it represents the final surrender of the Realist movement to an acquiescent mode of understanding with a strong bias toward the status quo.

SOCIAL SCIENCE AS POLITICS

The standard CLS claim is that the Legal Realists provided an invaluable service to legal scholarship when they exposed the indeterminacy and contingency of legal doctrine, but that they went seriously astray when they suggested that social research and policy science could replace the discredited formalist analysis and provide the necessary determinate answers. By opting for social science, most Critical scholars believe, the Realists merely replaced one equivocal form of discourse with another; they simply supplanted indeterminate doctrinal research with equally indeterminate exercises in social science and policy analysis. *Both* these forms of inquiry depend on arbitrary value judgments and political choice, CLS adherents stress, *both* seek to obscure that fact, and *both* should be discarded.

Mark Tushnet is a Critical scholar who is clearly of this mind. Tushnet rejects the social science program of Legal Realism because like doctrinal analysis it failed to provide finality. The Realists' embrace of social science, he believes, led them into a dead end:

> Realism was a simple and unproblematic attack on the idea that the body of legal doctrine provided an objective basis for decisions in specific instances. Some Realists tried to escape this conclusion by emphasizing the law's relation to social policy, but that route only opened the legal system to even more basic challenges. First, policies are more obviously controversial than the purely deductive arguments of case analysis. . . . Second, neither those policies nor indeed any others could be brought to bear on a specific problem to provide a single solution. Policies, like precedents, could always be used to argue for contradictory results.[11]

Thus, social science was even more unlikely than doctrinal analysis to provide the judge with a single, determinate solution to a legal problem. If the declared aim of the Realist adoption of the social scientific perspective was conclusive answers to legal questions, then their project was bound to fail.

The Realist critique of legal rules was "simple and deep," according to Tushnet. The Realists showed that because of the extreme variation of the available precedents and the flexibility of the accepted techniques of legal reasoning, a sound case could be made for almost any proposition.[12] This subversion of formalist jurisprudence was very successful in the United States, Tushnet argues, as was the Realist solution to this problem. Instead of arguing about disembodied legal concepts and rules, the Realists suggested that legal scholars should focus on the policy issues implicit in legal doctrine. In shifting attention to the policy goals of legal rules, plain and concrete aspects of social policy would become the focus of legal argument, not ephemeral legal abstractions.

This move to policy failed, however. When postwar legal scholars tried to implement the Realist program, according to Tushnet, the social sphere proved to be extremely complex and very difficult to adjust by legal means to reach policy objectives. Furthermore, Tushnet argues, "reforms that called for governmental intervention occurred in the face of adaptable and politically powerful interests, which placed stringent limits on politically tolerable and therefore achievable policy changes," while, for the same reason, "reforms directed at government itself were absorbed and trivialised." As a result, policy analysis acquired "an increasingly conservative cast," which boiled down to the insight "that nothing works, that reasoned interventions in complex processes are unlikely to have desirable effects." Moreover, Tushnet alleges, the political consensus which made policy analysis possible shattered. The liberal scholars advancing policy analysis in law after the Second World War found common cause in a Progressive New Deal reformist program. This political consensus ensured agreement about the broad goals that social policy should seek to achieve. Yet when this Progressive policy science was challenged by the conservative policy analysis of the Law and Economics movement, the social goals that had been taken to be uncontroversial became contested. Consequently, agreement about policy goals disappeared, and policy analysis in law became politicized. Hence, the policy analysts were back at square one. Just like formalist legal reasoning, policy science proved to be just an elaborate edifice to obscure the inescapable political character of law. Scientific research proved to be just another way to make legal doctrine look neutral and natural.[13]

In a similar vein, James Boyle argues that the focus on social policy in law, and on ways of improving it, did not solve the problems that the Realists had exposed but led them in the wrong direction. In an article with the revealing title "The Politics of Reason," Boyle argues that the Realist faith in the possibility to improve the social policies implicit in law were undergirded by a misguided belief in the objectivity and neutrality of social science data—"truth no longer resided in the law school; it had moved next door into the economics department." Much like Tushnet, Boyle maintains this did not offer any solution for the problem of legal indeterminacy. The factual data uncovered by the social sciences were too contentious and underdetermined to provide law with determinate answers. Hence, Boyle claims that "the choices that were to be made using these data remained just as politically loaded as they had always been" and that, consequently, "no amount of 'balancing' reified 'interests' and no amount of pro/con policy argumentation would put the Humpty Dumpty of legal neutrality back together again."[14]

Mark Kelman, finally, is also critical of the Legal Realist reversion to policy analysis and social science research. The ambiguity the Realists exposed in legal rules, according to Kelman, could hardly be corrected by a focus on the policy goals that rules were supposed to serve. The purposive understanding of legal rules, which the Realists believed would solve the problem of the inconclusiveness of legal language, assumed that such an understanding would be "far more determinate and less politically charged than the CLS adherents believe." Indeed, as Kelman points out, the CLS movement has expended a great deal of its energy in proving that a comparable belief in policy inquiry by "the most prominent consequentialist movement at today's law schools, the Law and Economics movement, does not deliver redemption from formalist indeterminacy."[15] Just like the efforts of the Law and Economics movement to translate legal problems into questions of wealth maximization, the Realist attempts to convert them into questions of social welfare are ultimately based on politically controversial assumptions and inconclusive empirical evidence. These do not offer the neutrality and certainty sought for, but merely obscure political choice with scientific rather than legal sophistry.

CRITIQUE OF SCIENCE AND REASON

This skepticism about the neutrality of scientific inquiry cannot be posited without argument, of course. Hence the criticism of the use of social science in law has involved CLS in epistemological theory and a comprehensive critique of science and reason. "As in the celebrated dispute between Galileo and the Italian establishment," the Critical scholar Alan Hutchinson observed, "it is not merely the truth of nature that is at stake, but the nature of truth itself."[16] Two broad lines of attack can be distinguished in this critique. Put crudely, Critical scholars have argued that (1) the very idea of science is fundamentally flawed, and (2) that science, like law, is politics.

To begin with the first of these two charges, CLS adherents believe that recent developments in philosophy—the linguistic turn, hermeneutics, Postmodernism—have dealt mortal blows to the idea that reason and science can provide us with objective knowledge about the world. Thus, in an evocative metaphor, the English Critical scholar Alan Hunt tries to explain what is ultimately at stake in CLS:

> As we approach the end of the century we are sitting anxiously on the edge of a glacier aware of its ultimate fate but impressed by its endurance. The seeming solidity of the main face, called the Enlightenment, continues to hold to the possibility of objective knowledge realisable through natural and social scientific procedures. Piling up behind and threatening to displace this longstanding and already fractured edifice are a complex intermeshing set of newer glaciers, each having their own distinctive origins. They have many and varied names: linguistic philosophy, phenomenology, post structuralism, deconstruction, pragmatism and relativism to name but a few.[17]

The central issue in these new movements in philosophy, sociology, and literary theory, according to Hunt, is the project of "pressing to their most disturbing implications the consequences of accepting the culturally constructed nature of social existence" and the challenge this poses to "those intellectual traditions since the Enlightenment which claim to offer the possibility of access to a verifiable truth." CLS is an integral part of this project. It aims to spell out what the insights of the "new movements" mean for law and is "engaged in confronting a very profound intellectual challenge to the conventional methods and preoccupations of legal scholarship."[18]

James Boyle argues in a similar vein that what CLS builds on in Legal Realism are the arguments that "deal on a very mundane level with rationality and the social construction of knowledge." Yet CLS holds that the Realists did not realize the full scope of their arguments about the social construction of knowledge. Their insight that concepts and structures of thought did not describe something inherent in the world but were contingent, cultural fabrications, the Realists believed, only had repercussions for formalist legal reasoning, not for scientific inquiry. Hence, Boyle notes, Realism could contain both "a *critique* of essentialist rationality in linguistic interpretation and a *defense* of the essential rationality of science." What the Realists did not consider, and CLS has since come to appreciate, however, is "the possibility that the same corrosion might be eating away at *both* language and science at the same time."[19] The critique of essentialism in law was an argument that ultimately turned against the Realist turn to social science, Boyle maintains. The Realist assault on the idea that words had a fixed, essential meaning that reflected something true about the world not only undermined formalist legal reasoning but also undercut the realm of purposes and policies that the Realists fell back on to remedy the inherent arbitrariness of the meaning of legal terms and concepts:

> After all, essentialism does not happen only in language. People want to believe that objects, events, science, social classes, genders, races, history, as well as words—that all these things have essential qualities. When we challenge the belief in essences we do more than change the direction of legal theory. We open ourselves up to the fragility of the stories we tell, the contingent, could-be-otherwise character of the film of meaning that we project onto the social world.[20]

If the abstractions of law were shown to be contingent social constructions that could not be considered to somehow represent the true nature of real-world phenomena, then there was no good reason to assume that the same could not be said of the premises and concepts of policy analysis and social science. In the end, social science was just a culturally constructed vocabulary with which to describe the world, without any privileged epistemological status. Hence, once the Realists brought their antiessentialist critique to bear on legal formalism, their turn to technocracy ceased to be a viable alternative.

Probably the most influential CLS critique of science, however, is Unger's *Knowledge and Politics*. In this book Unger sets out to uncover and demolish the "deep structure" of liberal thought. A central part of this "deep structure" is a liberal epistemology on which its faith in science and rationality is claimed to be built. The problem with this liberal epistemology is that it contains what Unger calls an "antinomy of theory and fact." On the one hand, Unger claims, the liberal commitment to science is based on a rejection of the preliberal doctrine of "intelligible essences," on the denial of the idea that things have apparent, essential features which determine whether they fall into one, rather than another, category of phenomena. Liberal thought, in other words, abandons the idea that facts speak for themselves, that facts are independent of the theoretical and linguistic concepts we use to study and interpret them. Yet at the same time liberal thought seems to be based on the very conception of the intelligible essences it rejects. Its faith in scientific progress and in the possibility of a rational choice between competing scientific theories presupposes a belief in plain facts, in facts that speak for themselves, in facts that can be used as a touchstone to see which of a given number of competing scientific theories is best. Hence, the antinomy of theory and fact in liberal thought is the contradiction that facts are at the same time manufactured by, and independent of, our theoretical framework. Or as Unger states: "The conception that there is a realm of things, independent of the mind, and capable at some point of being perceived as it truly is, seems necessary to the notion of science. Yet this conception also appears to rely on the doctrine of intelligible essences or plain facts, assumed to be inconsistent with the modern idea of science."[21] It would be difficult to overestimate the importance Unger accords to this antinomy. He suggests that it "appears to imply the incoherence of our idea of science, indeed of knowledge in general." To Unger the antinomy of theory and fact is proof that the idea of science is fundamentally flawed. The two sides of the antinomy "contradict one another, but to qualify either of them would seem to require a drastic revision of the view of nature and thought from which both are drawn."[22]

The CLS criticisms of science listed so far have been aimed at exposing the implausibility and incoherence of "liberal" epistemology. CLS does not only hold that this epistemology is incoherent, however; it also claims that it is political. Thus, according to Hutchinson, "there is no position of theoretical innocence or political neutrality" for CLS. Any form of interpretation is irreducibly political. Hence, the "question of what amounts to valid knowledge," Hutchinson maintains, "is itself a socio-political matter," and epistemology is just "ideological warfare fought by other, more esoteric means."[23] Alan D. Freeman claims that "crucial to the critical enterprise is the recognition, drawn from the Marxist tradition, that knowledge and power are inseparable, that the production of knowledge is connected with and dependent on realities of power." This does not mean Historical Materialism or a conspiracy theory about conniving capitalists, but it does mean that Critical scholars have a task "to liberate people from their abstractions, to reduce abstractions to concrete historical settings, and, by so doing, to expose as ideology what appears to be positive fact or ethical norm."[24]

James Boyle develops this theme more extensively. In an analysis drawing heavily on the Critical Theory of the Frankfurt School and dotted with references to the older works of Jürgen Habermas, Boyle tries to show that science and technocracy are not neutral but are methods heavily loaded against the transformative possibility of politics. "Much of the power of scientism lies in its claim to be free of any . . . utopian vision," Boyle asserts; "instead, technocratic thought claims merely to provide us with a means to an end." Scientific technique does not claim to be able to provide the goals that government should seek to achieve, which are assumed to be provided by prior public debate. It merely purports to provide the most rational and efficient way to achieve them. Yet the irony is, according to Boyle, "that the *presence* of the scientific analytic technique actually ensures the *absence* of the value decision on which the technique is supposedly premised." By focusing solely on means, the scientific approach creates a "vacuum" around the choice of ends, and this "vacuum," Boyle maintains, "is immediately filled by the uncritical assumptions of the existing power structure." In other words, when social issues are advanced in a depoliticized, scientific fashion, their open discussion in the public realm is all but precluded. As a result, existing conditions become the baseline for policy science, and imaginative political alternatives become difficult to voice. This circumspect affirmation of the status quo is especially insidious because the scientific approach disavows any substantive vision. Since it does not acknowledge that it supports any values, it cannot even be held accountable to its own standards.[25]

Roberto Unger strikes a similar note. In the introductory volume to his magnum opus, *Politics*, he asserts that "despite his claim to detachment, the positivist social scientist sees society with the eyes of a resigned insider, who takes the fundamentals for granted and shares his subjects' sense of reality and possibility even when he has claimed indifference to their interests and ideals."[26] The problem with positivist social science, according to Unger, is that it acquiesces in the existing formative structure of social life and within this framework cannot imagine the possibility of structure-changing, context-transforming political shifts. In this respect, Unger's analysis seems roughly analogous to Kuhn's distinction between "revolutionary" and "normal" science. In Unger's view, social scientists are mainly engaged in Kuhnian "normal science"; they do not challenge the paradigm within which they work but are merely engaged in solving the routine problems it generates. Indeed, they are so caught up in their conventional problem solving that they even forget that they are working within a paradigm. They start to believe that it is not a socially constructed framework of reference but reality itself that informs their research. Thus, Unger contends, social science "has a built-in propensity to take the existing framework of social life for granted and thereby to lend it a semblance of necessity and authority."[27] Unger therefore argues that social theory should become more attuned to the formative context that informs it. In Kuhnian terms, it should be more concerned with "revolutionary" science, with the potentiality of paradigm shifts that replace existing with alternative modes of understanding. Such a reorientation, Unger believes, can end the present state of "theoretical exhaustion and political retrenchment" and bring back the kind of transformative politics that is currently being smothered by the acquiescence of positivist social analysis.

Drawing on linguistic and literary theory, Gary Peller also argues that "representations of social life in rational 'disciplines' such as law, economics, or sociology, are actually contingent and political interpretations."[28] According to Peller, all observation, including the observation of the "rational disciplines," is mediated through language. Since contemporary linguistic and literary theory have revealed "that we are always in language and that language is always interpretation in the sense of a contingent social process of ascribing meaning to events," the "rational disciplines" should also be considered as forms of interpretation, as contingent ascriptions of meaning. The appreciation of this insight, Peller argues, precludes a clear separation of subject and object, of observer and observed: "Language . . . constitutes the sense of experience itself, even as we create the language for making sense of experience." Consequently, we can never think of ourselves as outside of the contingent, socially manufactured structures of meaning.[29] Experience is not something that happens to us apart from our language, our interpretive vocabularies, only to be represented and interpreted in them afterward. Our interpretive frameworks, instead, are always implicated in the way we perceive and act. They create their own instances. Thus, there is no untainted, preconceptual realm of experience that could be thought of as being represented more or less accurately. As a result, the "rational disciplines" cannot present their respective understandings of reality as something other than socially constructed, historically contingent, metaphoric systems, on a par with other nonrationalist metaphoric systems of understanding. Thus, according to Peller, the "rational disciplines" have no claim to special astuteness at explaining and representing the world. Rather, the "authority of the discourses of 'reason' depends on the subjugation of other knowledges of the world as inferior." Their appropriation of epistemological authority, Peller notes, constitutes "an act of power through which other ways of understanding and experiencing the world are marginalized as 'personal,' 'ideological,' 'emotional,' or 'primitive.'"[30]

THE POVERTY OF FUNCTIONALISM

The idea of the social construction of knowledge, so central in the CLS critique of social science and policy analysis, is also the most salient argument that CLS adherents have leveled against the idea of functionalism. Functionalism, as CLS adherents see it, proceeds from the idea that what is prior is society and what is posterior is law, which adapts and reacts to what goes on in society. Yet the social construction of knowledge thesis, as we saw, holds that what are seen as social facts by social scientists are better considered reified abstractions and objectified theoretical notions called forth by the conceptual vocabulary and theoretical framework that mediate observation. Hence, for CLS there is no untainted prior social world to be reflected in law. Law, through its conceptualizations of social relations, is already thoroughly implicated in the way the social world is perceived and experienced. Law is part of the "formative context" which forges exactly those social facts that the functionalist believes forge the shape of law. Hence, in important respects for CLS, law is prior and society posterior. Subsequently, the idea that law functionally adapts to changes in society provides a flawed picture of what legal systems do and how they change.

Thus Kelman maintains that the chief breach the Critical scholars have made with traditional legal sociology and adaptationist functionalism "has been to refuse to accept the ordinary distinction between epiphenomenal law and 'real' society." For CLS, Kelman argues, "law, in a sense, significantly *defines* the actors who are frequently pictured as the social base that influences law." While others have also objected "to positing a dividing wall between 'social' and 'legal' spheres," Kelman observes, the "point is bolstered once one defines *law* in terms of both state control over conduct and rhetorical understandings of the world."[31] When law is seen not only as a system that provides the basic order of society by its ascription of social status to people—as employer, owner, husband, shareholder—but also as a system that through its provision of "rhetorical understandings" determines the very outlook of people on the makeup of social life, then the functionalist picture of law simply accommodating social change becomes overly simplistic and misleading. Thus, Kelman argues, law is "poorly understood as a dependent variable," as a product of the interplay of external factors. Instead, the "supposedly external factors should be partly understood as dependent variables, altered by the internal peculiarities of legal practice." According to Kelman, "the 'world' will be different depending on how people sort out their experience, what they think of as just or inevitable, and the law helps define those expectations."[32]

The Critical scholar Robert Gordon, as we saw earlier, is firmly opposed to a functionalist approach to legal history. The arguments he mounted against functionalism in history also pertain to social science. According to Gordon, criticism of adaptive functionalism, in itself, is not distinctive for CLS. Crude forms of functionalism have also received strong opposition from mainstream legal scholarship. Yet, Gordon argues, even the severest critics of functionalism among mainstream legal scholars have still clung to its "skeletal frame, its division of the world into social and legal spheres"; they have still continued to assume "that at bottom the really basic terms of community life are set by conditions and relations we can, and should, describe independently of law: family ties, personal affections, power struggles, technology, consumption preferences, association in interest groups, and the organization of production." Mainstream scholarship has thus persisted in the assumption, he maintains, that the "*fundamental* operations of this world originate before law and go forward independently of it," in the belief that they "fashion in general outline (if not in tiny detail) the agendas and limits of legal systems and are beyond the power of law to alter."[33]

Gordon claims that CLS challenges this residue of functionalism in legal thought. Critical scholars doubt whether it is possible to describe even the most basic social operations without considering the legal elements that compose them. With this, CLS does not defend the position that law is successfully influencing people's conduct in accordance with its rules, that law is effective in bringing about conformity to its explicit regulation. It is not. Law, rather, is potent through its imposition of a conceptual scheme. It is influential because it is a constitutive element of people's consciousness of what the social world is like:

> Many critical writers would . . . claim not only that law figures as a factor in the power relationships of individuals and social classes but also that it is omnipresent in the very marrow of society—that lawmaking and law-interpreting institutions have been among the primary sources of the pictures of order and disorder, virtue and vice, reasonableness and craziness, realism and visionary naiveté and some of the most commonplace aspects of social reality that people carry around with them and use in ordering their lives. To put this another way, the power exerted by a legal regime consists less in the force that it can bring to bear against violators of its rules than in its capacity to persuade people that the world described in its images and categories is the only attainable world in which a sane person would want to live.[34]

This, of course, fundamentally undermines the functionalist picture of the legal system reacting to changes taking place in the social realm. Hence, to understand what is going on we primarily need to understand legal consciousness, not the social substructure that is erroneously supposed to be shaping law.

CONCLUSION

To sum up, the differences between CLS and Legal Realism with regard to the use of social science in legal research are basic and consequential. To begin with, the Legal Realists held that empirical study of the social operation of law and the social conditions it had to regulate would expose many legal illusions and provide numerous insights for legal reform. Yet Critical scholars expect that such a research effort will never be more than a circumspect form of political advocacy. Just like doctrinal analysis, empirical social research will fail to provide the lawyer with conclusive answers to legal issues. The only real purpose for social science research, CLS scholars believe, is to provide the political preferences implicit in law with an aura of certainty and objectivity. Second, the Realists were aware that cognitive frameworks necessarily guided and biased observation of the facts, but they still believed that scientific method could—at least to a point—transcend the raw subjectivity of undisciplined human perception. For CLS adherents, the privileged status of scientific knowledge has become suspect. Scientific knowledge, they believe, like all other forms of knowledge, is socially constructed and shaped by the contingent concerns of a certain time and place. Hence, science is just one among many discursive practices with which people ascribe meaning to the world, and there is no way to prove that it provides a more accurate representation of reality than any other form of understanding. As a result, the claim that science provides more dependable and accurate knowledge is disingenuous and political; it constitutes an imperialistic imposition of a certain perspective at the cost of others. Finally, for many Realists functionalism provided a useful framework for the study of law. A functionalist approach, they believed, could accommodate both law and social science, both empirical explanation and interpretive understanding, both a focus on the necessary social functions of law and on the historically and culturally contingent norms it embodied. Yet for CLS functionalism is a failure even in its own terms. It is fundamentally flawed because of its misguided stress on the supposed social basis of things legal and because of its complete lack of appreciation for the efficacy of law as an independent ideological structure.

 There are some serious problems with these points of criticism, however. By far the most serious of these is that most of the CLS critique is directed at a stark positivist and behaviorist conception of social science that the Realists never subscribed to and that only really gained currency among American social scientists after the Realist movement had disappeared from the scene. For the Realists, there simply was no debilitating antagonism between interpretivism and social science. They saw no problem in combining efforts to understand people interpretivistically and to observe their behavior scientifically. With this approach, the Realists were representative of what Richard Rorty has called the "middle ground" that Dewey proposed and that "inspired the social sciences in America before the failure of nerve which turned them 'behavioral.'"[35] The CLS movement, in turn, is part of the hermeneutic backlash against the social sciences that emerged after that "failure of nerve"—that is, after the behavioral revolution of the 1950s. CLS scholars are part of the broad movement in the humanities and the social sciences bent on replacing disengaged explanation of behavior with meaningful understanding of practices, on substituting positivism and behaviorism with hermeneutics and interpretivism. More specifically, they belong to the subgroup of the movement for hermeneutics which has politicized this methodological issue, the subgroup of interpretivist scholars that Rorty has aptly described as the "admirers of Habermas and Foucault" who "join in thinking of the 'interpretive turn' in the social sciences as a turn against their use as 'instruments of domination,' as tools for what Dewey called 'social engineering.'"[36]

With respect to the latter point, Rorty argues convincingly that the methodological and political issue should not be entangled. The contrast between scientific and interpretivist inquiry has no necessary parallel with the contrast between domination and emancipation. Dewey functions as Rorty's main example. It would be quite misleading to argue that a reformist liberal like Dewey was forwarding a conservative program of domination and preservation of the status quo with his appeal to social engineering and intelligent reform. A similar point can be made about present-day social scientists. Social science departments, whatever their faults, are hardly conservative think tanks. Their left-of-center political disposition is conspicuously evident. The equation of a scientific approach, such as the Legal Realists, with conservative politics is simply wrong.

More important, however, is the theoretical claim that a hermeneutic and a scientific approach are incompatible. CLS adherents seem to base this incompatibility thesis mainly on arguments derived from the polarized methodological debate between the proponents of behaviorism and the advocates of hermeneutics and interpretivism. Yet this debate completely ignores the "middle ground" that Dewey staked out for the social sciences and that the Realists tried to implement within the field of law. As Rorty states: "the recent reaction in favor of hermeneutical social sciences . . . has taken for granted that if we don't want something like Parsons, we have to take something like Foucault; i.e., that overcoming the deficiencies of Weberian *Zweckrationalität* requires going all the way, repudiating the 'will to truth.'"[37] The option that Dewey suggested, sharing many of the assumptions underlying the hermeneutic approach, was that although we are necessarily caught in a biased framework of reference we need not give up scientific inquiry and the search for truth. Indeed, his conception of science incorporated the idea that our cognitive structures were culturally and historically contingent. His notion of science was democratic and procedural. What was the best procedure for gathering knowledge was not a question that could be answered beforehand by theoretical reflection, but was something that had to be worked out in the process of inquiry itself.

In other words, the Pragmatist philosophers did not believe that giving up the idea that theory and fact were separable debarred them from advocating a scientific approach. For the Pragmatists, the possibility to test theories on a preconceptual realm of uncontaminated facts was not a precondition of science. What science required, instead, was a democratic community of scholars working within a shared conceptual framework, freely and openly testing and criticizing each other's work according to shared scientific standards, standards that themselves were open for discussion and change, and thus trying to achieve a level of intersubjective agreement on what theory worked best. Scientific truth in this approach was the idea that was destined to be confirmed in the long run by the democratic, responsible, and collaborative inquiry of a community of scholars; it was the end victory of reality slowly compelling and shaping thought in a context of open scientific inquiry. That these scientific truths, in the end, were relative to a certain conceptual framework did not worry the Pragmatists unduly. The Pragmatist solution to the problem of "loss of the world," the problem of not having direct, unmediated access to reality, according to Hilary Putnam, was "to be found in action and not in metaphysics." As Putnam points out, Peirce, James, and Dewey argued that "democratically conducted inquiry is to be trusted; not because it is infallible, but because the way in which we will find out where and how our procedures need to be revised is through the process of inquiry itself."[38] For the Pragmatists, in other words, the irreducible subjectivity of observation was not primarily a metaphysical problem to be solved by philosophical contemplation, but a practical problem to be dealt with in the practice of inquiry, in the actual confrontation of human thought with reality.

Indeed, the separation of theory and fact was one of the dichotomies the Pragmatist philosophy of Peirce, James, and Dewey sought to abandon. The only mode through which human beings could know things in their environment, Dewey explained, was through interaction with them. Thus interaction was a fundamental trait of human existence which slanted any mode of acquiring knowledge:

> [I]f man is within nature, not a little god outside, and is within as a mode of energy inseparably connected with other modes, interaction is the one unescapable trait of every human concern; thinking, even philosophic thinking, is not exempt. This interaction is subject to partiality because the human factor has bent and bias. But partiality is not obnoxious just because it is partial. . . . What is obnoxious in partiality is due to the illusion that there are states and acts which are not also interactions.[39]

Hence, just because scientific knowledge bears the imprint of our biased perspective does not necessarily mean it has no value or use. The worldview behind Newtonian physics, for instance, consists of quaint and contingent seventeenth-century ideas. Yet this does little to invalidate the practical use of Newton's theory of gravity, which is still heeded by anybody who wants to build a house in the twenty-first century. The partiality of knowledge becomes "obnoxious" only when it is held not to be the result of partial inquiry at all but to be absolute and certain. In other words, the hankering for absolute certainty that CLS imputes to science is exactly what Dewey thought detrimental to it. It would presume what Dewey seeks to deny, namely, that human beings are little gods outside, not limited creatures within nature.

Moreover, Pragmatism is not the only epistemology that can deal with the notion that observation is mediated through theory and that facts are theory-laden. The interpenetration of theory and fact has not caused any insurmountable problems for more contemporary advocates of science either. Many have made it part of their philosophies of science. The CLS argument is simply far too hasty with respect to this issue. The mere insight that facts are theory-laden certainly does not suffice as an argument to abandon science. William Ewald has severely criticized Roberto Unger for overlooking exactly this point in his analysis of the "antinomy of theory and fact," arguably the most authoritative CLS statement of the idea that the theory-ladenness of facts proves that the very idea of science is flawed. According to Ewald, "precisely the same considerations that militate against the separability of theory and observation can also be marshaled in favor of a robust scientific realism." Unger seems to be completely oblivious to this possibility, he argues, and "jumps straight from the contention that facts are theory-laden to the conclusion that the modern view of science is incoherent." Ewald concludes that Unger has "simply presented a crude variant of a familiar problem, labeled it an antinomy, and congratulated himself for having brought down the edifice of modern thought."[40] Philosophers of science like W. V. O. Quine and Karl Popper, to name only two of the most prominent, have argued that facts are mediated through theory and have subsequently based their respective philosophies of science on that assumption. Hence the claim that the interpenetration of theory and fact proves that science is a contradictory proposition needs to be supported, at the very least, by an argument concerning why the work of such distinguished philosophers is apparently wrong.

Finally, a few remarks need to be made about the CLS critique of functionalism. In Chapter 3 we saw that what the Realists meant by *functionalism* was much closer to contemporary meme theory than to the abstract and holistic functionalist theories we usually associate with the term *functionalism* today, such as Talcott Parsons's theory of the social system.[41] The Realists used the functionalist approach as a loose heuristic, not as something that could provide a universal template for legal systems anywhere. Moreover, they saw functionalism as something that operated on the legal system at a much more detailed level than the system as a whole. Their focus was not the functionality of the collective, the functional rigor of the anthill, but the adaptive fitness of the individual rule or concept.

But also this loose use of the functional framework is something CLS scholars find fault with. For them the very idea of privileging the social sphere over the legal sphere is mistaken. They believe the social world is the dependent variable that needs to be explained and the legal system the independent variable that should provide the explanation. It is the law that provides people with their basic notion of the social order, CLS adherents contend, and that determines what kind of social life we can imagine for ourselves. This aspect of CLS resembles the self-aggrandizement Susan Haack has criticized in the work of contemporary social scientists, scholars who have adopted a "fashionable linguistic idealism" and have fallen for the tempting belief that social science has called into being the very social institutions it studies. This position does not stand up to critical examination: "Yes, social institutions are partially constituted by people's beliefs and intentions; and yes, social-scientific theorizing can affect its objects. But social scientists no more brought child abuse or schizophrenia or homosexuality into existence by their intellectual activities than biologists brought anthrax into existence by theirs."[42] CLS scholars sometimes seem to suggest that, much like Athena, who according to Greek mythology was born out of the head of Zeus wearing full armor, the social world was born out of the head of the lawyer and legal scholar fully fitted out. Zeus, of course, was the master of the gods, the father of men, and the ruler of the universe. One wonders what place should be reserved for the lawyer in the Pantheon if his brainchildren are of such moment.

CHAPTER SIX

Night of the Living Dead: Legal Realist Anticonceptualism

> We live, think and act according to zombie-like notions; according to notions that have died, but continue to rule our thinking and our actions.
>
> —Ulrich Beck[1]

> A word is dead
> When it is said
> Some say.
> I say it just
> Begins to live
> That day.
>
> —Emily Dickinson[2]

An important element in the Realist critique of Classical American legal thought was its anticonceptualism. The Realists criticized their nineteenth-century predecessors and their more traditional contemporaries for engaging in barren legal reasoning on the basis of disembodied legal concepts and categories that had little relation to the economic and social realities of the day. In a much-quoted passage from the Legal Realist literature, Felix Cohen recounted Rudolf von Jhering's tale of the heaven of legal concepts to make this point more vividly:

> Some fifty years ago a great German jurist had a curious dream. He dreamed that he died and was taken to a special heaven reserved for the theoreticians of the law. In this heaven one met, face to face, the many concepts of jurisprudence in their absolute purity, freed from all entangling alliances with human life. Here were the disembodied spirits of good faith and bad faith, property, possession, *laches*, and rights *in rem*. Here were all the logical instruments needed to manipulate and transform these legal concepts and thus to create and to solve the most beautiful of legal problems. Here one found a dialectic-hydraulic-interpretation press, which could press an indefinite number of meanings out of any text or statute, an apparatus for constructing fictions, and a hair-splitting machine that could divide a single hair into 999,999 equal parts and, when

operated by the most expert jurists, could split each of these hairs again into 999,999 equal parts. The boundless opportunities of this heaven of legal concepts were open to all properly qualified jurists, provided only they drank the Lethean draught which induced forgetfulness of terrestrial human affairs. But for the most accomplished jurists the Lethean draught was entirely superfluous. They had nothing to forget.[3]

Cohen claimed, and most Realists agreed, that much of American legal thought moved in this celestial sphere of conceptual purity, far removed from the mundane concerns of life. The Realists believed legal scholars had been mesmerized by their own concepts and had lost touch with the social and economic conditions these had to regulate. Although legal concepts might have fitted social circumstances at their inception, in legal thought they tended to gain a life of their own and to develop into abstractions that were out of touch with social circumstances. Hence, the Realistic program was directed at exposing the discrepancy between the way social and economic relations were theoretically conceived of in American law and the way things actually proceeded in the social and economic realm. Empirical social science, they hoped, could shed more light on the relationship between legal concepts and economic and social practice. The goal of this critique was reform; it was aimed at providing the law with more up-to-date conceptual tools and at bringing legal reality more nearly in line with social reality.

From contemporary sources the Realists derived two basic strands of linguistic theory to inform this understanding of legal language: (1) a referential linguistics that sought to define meaning as a reference to observable real objects and behavior, and (2) a functional linguistics that sought to understand language primarily as a socially constructed tool designed to control and manipulate the environment within a given framework of social organization. The referential strand of linguistic theory was present in Oliver Wendell Holmes's writing, as well as in *The Meaning of Meaning*, a seminal work on linguistic theory by C. K. Ogden and I. A. Richards, which was hugely influential in the interwar period. In this referential view, most language was considered to be charged with emotion and ridden with preconceptions, ideals, and prejudices. As a result, it called for the reduction of linguistic confusion through strict definition of words in terms of a reference to observable, simple, and unambiguous empirical phenomena. The functional view of language, on the other hand, was present in the perspective on language afforded by John Dewey and in the work of contemporary anthropologists such as Franz Boas and Bronislaw Malinowski. In this view language was seen in an evolutionary framework as a tool developed by a given community to cope with its living environment. As such it could be more or less functional, more or less adapted to existing circumstances. Thus, the functional approach to language was concerned not with referential accuracy, but with the proficiency of language to bring about desired consequences within a given social and cultural setting.

Both of these sources taught the Realists that language did not reflect some order inherent in the world, but that it was an evolving, cultural artifact which represented reality in a contingent manner. Language did not correspond to some immanent makeup of the universe, but reflected the cultural experience of the given language community. Nevertheless, these two different strands of linguistic theory suggested two different ways to deal with legal language. The referential approach implied that legal concepts should be checked against the observable behavior and phenomena they purportedly described. Social science research, in that case, should uncover whether the real world accurately corresponded to the way it was depicted in legal concepts. The functional view, on the other hand, pointed toward an examination of the success of legal concepts in bringing about the projected results. Hence, it suggested that legal concepts should be checked not on their descriptive accuracy, but on their ability to deal with the problems that came before the courts and ultimately on their effect on the welfare of society at large.

Either way, the Realists were convinced that language was amenable to rational and empirical evaluation: vocabularies could correspond better or worse to the real world, or could be more or less functionally adapted to deal with its problems. Hence, they never rescinded the idea that legal concepts could be assessed on how well they fit social and economic circumstances. The referential linguistics they sometimes adopted seems largely outdated now. The functional view, however, is by no means indefensible or naive. The Realist idea that a conceptual framework can be appraised in terms of its success in dealing with reality—even though it predetermines the very perception of that reality—is still tenable after Wittgenstein. The final evaluation of the linguistic theory of the realists will need to wait until the Critical Legal Studies (CLS) views on language have been dealt with, however. In this chapter, the focus will be on contemporary sources of Realist anticonceptualism and the use to which these were put in Realist legal theory.

MEANING AS REFERENCE

One of the central elements of Legal Realism was a strong distrust of words and concepts. This distrust of words had already been present in Holmes's work. Holmes provided the Realists with many aphoristic statements about the equivocal relation between legal language and reality. Holmes was acutely aware of the pitfalls of language. Words did not simply describe real-world phenomena but were infused with emotion, replete with ideals and prejudices, and informed by the popular preconceptions and accepted social theories of the day. Holmes's solution to overcome all this equivocation was a single-minded focus on the real-world phenomena words referred to. His strategy for the clarification of concepts involved the reduction of meaning to the real objects they were supposed to describe—which were ultimately the only things that could be considered real and true. Once all the superimposed layers of emotion and opinion had been removed from a concept, only the bare facts it referred to remained, and concepts became more exact and accurate.

Thus, in his essay "Law in Science—Science in Law," Holmes emphasized the importance of "not being contented with hollow forms of words merely because they have been used very often and have been repeated from one end of the Union to the other." Words were merely labels for real-world phenomena. These phenomena were the important thing, not the categories and concepts used to define them. Hence, Holmes summoned: "We must think things not words, or at least we must constantly translate our words into the facts for which they stand, if we are to keep to the real and the true."[4] This statement captures Holmes's strategy for linguistic clarification, the type of referential linguistics he adhered to. It was a strategy in which the meaning of words was considered to be reducible to the observable, real-world phenomena they referred to. This approach bore a close resemblance to Jeremy Bentham's "paraphrastic method," in which words with an obscure reference were sought to be elucidated by paraphrasis into words that named real entities or that referred to simple ideas. Human knowledge, in the end, originated in sensual perception of real objects, Bentham believed. Hence, it should be possible to dissemble words that conveyed complex and abstract ideas into their component parts, that is, the elementary sense experiences that formed the basis of all knowledge. For Bentham—and equally it seems for Holmes—clarity of meaning could be achieved by going back to the building blocks of human ideas and concepts, to the experiences of real objects that were combined into the more complex notions and concepts denoted by words.[5]

Living language, of course, did not provide such a rigorous definition of its terms. Words embodied ideas of what the world was like, which is why they could so easily bewitch people and lead to a false sense of reality. They did not merely describe some real-world phenomena but contained a good deal of hypostatization. This hypostatization, moreover, was largely culturally determined and changed from one historical period to another. As a result, Holmes believed that the ideas embodied in legal concepts and categories changed through time. Thus, in his opinion in *Towne v. Eisner,* he claimed that "income" could mean different things in legal texts originating from different time periods: "It is not necessarily true that income means the same thing in the Constitution and the act. A word is not a crystal, transparent and unchanged; it is the skin of a living thought and may vary greatly in color and content according to the circumstances and the time in which it is used."[6] In *Gompers v. United States,* he expressed this same insight: "[T]he provisions of the Constitution are not mathematical formulas having their essence in their form; they are organic living institutions transplanted from English soil. Their significance is vital not formal; it is to be gathered not simply by taking the words and a dictionary, but by considering their origin and the line of their growth."[7] Thus, words, as they were used and applied by lawyers, did not have a true or timeless meaning for Holmes. Meaning was a function of the cultural experience of a society. Language expressed the idiosyncratic and historically contingent way in which a people creatively pieced together what they experienced in the world around them.

A more elaborate source for the idea of a referential linguistics was *The Meaning of Meaning* written by linguists Charles Ogden and I. A. Richards and first published in 1923, together with an influential supplement, "The Problem of Meaning in Primitive Languages," by anthropologist Bronislaw Malinowski. Although *The Meaning of Meaning* is not very well known today, it once was a seminal work. According to Edward Purcell, it was "one of the most widely read and discussed books of the interwar years" and enjoyed a "special prominence among many social scientists and legal theorists."[8] Ogden and Richards's theory of language and Malinowski's contribution to their book was influential among the Realists and figured prominently in many of their anticonceptualist diatribes.

The linguistic theory of Ogden and Richards was centered on the idea that there was no direct relation between words and the things they referred to. Between a word and the thing it referred to Ogden and Richards interposed the element of a thought construct. Thus, in their theory a word first referred to a mental concept, and that mental concept, in turn, described a real-world phenomenon.[9] Consequently, words did not have a natural or inherent meaning for Ogden and Richards. Meaning was the result of mental fabrication, of man-made conceptions of the world. The idea that there was a natural identity between words and things, "that words are in some way parts of things or always imply things corresponding to them," according to Ogden and Richards, was a superstition.[10]

This superstition, Ogden and Richards believed, had an insidious effect on human thought. If people forgot that words were merely shorthand symbols for human conceptions of reality and believed that words always stood for something real, then they would mistake those human conceptions of reality embodied in language for the real world. Because of this confusion of words and things, people engaged in all kinds of spurious, verbal speculation that had no direct connection with empirical reality. In Ogden and Richards's theory, entities inferred from words were "phantoms due to the refractive power of the linguistic medium; these must not be treated as part of the furniture of the universe, but are useful as symbolic accessories enabling us to economize our speech material."[11]

Moreover, words were used not only as symbols for empirical phenomena, but also as incitements to get an emotional response from the listener. Since Ogden and Richards defined meaning as a reference to something in empirical reality, they believed that this emotive aspect of words was entirely devoid of meaning, a point of view that resulted in some outspoken emotivist claims:

> Th[e] peculiar ethical use of "good" is, we suggest, a purely emotive use. When so used the word stands for nothing whatever, and has no symbolic function. Thus, when we so use it in the sentence, "*This* is good," we merely refer to *this*, and the addition of "is good" makes no difference whatever to our reference. When, on the other hand, we say "*This* is red," the addition of "is red" to "this" does symbolize an extension of our reference, namely, to some other red thing. But "is good" has no comparable *symbolic* function; it serves only as an emotive sign expressing our attitude to *this*, and perhaps evoking similar attitudes in other persons, or inciting them to actions of one kind or another.[12]

Especially in connection with the aforementioned tendency to assume that words always refer to something real, this emotive content of language led to theorizing that, in Ogden and Richards's view, was entirely empty of meaning and deduced entities from words that expressed only emotion and attitude.

The superstition, which equated the name of a thing with the thing itself, Ogden and Richards maintained, originated in "word-magic." Word-magic was "the primitive idea that Words and Things are related by some magic bond."[13] "To classify things is to name them," Ogden and Richards explained, "and for magic the name of a thing or group of things is its soul; to know their names is to have power over their souls."[14] This primitive attitude toward words could be found throughout Western history. From Plato's "Ideal World where the Name-souls dwelt,"[15] to the "monstrous symbolic machinery" of "the Hegelian Dialectic,"[16] word-magic had tricked thinkers into all sorts of specious arguments. "The persistence of the primitive linguistic outlook," Ogden and Richards believed, "not only throughout the whole religious world, but in the work of the profoundest thinkers, is indeed one of the most curious features of modern thought."[17]

To a certain extent, the emphasis on the arbitrary relation between word and thing—or in Ogden and Richards's terms, "symbol" and "referent"—is reminiscent of the familiar Saussurean distinction between signifier and signified. Yet, whereas in Saussurean linguistics this distinction ties in with a structuralist theory of language, with Ogden and Richards it is connected to a behavioristic outlook. They examined communication in terms of a psychology of stimulus and response within a given context. The cultural context might determine which phenomena of empirical reality were singled out for symbolization, but the symbolization process itself could still be looked at in behavioristic terms. One person communicating with another would use words—or symbols or signs—to refer to things. These words in the form of sounds were the stimuli that caused a conditioned response in the listener, that is, called up certain thought constructs. Within such a behavioristic framework, Ogden and Richards believed, it would be possible to study the efficiency of language as a tool for communication scientifically. Ideally language would minimize verbal misunderstanding through uniform paths of definition. Words should refer either to single objects in empirical reality, to unambiguous relations between these objects, or to compounds—however complex—made up of these objects and relations. If the paths of definition were standardized, then it would be clear to what object, or set of objects, a word referred and communication would reach a high level of efficiency. A degree of such a uniformity of definition had already been attained in the terminology of the natural sciences, but most language fell far short of this ideal. "In æsthetics, politics, psychology, sociology, and so forth," Ogden and Richards maintained, "the stage of systematic symbolization with its fixed and unalterable definitions has not been reached."[18]

Neither were these areas amenable to uniform definition yet. What was the right definition was determined by its place within a larger "symbolic system." And which was the preferable symbolic system, in turn, depended on its utility in dealing with empirical reality. Symbolic systems had to be adapted to the context in which they were used. Since, in Ogden and Richards's view, most areas of scientific inquiry outside of the natural sciences were not "far enough advanced for anyone yet to decide which system is most advantageous and least likely to exclude important aspects," it was still "an open question which symbolization is most desirable."[19] Consequently, for most topics the thought construct a speaker wanted to communicate with the use of a word might not correspond closely to the thought construct conjured up by that word in the listener. Hence, according to Ogden and Richards, we could never assume that words would have the same meaning for different people.[20] Such difficulties were no ground for "linguistic nihilism," however. If people acquired "a clear realization of the way in which symbols come to exercise such power, and of the various senses in which they are said to have meaning," then they could escape "from such skepticism as well as from the hypnotic influences [of words]."[21]

MEANING IN A FUNCTIONALIST FRAMEWORK

Bronislaw Malinowski's supplementary essay in *The Meaning of Meaning* tied in with Ogden and Richards's claim that "symbolic systems" were shaped by functional necessity. Malinowski—famous for his functionalist anthropology—believed, as did Ogden and Richards, that language was molded to satisfy the needs of a people in a certain environment, but he emphasized the functionalist theme to a much greater extent than they had done. Within the framework of his functionalist anthropology, Malinowski treated language largely as a social artifact framed to deal with a given social and physical environment. Thus, he contended: "Since the whole world of 'things-to-be-expressed' changes with the level of culture, with geographical, social and economic conditions, the consequence is that the meaning of a word must be always gathered, not from a passive contemplation of this word, but from an analysis of its functions, with reference to the given culture."[22]

Malinowski also agreed with Ogden and Richards that language did not always adjust harmoniously to changing conditions. Ogden and Richards had argued that when the environment changed, language did not always readily adapt to the new circumstances. As a result, language contained many relics of the past that were ill adjusted to meet the modern demands on language. "Tens of thousands of years have elapsed since we shed our tails," they wrote, "but we are still communicating with a medium developed to meet the needs of arboreal man."[23] Malinowski agreed wholeheartedly:

> Of course the more highly developed a language is and the longer its evolutional history, the more structural strata it will embody. The several stages of culture—savage, barbarous, semi-civilized, and civilized; the various types of use—pragmatic, narrative, ritual, scholastic, theological—will each have left its mark. And even the final powerful, but by no means omnipotent purification by scientific use, will in no way be able to obliterate the previous imprints. The various structural peculiarities of a modern, civilized language carry, as shown by Ogden and Richards, an enormous dead weight of archaic use, of magical superstition and of mystical vagueness.[24]

Language was not primarily constructed to serve the needs of science, and to assume that words were endowed with accurate and precise meanings could only lead to error and confusion.

The ideas conveyed in *The Meaning of Meaning* had some affinity with another important intellectual source of Legal Realism, namely, American Pragmatism. Indeed, in a review of *The Meaning of Meaning*, John Dewey called it a book "which lacks little of being of first-class importance."[25] Dewey seems to have been attracted especially to the contextual view of language, however, and much less so to the referential linguistics of Ogden and Richards. His references to the work were mainly confined to the concluding essay by Malinowski, who predominately stressed the importance of the cultural context and the need for a functional perspective. The importance of context for the meaning of words complemented Dewey's overall view that certain knowledge could not be had in a transitory and changing world. It showed that not only knowledge had to be adjusted to changing conditions, but also the linguistic tool in which knowledge was embodied, developed, and communicated. In his essay "Context and Thought," which starts with a discussion of Malinowski's supplementary essay, Dewey underscored this importance of context:

> We grasp the meaning of what is said in our own language not because appreciation of context is unnecessary but because context is so unescapably present.

It is taken for granted; it is matter of course, and accordingly is not explicitly specified. Habits of speech, including syntax and vocabulary, and modes of interpretation have been formed in the face of inclusive and defining situations of context. The latter are accordingly implicit in most of what is said and heard. We are not explicitly aware of the role of context just because our every utterance is so saturated with it that it forms the significance of what we say and hear.[26]

Moreover, the contextual view of language lent support to Dewey's view that knowledge should result from experience, from an active, practical posture, rather than from passive reflection. Language, after all, had developed within the practical world of social behavior. Thus, in *Experience and Nature,* Dewey asserted that "nothing more important for philosophers to hearken to has been written than Dr. Malinowski's conclusion: 'Language is little influenced by thought, but Thought on the contrary having to borrow from action its tool—that is language—is largely influenced thereby.'"[27] Words acquired meaning in the social struggle to cope with a changing world. To lift language out of this practical context and apply it in a theoretical search for timeless and certain knowledge was a mistake.

Language was one of the greatest inventions of humankind, Dewey believed. It was the "tool of tools," "a wonder by the side of which transubstantiation pales."[28] Language developed in the evolutionary process of adaptation; it was a tool developed to coordinate the actions of human beings in their effort to cope with their environment. With language defined as the "tool of tools" aimed at the transformation of raw experience into manipulable form, Dewey distinguished two basic functions: (1) an aesthetic function directed at the enhancement of experience in art, play, and ritual; and (2) a scientific function concerned with prediction and control of the objects of experience.[29] It is mainly the second function of language that concerns us here. When language was seen as a tool for prediction and control, it was determined by the success with which it brought about desired consequences. New conceptions were tried out and the application of existing conceptions was widened experimentally to see whether they produced expected results. In this way, language developed and was fine-tuned to deal with the outside world.

This process was not something that depended on individual effort. Language always implied a social setting, according to Dewey: "Language is specifically a mode of interaction of at least two beings, a speaker and a hearer; it presupposes an organized group to which these creatures belong, and from whom they have acquired their habits of speech. It is therefore a relationship, not a particularity." Language was based on interaction between members of a group, who developed common understandings of the objects words referred to within the framework of collective effort. Language developed in use; it was relational not objective, dynamic not static. Moreover, meaning was understood inclusively in Dewey's conception of language. Meaning was not something limited to what the speaker intended to express, according to Dewey: "When we attribute meaning to the speaker as *his* intent, we take for granted another person who is to share in the execution of the intent, and also something, independent of the persons concerned, through which the intent is to be realized. Persons and thing must alike serve as means in a common, shared consequence. This community of partaking is meaning."[30]

In Dewey's view, in other words, language should not be looked upon as a thing, a given set of labels cataloging a given set of real-world phenomena. Indeed, Dewey claimed that "it would be difficult to imagine any doctrine more absurd than the theory that general ideas or meanings arise by the comparison of a number of particulars, eventuating in the recognition of something common to them all."[31] Words and symbols acquired meaning against the background of social efforts to deal with the environment, not through a disinterested taxonomy of real-world objects. Nor was it right to assume, like the ancient Greeks had done, that "things, meanings, and words correspond," that "the universe was an incarnate grammatical order constructed after the model of discourse."[32] Language was "a work of social art" and could not be taken to reflect anything as grandiose as the order of the cosmos.

This Pragmatic view of language should not be mistaken for nominalism, Dewey warned, for the idea that all meaning and order emanated from the human intellect. What nominalism left out of consideration, Dewey argued, was association and interaction. Nominalism, he observed, "regarded the word not as a mode of social action with which to realize the ends of association, but as an expression of a ready-made, exclusively individual, mental state." Yet, Dewey maintained, a word "does not become a word by declaring a mental existence; it becomes a word by gaining meaning; and it gains meaning when its use establishes a genuine community of action." He emphasized that language developed in a social exchange: "Language and its consequences are characters taken on by natural interaction and natural conjunction in specified conditions of organization." Nominalism, however, Dewey observed, "ignores organization, and thus makes nonsense of meanings."[33] If the social setting and the purposive, result-oriented character of communication were ignored and language was only considered to

[margin note: contra nominalism]

reflect the private sense impressions, thoughts, and feelings of people, then language could never be seen for what it was: an ongoing, experimental, and intersubjective understanding of the world and the way desired consequences could be brought about in it. Dewey, to sum up, believed language was based on social convention and could not be assumed to mirror reality objectively. Yet language was still confronted with reality and was judged by how well it brought about anticipated consequences within it. Language contained warranted and tested conceptions that, for the purposes of a given community, allowed for effective dealings with the real world.

LEGAL REALISM AND LANGUAGE

When they fashioned their linguistic background theory, the Realists seem to have borrowed eclectically from, among others, Holmes's work, Dewey's Pragmatism, the emerging discipline of American anthropology, and Ogden and Richards's linguistics, without giving much thought to the different directions in which these diverse views of language were pulling. When the Realists talked the language of social science, they usually advocated a referential linguistics, and legal concepts became research variables that were defined in terms of observable behavior and facts—for example, their central definition of law as what the courts did in fact. When they wanted to criticize the conceptualism of their formalistic colleagues, Ogden and Richards's concept of word-magic often appeared, and traditional lawyers were accused of inhabiting a world of disembodied abstractions. When they discussed law from the perspective of social policy, they reverted to the language of Pragmatism, and the notions of "functionality" and "consequences" were applied to legal concepts. When they looked at the historical evolution of law, they stressed the contextual understanding of language, and concepts were seen to embody the evolving cultural experience of a society. Hence, the two basic strands of linguistic theory, which have been called the "functional" and the "referential" view of language, did not exist as distinct notions in Realist thought but were woven together in a multi-faceted patchwork.

The Realists were clearly much taken by Ogden and Richards's *The Meaning of Meaning*. Jerome Frank's discussion of language in *Law and the Modern Mind* is based to a considerable extent on the linguistic theory of Ogden and Richards. Frank subsumed their linguistics in his overall Freudian view, however. The idea that words had a fixed, natural meaning did not derive from word-magic, he believed, but stemmed from the same longing for a father-controlled world that shaped people's attitudes toward law. Thus, with regard to verbalism, word-magic was not the disease but a symptom of "emotional infantilism unduly prolonged."[34] Nevertheless, Frank contended, "the work that Ogden and his associates have begun, even though it may not be striking at the roots of the evil which they hope to eliminate, is of great importance."[35]

Frank believed, like Ogden and Richards, that words suggested something real they referred to. Consequently, words could blur our vision of empirical reality. If they dominated the way we came to grips with the outside world, they would give us a distorted view of what that world was like:

> In order to save time, we contract and condense language. We therefore make up words like Virtue, Liberty, Democracy, Freedom, and then forget that they are merely handy abbreviations. So we come to treat them as if they were independent entities, more real than the aspects of the circumstances they were used to describe or classify. But if we view them as mere symbols or labels we shall be rid of all the troubles such bogus entities have cost mankind.[36]

In Frank's view, all this was true of language generally, but especially of legal terminology. Since people projected their longing for a father-controlled world on law, law tended to exacerbate the proclivity to treat words as if they had a fixed and certain meaning. "Adults of keen mind become 'scholastic' and verbalistic in dealing with the law," Frank stated, because "confronted by the law, men tend to be baffled by feelings stimulated by the father-substitute which law represents, and therefore use narcotizing and paralyzing words to pursue what are relatively childish aims." Hence, Frank thought a "war on words" would be welcome particularly in law and would "assist in demolishing many a legal myth."[37]

The Realist Charles Clark was also inspired by Ogden and Richards to attack the conceptualism of law. In his critique of the restatement of the law of contracts by the American Law Institute, Clark objected that the enterprise was too focused on refining barren legal concepts. A list of suggested definitions to accommodate discussion had come to absorb all the attention of the lawyers involved in the Restatements, Clark believed, and had turned the project into sterile verbal theorizing, which had little relation to the realities of contract cases. "Lawyers live by words," he claimed; "here is their capital, their servant and too often their master. Word-magic is the bane and life of the law. With the Institute a formula as to the way in which words were to be used, briefly stated in its initial plan, has come to dominate its operations so as to press the fruitful activities of its scholars into the dry pulp of the pontifical and vague black letter generalities."[38]

The Realist Thurman Arnold drew on Ogden and Richards to fashion a social theory that focused on the importance of "symbols" and "magic words" in maintaining social and institutional cohesion. The values and ideals of a social institution, Arnold contended, were embodied in a set of "magic words" that ingrained trust, enthusiasm, and affection for that institution. These "magic words" were so effective in stimulating attachment to an institutional practice that they could even outlast the institution. Arnold's description of the troubles caused by the emergence of new social institutions provides a colorful illustration of this use of the concept of word-magic:

> The reason for th[e] confusion which attends the growth of new organizations in society lies deep in the psychology which concerns the effects of words and ceremonies on the habits of men in groups. Men always idealize these habits and the structure they give to society. The idealizing is done by magic words which at first are reasonably descriptive of the institutions they represent. At least they represent the dreams which men have of those institutions. When the institutions themselves disappear, the words still remain and make men think the institutions are still with them. They talk of the new organizations which have come to take the place of the old in terms of these old words. The old words no longer fit. Directions given in that language no longer have the practical results which are expected. Realists arise to point this out and men who love and reverence these old words (that is, the entire God-fearing, respectable element of the community) are shocked. Since the words are heavily charged with a moral content, those who do not respect them are immoral.[39]

Words could dominate thinking about institutions, even if they no longer fit with institutional practices. Thus, the mere existence of a concept did not mean that there was something real for it to refer to. Language could very well endure and condition thought even though the realities on which it was once modeled had changed dramatically. Note, also, the evaluation of language in terms of "the practical results that are expected," which is a clear reference, not to Ogden and Richards, but to Dewey's Pragmatic view of language.

Llewellyn also stressed that legal terminology colored the perception of the facts. He emphasized that *"no case can have meaning by itself."*[40] Legal concepts and categories shaped the way in which the bare facts were interpreted and became meaningful. In his article "A Realistic Jurisprudence— The Next Step," Llewellyn observed that, "although originally formulated on the model of at least some observed data, [categories] tend, once they have entered into the organization of thinking, both to suggest the presence of corresponding data even when these data are not in fact present, and to twist any fresh observation of data into conformity with the lines and shape of the category."[41] Categories and concepts were not inherent in the structure of the world for Llewellyn. Rather, they were malleable, arbitrary, and crude classifications of the infinite diversity of fact situations of real life. Consequently, there was always an element of distortion when the facts were recast in legal terminology. And Realism, as Llewellyn understood it, was all about "a narrowing as far as the present state of knowledge will permit, of the field for obstructing eyes with words that masquerade as things without a check-up."[42]

Llewellyn did not argue for the abolition of all concepts. Concepts were unavoidable: "Behavior is too heterogeneous to be dealt with except after some artificial ordering. The sense impressions which make up what we call observation are useless unless gathered into some arrangement."[43] Yet Llewellyn believed that words should never be treated as anything else but arbitrary classifications of our sense data. And the trouble with words was that they were taken to mean something definite and that arguments were built on the basis of these illusory, definite meanings. "The traditional approach is in terms of words," Llewellyn asserted; "it centers on words; it has the utmost difficulty in getting beyond words. . . . Here lies the key to the muddle."[44]

The Realist Leon Green struck a similar note. With regard to the concept of negligence, Green observed that the combinations of factors pertaining to negligent behavior were "literally infinite, as infinite as space and time." Law, therefore, provided only an arbitrary and narrow classification of negligent behavior, Green maintained, in order to keep the amount of incidents of negligence manageable:

> The number of instances of conduct which could be labeled either as negligent or non-negligent is beyond the limits of any catalog the law can make. So it is not surprising that in the face of infinity the law does exactly what other sciences do in like situations. It adopts a formula; a formula in terms which will permit its problems to be reduced to a graspable size. This formula, like many other formulas, tends quickly to become ritual and it would seem that it is only this ritual which holds the law's interest.[45]

Although this was deplorable, it was also necessary, Green believed. "[A]nalysis and classification are indispensable," he asserted. "Though they retard the very progress they would promote, they are nevertheless the machinery through which the law and lawyers function."[46]

Thurman Arnold even applied the suspicion of words to his own writing. In *The Folklore of Capitalism,* he warned that his conceptions of society should be taken as only "half truths" because "any classification of the tumbling stream of events which is not actually separable into classified elements represents only an emphasis on some particular phase of the scene and ignores other phases."[47] Any conceptualization or classification was a fib, a slanted and attenuated ordering of the facts that furnished a deceptive representation of a phenomenon.

This distrust of words had serious implications for law, of course. If the meaning of words was not precise, then what was the status of legal rules made up of these imprecise terms? If a legal decision was the application of a set of rules to a set of facts by means of formal logic, then it was of the utmost importance that the set of facts would readily fall into one of the generalized categories of law. Otherwise, the beginning of the logical chain of reasoning would rest on an arbitrary designation of the facts, and the whole logical structure of the legal argument would be built on quicksand. Moreover, if the legal rules to be applied were inferred from precedent, then again it was important to know what the words in which these precedents were phrased meant. If the language of these precedents was ambiguous or unclear, then what direction could they give lawyers in later cases? Thus, suspicion of words and concepts was one of the central arguments for the renowned "rule-skepticism" of the Legal Realists. As Frank put it in *Law and the Modern Mind*:

> Formal logic is what its name indicates; it deals with form and not with substance. The syllogism will not supply either the major premise or the minor premise. The "joker" is to be found in the selection of these premises. In the great run of cases which come before the courts, the selection of the principles, and the determination of whether the facts are to be stated in terms of one or another minor premise, are the chief tasks to be performed. These are the difficult tasks, full of hazards and uncertainties, but the hazards and uncertainties are ordinarily concealed by the glib use of formal logic.[48]

If words did not have a definite meaning, then the logical application of legal rules to the facts of a case became a precarious enterprise.

Llewellyn was of a similar opinion. In *The Bramble Bush,* he presented the image of a legal argument as "a sound technical ladder" from the legal rules and facts to the final decision.[49] The problem, according to Llewellyn, was not with the logical coherence of this ladder, but with the ground it stood on—arbitrary categories and unclear precedents:

There is judgment to be exercised, then, first, in selection of raw evidence; second, in interpreting or transforming what has been selected; third in classifying for legal significance the material after its *fact*-meaning has been assured. And for the advocate there is persuading to be done not only on the side of induction from ambiguous precedents, but also on the side of deduction, of classifying any concrete facts into the abstract fact-categories which are all that rules at law can hope to deal with. Of a truth the logic of law, however indebted it may be to formal logic for method, however nice it may be in its middle reaches, loses all sharp precision, all firm footing, in the two battlegrounds in which the two feet of the ladder stand.[50]

Since the "abstract fact-categories" of law did not reflect some objective order of the real world, but were ambiguous and arbitrary classifications of an infinite diversity of fact-situations, correspondence between the facts of a case and a legal category was almost never a straightforward matter. Hence, usually the lawyer had latitude in fitting the facts of a case to a relevant legal category. Consequently, the idea that the logical application of legal rules would make law certain and predictable was a chimera.

The problem of imprecise legal terminology was exacerbated by the tendency in law to look for broad and embracing concepts and categories. "The old categories are imposing in their purple," Llewellyn observed, "but they are all too big to handle. They hold too many heterogeneous items to be reliable in use."[51] Indeed, Llewellyn, together with Frank, listed the need for narrower categories as one of the nine central characteristics of the Realist approach in their programmatic article "Some Realism About Realism." Realists, they claimed, embraced "the belief in the worthwhileness of grouping cases and legal situations into narrower categories than has been the practice in the past," and shared "a distrust of verbally simple rules" which often covered "dissimilar and non-simple fact situations."[52]

Arnold also believed that when too many different facts were covered by a single legal term, it lost all the precision it might have had. He explained the problem of broad concepts in law with a fictitious example:

Originally the word "trunk" was applied to trees. Suppose later a writer on the science of things in general classifies "elephants," "trees" and "tourists" under the same heading. The reason for such a classification is that all three possess trunks. The answer to the objection that the trunks are of different kinds can easily be met by saying that to a nicely balanced analytical mind, they all have one inherent similarity, i.e. they all are used to carry things. The elephant's trunk carries hay to the elephant's mouth. The tree trunk carries sap to the leaves and the tourist trunk carries clothing. The soundness of the new abstraction cannot perhaps be disputed but nevertheless the classification would create at least verbal confusion and the necessity for a great many fine distinctions.[53]

The construction of legal abstractions often proceeded along similar lines, resulting in perplexing conceptual muddles and the need for elaborate explication. Arnold believed the legal term *trust* to be such a confused concept. He observed that *trust* was "an abstraction which cuts across a large number of complicated situations, changing its content with each one of them, and used in varying ways."[54] "Trust," Arnold maintained, as a result, "is not the name of an organized philosophy; it is simply a bad piece of indexing."[55]

Legal terms became such convoluted arrangements of heterogeneous elements, according to Arnold, because of the inherent conservatism of the judiciary. The courts preferred the use of old concepts to the invention of new abstractions. As a result, the old concepts were retained and applied to more and more diverse new cases, stretching their field of application to an ever wider range of heterogeneous fact-situations:

> Judges never feel secure in abandoning an ancient way of talking, because they fear destructive effects on some other part of the law's "seamless web" if they do so. A long list of archaic concepts such as the law of criminal attempts, the fiction of the lost grant, the distinction between trespass and case, local and transitory actions, the Statute of Uses, the distinction between resulting and constructive trusts and many others surviving in spite of their present ineptitude, bear witness to this fact. The occasional opinion which attempts to say that there is no utility in some so-called "well settled principle" is looked upon as an example of daring originality. It is usually followed by a concurring opinion which agrees with the result, but sternly points out the duty of the court to use the same language as its predecessors, no matter how far from reality that language may be.[56]

Law was full of old terms that had acquired a heavy load of diverse meanings and were applied to a great number of unlike situations. It was fruitless to try to cover all those different applications in vague and inclusive generalizations, as orthodox legal scholars had tried to do. Realism, instead, sought to narrow the meaning of legal terms on the basis of a functional understanding of the social and economic circumstances they were meant to govern.

The Legal Realists' skepticism regarding words also had consequences for legal scholarship. If the meaning of words was accepted at face value, then thinking about law could easily devolve into the kind of specious theorizing that Ogden and Richards had warned against. If words were taken to mean something definite and real, then it was easy to start making specious arguments on the basis of these arbitrary meanings of words. Thus, in a paper on social science and law, Llewellyn reassured an audience of social scientists: "I have no intention of framing a *definition* of law, of laying a foundation for argument, of inveigling you into acceptance of something for me to pull conclusions out of later on."[57] It was this kind of theorizing, which built a whole structure of verbal argument on the basis of definitions without any clear relation to empirical reality, that the Legal Realists reacted against. Instead, they believed that legal scholarship should get past words and focus on the actual facts and on actual behavior. "What looms large," according to Llewellyn, is "the difference between the *words* and the *practices* of officials." And the focus of the legal scholar should be on actual behavior and not on conceptualizations of that behavior; "not what stands on the books, but what happens," Llewellyn maintained, should be "the center of attention."[58]

This was even more true because words usually have not only a purely descriptive but also an evaluative content. Like the ethical use of *good* for Ogden and Richards, the legal use of *right* for Llewellyn added "nothing to descriptive power" but gave "a specious appearance of substance to prescriptive rules." Rights, according to Llewellyn, were "idealized somethings which may not, which mostly do not, accurately reflect men's actions." A concept like "rights," he believed, introduced "the additional notion of 'rightness' (in the sense of what ought to be)," which made the concept all but useless as a descriptive tool for scientific research.[59]

In an article on real property mortgages, Wesley Sturges and Samuel Clark repeated this theme. The main purpose of this article was to prove that the different conceptions of "mortgage" in traditional legal doctrine were confused and self-contradictory and did not account for the disparate hodgepodge of legal decisions arrived at in mortgage cases. Sturges and Clark wondered, however, why judges in legal opinions nonetheless constantly appealed to these doctrinaire conceptions. Referring to Ogden and Richards's work, they suggested that the continued use chiefly served an emotive purpose. Thus, they concluded that "the words reporting the theories, doctrines and generalizations which are under consideration are not used as symbols designed to be *descriptive*, but rather to be *emotive*. They are 'one more word' in soliciting approval, in urging plausibility, for a particular judgment."[60]

Legal categories and concepts were not arbitrary conventions for the Legal Realists, however. The meaning of words was not dependent on mere taste or preference. The Realists, instead, thought that the meaning of words derived in large part from a constantly evolving context. Social and economic conditions, cultural background, prevalent social and economic theory molded the meaning of words. Frank, for instance, regarded language from a Pragmatic point of view; it was a tool that had to be adjusted to fit changing circumstances. Thus, he reflected in *Law and Modern Mind*:

> Our legal abstractions can only be approximations. They are, by definition, drawn off—abstracted—from the facts. Hence, the results can never be precise, perfect. They must be inexact. If the "environment" were stable, the degree of inexactness could become more negligible and remain relatively fixed. But the economic, political and social problems are ever-shifting. So that, in the very nature of the situation, the approximation must be revised frequently and can never be accepted as final in terms of satisfactory consequences. We must be content with modest probabilities, as Dewey puts it, and not foolishly pretend that our legal abstractions are mathematically accurate, for that pretense obstructs the will to modify and adjust these abstractions in the light of careful observation of their working results.[61]

Hence, Frank argued that words could outlive their use. Society was in perennial flux. Today's accurate concept was tomorrow's outdated notion. Legal terminology had to prove its utility in coping with social, economic, and political problems. If a term was no longer useful in coming to grips with new circumstances, it had to be adjusted or replaced. Thus, social and economic circumstances shaped and conditioned the use of language.

Cohen understood the functional approach in science as a method of ascertaining the significance of a fact "through a determination of its implications or consequences in a given mathematical, physical or social context."[62] For law, this meant that "the meaning of a definition is found in its consequences."[63] Realism, he believed, was about ridding the law of "supernatural concepts" and redefining them "in terms which show the concrete relevance of legal decisions to social facts."[64] Legal terms should be understood as tools to bring about desired results, not as words reflecting something true or real. Thus, for instance, he maintained that a "definition of law is *useful* or *useless*. It is not *true* or *false*, any more than a New Year's resolution or an insurance policy."[65]

Arnold also considered language from a Pragmatic perspective. The conceptual vocabulary with which people approached social problems should foster and stimulate progress, he believed, not hamper practical problem solving. Thus, he discussed many Americans' resistance to the reformist, New Deal legislation of the 1930s as a case in which old conceptions prohibited the affirmation of necessary policy. For Arnold, much of the resistance to the New Deal was the result of the preindustrial concepts in terms of which people thought of their society and economy. Yet society had changed. The economy had been organized in large corporations and huge, new industries, and the concepts that were once relevant in a commercial society of small tradespeople and manufacturers were no longer applicable. The economy, Arnold remarked, was "much more like an army than the group of horsetraders which it is supposed to be." This disjunction between nineteenth-century conceptions and twentieth-century circumstances created a lot of social apprehension. If people tried to make sense of their world with concepts that had outlasted their relevance, things were bound to look askew. "Men believe that a society is disintegrating when it can no longer be pictured in familiar terms," Arnold commented. "Unhappy is a people that has run out of words to describe what is going on."[66]

In other words, Arnold believed that the conceptual vocabulary that people used to come to grips with reality was informed by their worldview, their vision of society. These vocabularies were never accurate in their descriptions of reality, but it was essential that they fostered progress and the tackling of social problems. With regard to legal and economic theory, Arnold remarked that they were "nothing other than a way of talking about organizations"; they were "nothing more than huge compound words with high emotional content." Legal and economic theories never described economic and legal behavior accurately. They were ridden with arbitrary abstractions, preferences, and values. Yet social institutions, like the economy or the law, needed such theories to give them coherence and sense of purpose. They provided words to talk about those social institutions. And words, according to Arnold, "affect the attitudes, crystallize them, make them stereotyped, and finally form the cement which binds the organization together."[67] The need for such theories was undeniable; the only question was which words were best suited under the circumstances to bring about desired results.

Llewellyn also conceived of legal language as something that acquired meaning in a context of historical experience. In *The Bramble Bush,* he advised first-year law students to use the dictionary to master legal terminology, but at the same time he cautioned them not to put too much stock in dictionary definitions: "Can you trust the dictionary, is it accurate, does it give you what you want? Of course not. No dictionary does. The life of words is in the using of them, in the wide network of their long associations, in the intangible something we denominate their feel."[68]

In Llewellyn's work this contextual view of language developed into an argument that undercut the idea that the meaning of legal concepts and legal rules was equivocal. Although Llewellyn had argued that certainty in law could not be brought about by the logical application of legal rules to the facts of a case, he did not argue that law was, therefore, erratic and unpredictable. For Llewellyn the supposedly compelling character of legal rules did not bring about the predictability of law, however, but the circumstances that conditioned lawyers to favor certain interpretations of the rules over others. That a definite outcome somehow followed logically from the operation of the pertinent legal rules on the relevant facts was a fiction. Yet, even though in principle all kinds of legal conclusions could be drawn from the facts of a case, social and institutional constraints ensured that lawyers would find only some of these conclusions acceptable and thus limited lawyers in their interpretation of the rules. In "My Philosophy of Law," Llewellyn sketched his understanding of law in familiar terms; it was a body of rules, principles, and concepts. Yet on top of these he added: "the going institution of our law contains an ideology and a body of pervasive and powerful ideals which are largely unspoken, largely implicit, and which pass almost unmentioned in the books. It contains also a host of sometimes vagrant, sometimes rigid practices, of ways of doing what is done, without which such things as rules would have no meaning in life."[69] What gave meaning to the body of legal rules and concepts was this mute consensus of hidden assumptions, ideological standpoints, ideals, and practices. It was this unexpressed, shared ethos that made the decisions of lawyers predictable, not the legal rules themselves. Thus, for Llewellyn, it was of the utmost importance that the people applying American law were Americans, "and not only Americans, but American lawyers," and that they were "judges, and of the American tradition, and in or about the present time." These were the unifying factors that ensured that there was predictability in the administration of law. These factors, as Llewellyn put it, "give the wherewithal for getting far closer to accurate prediction than do any but the rarest rules alone."[70]

CONCLUSION

Two broad strands of linguistic theory are combined in the Realist conception of language. First, a referential strand inspired by Holmes and Ogden and Richards in which words were considered to mean something only insofar as they referred to an empirical phenomenon. Second, a functionalist strand mainly inspired by Dewey and Malinowski in which words were considered to be meaningful when they brought about expected and desired consequences. The Realists used both approaches interchangeably, without worrying whether they could be made to cohere. Moreover, the two approaches were combined, both in their original sources and in their use by the Realists, with the notion that meaning also depended on context, with the idea that language was a socially constructed tool reflecting cultural idiosyncrasies and social environment. Yet, while the functionalist strand in their theory of language allowed for such a combination, the referential strand did not blend easily with such a contextual approach to language.

"What looms large," Llewellyn was quoted above, "is the difference between the *words* and the *practices* of officials." This statement contains the contradiction in a nutshell. It suggests that the behavior of officials and the words that label that behavior can be separated, and that the meaning of a word can be checked against the actual behavior it is supposed to describe. Yet if you argue that the meaning of words is socially constructed and that this socially constructed meaning conditions the way people perceive reality, then words and practices become intertwined and can no longer be separated that way. Once you hold that concepts shape the way people understand their world and the way they behave, you can no longer argue that observable behavior is a neutral and independent category of facts against which the accuracy of concepts can be checked.

The Pragmatic strand in the Realist view of language did not suffer from this contradiction. Dewey had not been concerned with reference, with the accuracy with which concepts and categories corresponded to real-world phenomena, but with consequences, the effectiveness with which concepts dealt with the real world. What interested Dewey was not so much whether a given vocabulary truly and objectively mirrored empirical reality, but whether it was useful as a tool to bring about desired outcomes. Whether language corresponded with objective reality was a pointless question from a Pragmatic perspective; whether language was successful in bringing about desired goals was not. Hence, Dewey's approach did not call for the checkup of words against the objective facts they referred to, but only against the results that could be achieved with them. The choice between conceptual vocabularies was a question of Pragmatics, not a question of ultimate truth. Thus, there was no contradiction with the contextual view of language in which meaning derived from the social and cultural context. For Dewey, this was simply true for everybody, including the scientist. He did not believe that scientists could uncover objective truth, in any final and ultimate sense, and use that as a standard to judge the accuracy of language with; they could only experiment, try out novel conceptions of reality, and see how well one compared to another in terms of consequences. Put differently, Pragmatism was not about investigating how well a given vocabulary corresponded to objective reality, but about comparing how successfully different vocabularies dealt with that reality. Dewey knew that knowledge was produced within the confines of a given conceptual paradigm, but he rejected the idea that any paradigm was as good as another. People still could, and still should, try to figure out experimentally which vocabulary was most effective in dealing with the real world.

CHAPTER SEVEN

The World Well Lost:
Variations on the Linguistic Theme

> "When I use a word," Humpty Dumpty said in rather
> a scornful tone, "it means just what I choose it to
> mean—neither more nor less."
> "The question is," said Alice, "whether you can make
> words mean so many different things."
> "The question is," said Humpty Dumpty, "which is
> to be master—that's all."
>
> —Lewis Carroll[1]

This chapter will discuss the views of language current in Critical Legal
Studies (CLS) theory. As we shall see, these views are both more radical
and more fundamental to the overall theory of law propounded by CLS
adherents. If for the Realists linguistic theory mainly provided a sensitivity
to the pitfalls of legal language, then for Critical scholars it is a comprehensive and indispensable component of their legal theory. CLS is saturated
with linguistic philosophy. Like the Realists, Critical scholars claim that
language mediates the observation of reality. What the social world looks
like is in large measure determined by the conceptual vocabulary employed.
Yet, unlike the Realists, CLS adherents do not believe that there is any way
to judge conceptual frameworks, or paradigms, or language games, rationally and empirically. Consequently, CLS presents a much more solipsistic
view of language, in which language groups are believed to manufacture
their own reality through their shared language, their shared conceptual
paradigm, and not to have any direct access to the real world. Thus, to borrow a phrase from Richard Rorty, CLS seems to adhere to the notion of a
"world well lost."[2] For CLS adherents, in other words, reality can no longer
be thought of as an independent arbiter of truth. People are imprisoned by
their own linguistic conventions. The only reality they know is the one created by their conceptual paradigm, and there is no way to step outside of
this paradigm to see the world plain and pure.

But how can they know this

In one of the most influential books in the CLS literature, *Knowledge and Politics*, Roberto Unger explains how this predicament has come about. According to Unger, we have lost the world, because we have given up the ancient idea of "intelligible essences." This notion of "intelligible essences" held that everything "has a feature, capable of being apprehended, by virtue of which it belongs to one category of things rather than another category." Hence, people that subscribe to the notion of intelligible essences believe that objects have essential properties that are immediately graspable and that make it instantly clear to which class of things they belong. This idea, Unger maintains, was central to theories of knowledge in ancient and medieval Europe. These theories were premised on the idea that science merely uncovered and recorded an innate order of reality; on the idea that "because everything has an essence, everything can be classified under the word which names its category."[3]

In the modern conception of nature, however, the idea that things and events have essences that can readily be observed and distinguished is rejected. Instead, Unger claims, the modern view holds that categories are man-made, that it is us who divide up the world and group things together as the same. Consequently, there are "numberless ways in which objects and events in the world might be classified." This modern "denial of intelligible essences, leaves no stone of the preliberal metaphysic standing," Unger contends, and its "consequences for our moral and political views are as far-reaching as they are paradoxical."[4]

One of those "far-reaching" and "paradoxical" consequences, Unger maintains, is that without intelligible essences it has become impossible to still make sense of the relation between our theories and reality:

> If there are no intelligible essences, there is no predetermined classification of the world. We can distinguish among objects-events only by reference to a standard of distinction implicit in a theory. It is the theory that determines what is to count as a fact and how facts are to be distinguished from one another. In other words, a fact becomes what it is for us because of the way we categorize it. How we classify it depends on categories available to us in the language we speak, or in the theory we use, and on our ability to replenish the fund of categories at our disposal. In whatever way we view the play of tradition and conscious purpose in the manipulation of the categories, there is no direct appeal to reality, for reality is put together by the mind.

This condition leads to what Unger calls the "antinomy of theory and fact"; that is, the paradoxical situation that, on the one hand, facts are considered to be creatures of our theories, while on the other hand, facts still need to be understood as independent of our theories for them to function as independent touchstones to those theories. Unger suggests that this is a "conundrum" which seems to imply nothing less than "the incoherence of our idea of science, indeed of knowledge in general."[5]

CLS skepticism does not stop there. CLS adherents do not only maintain that there is no recourse to reality to check how well a conceptual paradigm conforms to it, but they also argue, in familiar Kuhnian fashion, that it is impossible to compare alternative conceptual paradigms because such a comparison necessarily proceeds from within one, or the other, paradigm and is therefore always partial and biased. Thus, Unger observes that we cannot decide between such "radically different theoretical systems" as "Newtonian and quantum mechanics" by comparing how well they can predict and control events: "We must still interpret the results of the experiments we perform and justify the methods of proof we have chosen. If there are no intelligible essences, the facts of the test experiment may mean different things in different theoretical languages."[6] Since facts take on a different character when looked at from different theoretical perspectives, they cannot form an impartial basis for deciding between competing paradigms, and there is no neutral procedure we can turn to, to decide between different conceptual vocabularies, different ways of constructing reality.

The Critical scholar Joseph Singer phrases the same notion in plainer language: "We have no antecedently existing rational method to determine whether people are justified in accepting the criteria they accept. We can judge the criteria that others accept only by whatever criteria we accept. If they do not accept our criteria, there is no way to prove that they are wrong."[7] Just as we are incapable of stepping outside of our conceptual paradigm to see the world unmediated by the categories and concepts we happen to have inherited, it is also impossible to step outside of our paradigm to some transparadigmatic vantage point from which we can judge the relative value of different paradigms. Hence, one paradigm cannot be shown to be better than any other, and the choice for one, rather than another, paradigm, or legal vocabulary, is irreducibly political. As a result, how the social and economic world is, or should be, conceptualized in the law is a question of ungroundable moral and political choice, not a question that can be decided neutrally by empirical research and rational deliberation.

With views such as these, it should come as no surprise that Critical Legal scholars express a great deal of sympathy for Realist anticonceptualism. Nor should it come as a surprise that they typically argue that Realist anticonceptualism does not go far enough. Realist skepticism about concepts cannot be confined to just legal reasoning, CLS adherents tend to claim, but extends to all conceptualizations and to any vocabulary with which we talk about reality. Hence, it applies with equal force to the social sciences that the Realists turned to, to check whether legal concepts conformed to the social phenomena they were supposed to regulate. Once you cast doubt on the relation between words and the things they refer to, once you start to see concepts and categories as arbitrary conventions rather than labels for existent real-world phenomena, it becomes impossible to argue, according to many Critical Legal scholars, that concepts can be checked on the accuracy with which they reflect the phenomena they describe. There is no way to avoid using a language and to see the world unmediated by linguistic conventions. There are just different conceptual paradigms reflecting different modes of understanding real-world phenomena. Hence, when the Realist enlisted the social sciences to examine the veracity of legal concepts, they did not really leave Rudolf von Jhering's heaven of legal concepts to return to earth, but merely moved into an alternative heaven, a heaven populated with equally disembodied social science concepts. What the Realists failed to realize was that their skepticism about concepts was just as unsettling for the abstractions of empirical science as it was for the abstractions of law.

Thus Critical scholars take the anticonceptualism of Legal Realism much further than did the Legal Realists. This is usually explained as a resolute extension of the intrinsic logic of the linguistic background theory of the Realists. The Realists simply did not realize that their linguistic insights had such far-reaching implications. Or they did realize but shied away from the corrosive consequences they would have had for law and legal scholarship. Critical scholars, however, claim to have profited a great deal from what is often called the "linguistic turn" in philosophy. In this post-Wittgensteinian era they believe to have the benefit of a much more profound understanding of language than was available to the Realists. Hence, Critical scholars claim to be in a much better position to spell out the wide-ranging implications of the linguistic background theory of the Realists than did the Realists themselves.

What exactly Critical scholars believe has become clear about language since the Realists left the scene will be the topic of the current chapter. This will not add up to a tidy picture. What goes under the name of the "linguistic turn" is not a single coherent theory, but a diverse collection of views that converge on a deep suspicion about the relation between language and reality. The CLS understanding of language seems to draw on several strains of theory within the "linguistic turn." Consequently, the discussion will fall into three sections. The first will discuss the way Mark Tushnet and

James Boyle have applied the insights of Ludwig Wittgenstein to law. The second section, in turn, will focus on Gary Peller and Clare Dalton, who have articulated a Post-structuralist critique of law, which draws on Michel Foucault and Jacques Derrida. Then, in the third section, we will move on to more contemporary work by Critical scholars, which shows that the destabilizing linguistic critique of CLS has made it well-nigh impossible to still formulate a coherent alternative to the status quo. Finally, in a concluding section the linguistic theories of CLS will be evaluated and confronted with the Realist view on language.

A PORTRAIT OF WITTGENSTEIN AS A RADICAL PHILOSOPHER

More than any other thinker, Wittgenstein is responsible for a focus on the problematic nature of language characteristic of the linguistic turn. Several CLS adherents have drawn on his work. One of the most important among these is Mark Tushnet. In an article on the plight of contemporary legal scholarship, in which Tushnet claims that Postrealist legal scholarship has chosen to ignore, rather than face, the profound Realist critique of rules, he suggests that their case against the efficacy of legal rules has only become more compelling. Many Realists, according to Tushnet, considered the problems with respect to the subjectivity of judges in interpreting rules as "merely difficulties encountered in executing a program grounded in the rule of law." Yet, he argues, since "the Realists wrote, we have come to understand that the problems they described arose from the concept of rules and from the characteristics of language itself." Subsequently, he remarks in the accompanying footnote, "the fancy citation for this is L. Wittgenstein, *Philosophical Investigations.*"[8]

Tushnet does not provide page or paragraph numbers in his reference, but he is probably alluding to Wittgenstein's famous "rule paradox" in *Philosophical Investigations.*[9] In his work on constitutional law, Tushnet provides a more elaborate analysis of rule-following that can shed more light on his allusion to Wittgenstein. To explain the problems with the concept of rules, Tushnet borrows an example from Peter Winch roughly similar to one of Wittgenstein's own in *Philosophical Investigations*:

Consider the following multiple choice question: "Which pair of numbers comes next in the series 1, 3, 5, 7 . . .? (*a*) 9, 11; (*b*) 11, 13; (*c*) 25, 18." It is easy to show that any of the answers is correct. The first is correct if the rule generating the series is "List the odd numbers"; the second is correct if the rule is "List the odd prime numbers"; and the third is correct if a more complex rule generates the series. Thus, if asked to follow the underlying rule—the "principle" of the series—we can justify a tremendous range of divergent answers by constructing the rule so that it generates the answer we want. As the Legal Realists showed, the result obtains for legal as well as mathematical rules.[10]

The point that Tushnet wants to make with this example is that legal rules cannot control judges. If the decisions of judges are to be consistent with earlier cases, and the rule underlying these earlier cases can be construed to support several different conclusions, then judges have a great deal of leeway in determining how a rule pertains to the case at hand.

Tushnet immediately qualifies this conclusion, however. He notes that there is something odd about the example: "After all, we know that no test maker would accept (*c*) as an answer, and indeed we can be fairly confident that test makers would not include both (*a*) and (*b*) as possible answers, because the underlying rules that generate them are so obvious as to make the question fatally ambiguous." These limitations of possible test answers do not follow from any logical constraints, however, but from the practice of intelligence testing. People who make intelligence tests, as well as people who take them, know that the obvious rules that underlie (*a*) and (*b*) are the kind of rules asked for in intelligence tests, but that more complex rules that could generate an answer like (*c*) are not. Hence, even though the numbers sequence can be interpreted to produce an answer like (*c*), it would not be accepted as a valid answer, because within the practice of intelligence testing such a rule would be considered nonsensical.[11]

The same is true for law, Tushnet maintains. Thus, he claims that American lawyers can arrive at the conclusion that the Constitution prescribes a drastic redistribution of wealth by using standard techniques of legal argument. Yet it is clear, according to Tushnet, "that no judge will in the near future draw that conclusion." This is not because of any constraints the rules and principles put on judges, he believes, but "because judges in contemporary America are selected in a way that keeps them from thinking that such arguments make sense." The instruction to "follow the rules" is largely empty. If such a demand binds judges, he claims that "it does so only because they have implicitly accepted some version of what the rules in some controverted cases ought to be before they apply those rules in the case at hand."[12] This appreciation of the crucial importance of the legal community in constructing the meaning of rules is supported by contemporary work in literary theory, Tushnet argues. This is work which not only "emphasizes the role that interpretive communities play in determining the authoritative meaning of texts," but which also "questions the basis on which an interpretive community gains its authority."[13]

As we saw in Chapter 3, Tushnet employs these insights to criticize two theories that seek to present the language and rules of constitutional law as controlling and detached: "interpretivism" and "neutral principles." The notion of interpretivism, we noted there, shatters on the impermanence of meaning and the historicity of legal understanding. The dogma of neutral principles, in turn, founders on the pluralism of liberal society. If the interpretive community determines meaning, then the *rule of law* becomes the *rule of those interpreting law*. This would not be problematic if the interpretive community coincided with society as a whole, if everybody shared an understanding of what legal language meant. But because there is no shared way of life in liberal society, there can be no shared understanding of the meaning of legal language. In a pluralistic, liberal society, uniformity of legal interpretation in the judiciary can be achieved only through the institutional exclusion of people with other points of view.

Tushnet's understanding of language games is common in CLS and is often combined with the Kuhnian idea that different conceptual paradigms are fundamentally incommensurable. Different ways of talking about the world cannot be objectively evaluated, because all our knowledge and observation is mediated by them and we have no independent criteria outside of our interpretive schemes to assess their relative worth. Hence, CLS adherents tend to believe that there is no rational, or objective, or authoritative way to support the manner in which the legal system currently conceives of social and economic relations. In the end it is just a contingent vocabulary to talk about society that cannot be proved to be more true, or natural, than any other vocabulary. If the way legal rules are presently understood is in no way justifiable as more true or objective than any other understanding, legal doctrine can be nothing more than the imposition of a certain political point of view at the cost of other perspectives. Things could very well be conceived of differently in the law, with very different results. Consequently, the conventional understanding of legal language is not innocent, but political through and through, if not downright oppressive of other points of view.

This view is prominent in the approach of Critical scholar James Boyle. Like Tushnet, Boyle builds on Wittgenstein to undergird his understanding of law. He argues that legal scholarship, "like most areas of human knowledge, is slowly assimilating to the post-Wittgensteinian view of language."

This post-Wittgensteinian view consists of four basic elements, according to Boyle:

(1) Words do not have "essences."
(2) Words do not have "core meanings."
(3) Language is, or *can* be, used in an infinite number of ways: it is a malleable instrument for communication.
(4) That a word is commonly used to mean X does not mean that X is the "core," or "plain," or "essential" meaning of that word. To look to the "plain meaning" of a word as its "real meaning" is a special type of reification, since it ignores the purpose for which the word is actually being used.[14]

Central in these points is the idea that language "*can* be" used in myriad ways. Boyle's critical argument revolves around this insight. If most people conventionally understand a word to have a certain meaning, then the appreciation that the same word *can* potentially be understood differently has important consequences. Once we realize that we can conceive of the world differently and that we can endow the words we use with alternative meanings, the accepted meanings of words lose their artless, uncontrived quality. Accepted meanings can then be seen for what they are: arbitrary designations of meaning that imply political choice.

Thus, for example, Boyle argues that "the ordinary language meaning of 'woman' may contain sexist assumptions."[15] The word *woman* as it is commonly used is not simply a neutral designation for a female member of the human species. It carries with it manifold preconceptions about what such a member of the human species is like, preconceptions that can be discriminatory. Consequently, as Boyle claims under point (4), the way a word is commonly used cannot simply be accepted as its plain or true meaning, because that would leave the "purpose for which the word is actually being used" out of the picture; that is, it would fail to consider the politics that went into the construction of its meaning. An approach in which the ordinary understanding of words, as a matter of course, was accepted as their true meaning, would acquiesce in the political biases of discourse.

The people that first opened up the Pandora's box of discursive politics in law, Boyle argues, were the Realists. They were instrumental in the destruction of the idea that legal language had an "essential" or "objective" meaning, independent of the contingencies of time and place, which the judge merely had to uncover and apply to the case at hand. They replaced the formalistic semantic theory with a functionalist procedure for elucidating legal terminology. Judges, they believed, should not try to determine, once and for all, what a legal term truly and objectively means, but should look for the intention, the purpose, the policy goal behind it, so that its meaning for the case in question could be determined in light of the purpose it was meant to serve. However, this Realist alternative did not prove to be viable, according to Boyle. Purposive interpretation did not provide judges with a conclusive method for ascertaining legal meaning, but moved them into the politically contentious world of the competing social theories and conflicting visions of the good life that informed legal language. Thus, Boyle claims, the Realist view of language in the end shut the door on "the possibility of a method of adjudication that is separable from political argument in general, since the court must go beneath the words into the political struggles producing them."[16]

Once the antiessentialist genie was out of bottle, Boyle maintains, there was no going back. Antiessentialism had corrosive effects that went far beyond the intended eradication of formalism in legal thought. The critique of essentialism, he contends, was a tool that "had a nasty way of turning on its users":

> After all, essentialism does not happen only in language. People want to believe that objects, events, science, social classes, genders, races, history, as well as words—that *all* these things have essential qualities. When we challenge the belief in essences we do more than change the direction of legal theory. We open ourselves up to the fragility of the stories we tell, the contingent, could-be-otherwise character of the film of meaning that we project onto the social world.[17]

When you give up the idea of "essential meaning," Boyle argues, not only words become equivocal, but also the preinterpretive notions about society and social policy that were supposed to shape the meaning of words in the Realist-inspired solution for linguistic indeterminacy—purposive interpretation. Hence, once essences go, the plain meaning of words, as well as the shared preconceptions of social policy, become too elusive to provide legal rules with a clear and fixed meaning.

CLS AND POST-STRUCTURALISM

The idea that language, knowledge, and theory are all inherently political is also a central tenet of French Post-structuralist philosophy. Several CLS adherents have drawn on this intellectual source to inform their theory of law. Post-structuralism shares with Structuralism—the theory it superseded—the notion that people's thought is in large measure determined by structures of cultural and linguistic meaning. What we think and do is profoundly conditioned by the structures of meaning we are socialized into when we grow up. These structures of social meaning arbitrarily invest the world around us with significance and shape what we can think and believe. Yet, whereas the Structuralists traditionally believed these linguistic and cultural structures were largely stable and determinate, Post-structuralists doubt their fixity. For the Post-structuralist, structures of cultural and linguistic meaning are inherently impermanent, unstable, ambiguous, and indeterminate. Consequently, they cannot provide us with a stable medium for the communication of ideas, the production of knowledge, or the regulation of society.

Such ideas are central in the thought of Critical Legal scholar Gary Peller, a representative of what is known as the "irrationalist" strand of CLS. Peller borrows heavily from French Post-structuralist thought. Inspired by the work of Jacques Derrida, Peller seeks to deconstruct the "metaphysical assumptions" on which legal thought has purportedly been based and in Foucauldian fashion he attempts to expose the pernicious politics involved in legal discourse. Legal discourse cannot be neutral, Peller contends; "representational practice, whatever its form, inevitably is ideological." For Peller representations of the world, in legal or any other type of discourse, are inherently narrow and arbitrary and therefore necessarily present a politically biased view. Thus, law exerts political influence through its representational scheme. It imposes a certain understanding of the world as sound and rational, to the detriment of other points of view, which are marginalized as emotional and irrational.[18]

According to Peller, the way legal discourse manages to institutionalize a certain view of the world is by providing a set of "underlying structures of meaning" or "instituted codes of 'common sense,'" which "freeze the argumentative play of analogy by providing categories that form boundaries for 'real' similarity and difference." By predetermining what are the salient aspects of social phenomena, by foreordaining on what grounds certain things can be grouped together as similar and others can separated as different, legal discourse provides "metaphors for organizing perception and communication," metaphors that "cannot themselves be justified as rational rather than rhetorical."[19] Reality can be cut up in myriad ways. Hence the demarcation lines provided by legal discourse, which arbitrarily organize the world for us and decide what is the same and what is different, are at once completely arbitrary and fundamentally important.

This idea of "difference" as the source of linguistic meaning originates from Derrida, of course, and ultimately from the Structuralist linguistics of

Ferdinand de Saussure on which he builds. In Derrida's and De Saussure's understanding of language, the meaning of a word does not derive from some manifest or inherent quality of the phenomenon it refers to, but as Peller puts it, from its "relationship to other words within the socially created representational practice." If a representational practice does not label preexisting classes of objects, but carves up the world in arbitrary ways, if the order of things is constructed rather than reflected in language, then the lines drawn between the constituent terms of the representational scheme are the primary sources of meaning, not any manifest qualities in the real-world objects referred to. A word like *tree*, Peller argues, does not capture some obvious quality of tree-ness, but "acquires its meaning from not being another word, say 'bush' or 'woods.'" In other words, if we divide up vegetation along such arbitrary distinctions, then the meaning of a word like *tree* depends on its place in relation to the other categories in our taxonomy of greenery. Meaning is something that emerges from the opposition of a term to the other terms in the representational structure. As a result, a word can be defined only in terms of its difference to other words. Consequently, Peller claims, that "it is not some substantial plenitude which determines the meaning of a representational term, but rather a lack of meaning which points elsewhere, outside of itself, to other terms of signification which it is not."[20]

This understanding of meaning as a product of the differentiation of terms within the framework of a representational structure forms the basis for Derrida's technique of "deconstruction." When the meaning of concepts is elucidated in terms of differentiation, this is usually done with conceptual pairs that are polar opposites. *Public* and *private*, to borrow one of Peller's examples, form such a pair within the context of law and seem to label diametrically opposed realms of life. Deconstruction proceeds from the assumption that there is usually a hierarchy within conceptual dichotomies, that one side of the dichotomy is privileged at the cost of the other. With the public/private distinction, it is the private—associated with the free and natural relations between individuals—that is privileged, and the public—associated with government intrusion—that is subordinate in the conceptual framework of law. Nevertheless, the two sides of the conceptual dichotomy are deeply implicated in each other's meaning. Both sides can be defined only in reference to the other—public is public, because it is not private; and private is private, because it is not public. This intimate relationship between dichotomous concepts ensures that there are always traces of the suppressed concept in its privileged counterpart, that each privileged concept contains aspects of its suppressed negative. This is where deconstruction comes in. It is a technique aimed at uncovering those suppressed elements, at exposing the concealed tensions within a concept and destabilizing its accepted meaning.

Peller claims that many Realists engaged in this type of deconstructive critique, decades before Derrida provided it with a name. The public/private distinction again is a good example. Classical legal thought, with its embrace of laissez-faire economics and freedom of contract, depended heavily on the public/private distinction. It claimed to defer to a natural private sphere in which independent individuals owned property, acted according to their own free will, and decided under which conditions they wanted to cooperate and contract with each other. For Classical legal scholars, this private sphere was the mainspring of legal categories; law reflected rather than created the social and economic relations that developed from the genuine intentions of free individuals. This authentic sphere was separate from, and needed to be protected against, the public sphere, which stood for contrived governmental coercion and intrusion in the unconstrained play of social life. The Realist critique against this traditional perspective was, basically, that no such pristine private sphere existed and that the terms on which people engaged with one another in the private sphere were largely publicly defined through the legal system.

Peller uses Felix Cohen's analysis of the legal protection of trademarks to illustrate the Realist deconstruction of the public/private distinction. A trademark is a thing of value, the traditional legal argument went, and therefore it constitutes property. Property arose from the free play of economic forces in the private sphere and is therefore protected by law. Thus, if a third party uses the trademark, this is essentially treated as a taking of property. Cohen, however, argued that this argument was circular. What made a trademark property, he claimed, was exactly its protection by the courts. If the courts would not protect a trademark, it would simply be a piece of advertising without any special economic value. "In other words," he argued, "the fact that the courts did not protect the word would make the word valueless, and the fact that the word was valueless would then be regarded as a reason for not protecting it."[21] Hence, private property was not some preexisting entity out there in the real world that the legal system merely protected. Rather, property was a creature of the legal system; it depended on *public* recognition by the legal system for it to become *private* property. This showed that law did not mirror some natural social order, but was a closed, self-referential set of symbols. Legal Realism produced a great many similar deconstructive arguments, Peller claims, which sought to show that the basic conceptual divisions of law did not reflect some given, natural order of society, but constructed that order with paired concepts that only referred back and forth to each other.[22]

Yet Peller not only praises but also criticizes the Legal Realists. He rejects their efforts to ground law in a scientific understanding of society, a project that suffered from the same fundamental flaws as the Classical legal thought it tried to displace. Much like Classical legal thought, Peller claims, the constructive program of Realism involved a "metaphysics of presence." It was predicated on "the concept of a self-present origin, a stable and positive ground for the representation of social life existing apart from the social process of differentiation."[23] Where Classical legal thought had grounded its categories in the "transcendental subject" of the free and autonomous individual that was thought to originate legal relations, constructive Realism located meaning in the "transcendental object" of an accessible and knowable social world that could be studied separate from its representation in discourse and used as an independent foundation for legal concepts and categories. As a result, Peller argues, constructive Realism fell victim to the illusion that the representation of social life in law could occur "free from the indeterminate play of rhetoric and metaphor, free from socially contingent ways of projecting similarity and difference, free, in short, from the contingencies of language."[24]

This is not to say that Peller rejects the type of social-scientific reformism the Realists aspired to. He is not averse to proposing a constructive political program himself. Thus, for instance, he applies deconstructive analysis to argue for the extension of the concept of rape. Peller claims that "'rape' is an artifact of the legal representational process whereby some sexual relations are called coercive and others are called consensual."[25] The "mind/body dichotomy" is the distinction that mediates the difference between the coercive and the consensual in this case. According to Peller, this leads to an arbitrary narrowing of the definition of rape to physically coerced sex, at the expense of more subtle, nonphysical forms of sexual coercion that might take place within the workplace or a marriage. In other words, Peller aspires to extend the present legal concept of rape to cover more cases and uses deconstruction of its arbitrary rhetorical distinctions as a way to achieve that goal.

In another article, he makes a similar claim with reference to the project of integration. Integrationism is mediated by the convergence of two dichotomies: on the one hand, the distinction *universalism/particularism* and, on the other, the distinction *truth/prejudice*. Truth is equated with the universal and prejudice with the particularistic. Prejudice involves stressing supposed irreducible differences—blacks are just plain lazy—while truth proceeds from the acknowledgment of our common humanity. Within this framework integration is a process of reducing particularism and distinction; so everybody is treated equally and our universal human equality is recognized. Yet the universals of American society are not neutral; they are slanted toward the white majority. Consequently, an eradication of particularism, of white supremacist prejudice, will not bring about justice for blacks. Hence, as long as the difference of blacks is not recognized, policies that promote a pure equality of opportunity will not redress some of the inequalities endemic in American society.[26] Such barely concealed political preferences are quite problematic in conjunction with the corrosive acid of Post-structuralism, as we shall see.

A second Critical scholar who applied Post-structuralist insights to the analysis of law is Clare Dalton. In her critique of American contract doctrine, Dalton proceeds from a deconstructive framework that is fairly similar to Peller's. Dalton acknowledges right from the start that she has "benefited from the deconstructive textual strategies developed by Jacques Derrida"; from his notion "that all discourse tends to favor one pole of any duality over the other creating a hierarchical relationship between the poles," as well as from his method of undermining these hierarchies by making the meaning of the suppressed pole resurface, "revealing to us that things are not, after all, what they seem."[27]

Dalton has a narrative perspective on law. Law, Dalton believes, "like every other cultural institution, is a place where we tell one another stories about our relationships with ourselves, one another, and authority." This narrative conception should not be taken to suggest that there is presently a great deal of freedom in law to conceive of our relationships with others. Dalton is firmly located within the Post-structuralist framework and every bit as convinced as Peller that people's thought is shaped and limited by legal discourse. Hence, what Dalton is mainly interested in is not the unbounded and open-ended character of law's narratives, but the "particular limits law stories impose on the twin projects of self-definition and self-understanding." She wants to expose "the way law shapes all stories into particular patterns of telling, favors certain stories and disfavors others, or even makes it impossible to tell certain kinds of stories."[28]

The way the law accomplishes this feat is something that brings us back to the Post-structural understanding of language. The overarching themes in the story of contract doctrine, Dalton claims, are issues of knowledge and power. Law stories are preoccupied with what separates people from and connects them to others—the power aspect—and with how people can know and understand what others intend and want—the knowledge aspect. This fundamental opposition between self and other, subject and object, in Dalton's view, profoundly structures contract doctrine, which "devotes its energies to describing, policing and disguising the divide."[29] The problems thrown up by this basic split between self and other, subject and object, are irresolvable. As a result, in the realm of contract doctrine the intractable issues of knowledge and power are displaced; they are translated into "doctrinal structures that depend on the dualities of public and private, objective and subjective, form and substance," in order to manage and contain the problems they cause.

This should now begin to look like the familiar territory of deconstructive analysis, and Dalton's next claim should no longer come as a surprise— namely, that contract doctrine "consistently favors one pole of each duality," that it "describes itself as more private than public, interpretation as more about objective than subjective understanding, consideration as more about form than about substance." This method of "hierarchy in duality," Dalton maintains, allows "doctrinal rhetoric to avoid the underlying problems of power and knowledge." By privileging one side of each conceptual dichotomy, the suppressed negative is turned into a harmless exception to, or qualification of, the privileged concept. Yet the problems are merely displaced by rhetorical fiat. The method of "hierarchy in duality" amounts to little more than a rhetorical smoke screen that leaves the underlying dilemmas unresolved.[30]

The goal of this critique is not to clear the ground for some grand alternative that can replace present contract doctrine. Dalton does not provide her own substantive view on contract law. Rather she suggests a different general approach to deal with contract issues that is more sensitive to the complexities and ambiguities of social life. Law, to Dalton's mind, severely truncates the intricacies of human relations by forcing them into the standard categories of law and often abruptly cuts disputes short before they can be fully worked out by the interested parties. Cast in narrative terms, this leads to the conclusion that contract doctrine tells a greatly impoverished story about human relations. "The infinitely rich potential that we call reality," Dalton observes, "is stripped of detail, of all but a few of its aspects."[31]

Thus, unlike Peller, Dalton is not tempted to propose an alternative to mainstream legal thought that would be vulnerable to the very same deconstructive arguments used to displace that thought in the first place. This avoidance of self-contradiction comes at a price, though. To be a consistent deconstructivist, Dalton must claim not only that legal thought can no longer be based on a misguided belief in reason and the transparency of language, but that nobody's thought can, including her own. Consequently, she can no longer believe that any sound reasons can be provided to prefer an alternative to the going conception of law, nor can she any longer have faith in the medium of language to communicate such an alternative to others accurately. Without the possibility of intersubjectively valid arguments, or even the assurance of intersubjective understanding, the only thing that remains for Dalton is to add her story of law to the ones already circulating in the legal tradition and encourage others to do the same in the hope that such a kaleidoscopic collection of stories will enrich legal understanding.

THE FRAGMENTATION OF CLS

The problem that Peller ignores and Dalton tries to resolve with her narrative approach is elevated to a defining characteristic of recent Critical work in law by Duncan Kennedy. According to Kennedy, there is a basic tension within the recent theory that has developed out of the CLS movement. He has introduced the term Left/MPM (Modernism-Postmodernism) theory to describe the kind of intellectual position that much of the work proceeding from CLS occupies. This composite term explains a great deal about the intellectual disintegration of CLS. It juxtaposes a reformist, even revolutionary political program of emancipation with an academic genre of "viral critique" aimed at undermining any claim to rightness and objectivity, including those from the left. In the section below, Kennedy's analysis of what happened to CLS will be elaborated upon, and his conclusions about the rapid recent bifurcations of Critical Legal theory will be highlighted with some examples.

In a nutshell, Kennedy asserts that there was always a degree of theoretical multiplicity in Critical Legal Studies. On the one hand, CLS adherents placed themselves in a leftist tradition of social reconstruction in the service of the disadvantaged. This leftist tradition called for a theory, a plan, a program of reform, a consistent analysis of present woes. On the other hand, CLS scholars embraced the cultural critique of Modernist and Postmodernist theory. This critique was aimed at the pretense of science and rationality, the pomposity of theory, the treacherousness of language, and the intolerance of political theories and programs. In *A Critique of Adjudication*, the most comprehensive elaboration of his theoretical position, Kennedy describes this tension vividly:

> The notions of leftism and mpm are helpful in understanding many of the debates that occurred within cls when it was a life movement and that still arise about cls understood as a school and a theory of law. Attacks from the left, internal and external, often focus on its mpm quality. "Being right" in the rationalist sense has been a crucial part of leftism, and the mpm strand in the project is hostile to rightness in all its forms. Other critiques of the project from the left come from the demand that theory contribute to a particular model of action in the world, whereas the dandyish, aestheticist, politically quietist mpm strands rebel against that image.[32]

Kennedy seems quite prepared to live with this tension. Indeed, you get the sense that, much as in psychoanalysis, it is more important to understand your innermost drives, to see how they cause the trouble they do, than to resolve them one way or the other. Understanding is enough. There is no need to choose, to suppress any part of what you are.

This embrace of the internal tension within CLS and the undirected nature of its critique is something that Wendy Brown and Janet Halley have much sympathy for. In an overview of recent trends in leftist legal theory, Brown and Halley try to answer the question head-on: What good is critique for, from a perspective of left politics? Their answer is that critique is very adept at exposing structures of power:

> Critique offers possibilities of analyzing existing discourses of power to understand how subjects are fabricated or positioned by them, what powers they secure (and disguise or veil), what assumptions they naturalize, what privileges they fix, what norms they mobilize, and what or whom these norms exclude. Critique is thus a practice that allows us to scrutinize the form, content, and possible reworking of our apparent political choices; we no longer have to take them as givens.

Brown and Halley accept that such a technique of unmasking the political power behind the dominant discourses of the day is a procedure very difficult to contain to just established creeds and right-wing ideologies. It might very well undermine some cherished left-wing ideas as well. Indeed, according to Brown and Halley, it is difficult to predict where the critique will lead: "Yet, rather than apologize for this aspect of critique, why not affirm it?" they assert confidently. "For part of what it means to dissect the discursive practices that organize our lives is to embark on an inquiry whose outcome is unknown, and the process of which will be radically disorienting at times."[33]

One of Brown and Halley's examples of such a "radically disorienting" dissection of discursive practices is the feminist critique of pornography. At one point, this critique was a coherent, straightforward, wholesale rejection of pornography as a degrading and misogynous practice. Yet once women started to subject pornography to a critical discursive inquiry, they developed a confusing array of responses:

> [W]omen found themselves having all kinds of responses to porn that could not simply be classified as for or against: some were distressed by it but grasped their distress as an index of the sexual shame their gender construction entailed; others were drawn to it and flatly delighted to be let into a sexual order previously designated for men; others were more ambivalent, liking the idea of porn or liking bits of it but troubled or turned off by the misogynistic (or racist or colonial) strains in it (some were confusingly turned on by these very same strains); still others were inspired to try to make good porn for women. What was the political cache of this rich array of responses? It produced a wave of new feminist work on sexuality: new questions, new theories, new domains of research, new practices, new arguments, new positions in every sense of the word.[34]

Compared to the dry and narrow liberal-legalistic view on pornography, focused on equality, civil rights, and free speech, Brown and Halley celebrate this as an example of "marvelously fertile political contestation and intellectual exploration."[35] It is fair to say, however, that few conclusions can be drawn from this cornucopia of feminist opinion.

Yet where Duncan Kennedy makes no apologies for the contradictions of his position and seems to suggest that only sticklers for coherence could object to his intellectual dandyism, Brown and Halley shy away from such an unapologetic stance. For them the end goal is still to arrive at a constructive political program. They treat the recent disorientation not as a permanent condition but as a necessary preparatory period for the formulation of a new leftist position: "Surely we should not disavow a left critique of the tensions and contradictions in affirmative action simply because that critique does not deliver in advance a blueprint or set of strategies for achieving racial, gender, or class justice in America." Even Marx himself was unsure where his critique might lead when he marshaled his intellectual powers against the dominant Hegelian tradition as a young man, they claim. It was only at a later stage that his critique evolved into a comprehensive program for social and political change. Yet he would never have reached that point without the disorienting and open-ended critique of his early work.[36]

The development of such a new comprehensive approach seems an elusive dream to Richard T. Ford, at least in the field of racial justice. Ford argues in "Beyond 'Difference'" that "racist discourse is Janus-faced: it articulates difference with one mouth and condemns it with another." Hence, it is well-nigh impossible to develop a coherent and effective solution to the problem of racism. Of course, Ford admits, he could try to "negotiate the tightrope of production and punishment of difference more effectively than either contemporary antidiscrimination law or cultural rights type proposals do," but that would still amount to no more than a negotiation of the contradiction. Indeed, he does not believe that "law is capable of resolving or banishing this contradiction."[37]

Meanwhile, Ford contends, both liberal integrationism and race consciousness fall far short of providing a solution for the prejudice and discrimination of American society. Integrationism is an impoverished version of the call for racial justice from within the black community. Its ideals of universalist humanism have been hijacked and used cynically to curtail racial equality. As a result, Ford argues, "color blindness was deployed against affirmative action, integration was used to undermine any form of racial solidarity, assimilation became a bludgeon to discipline any practice that made the milquetoast mainstream uncomfortable."[38] Also the "politics of difference," however, which developed as a reaction to the sellout of integrationism, failed to live up to the call for racial justice. Indeed, Ford wonders: "What if the politics of difference threatens to become another hegemonic discourse, no less total, no less obsessive, no less myopic than the universalist ideal that preceded it?"[39] The problem with the politics of difference is that it ends up freezing a cultural identity in its present form and defending it against any outside influences. Anything that would force change on a minority culture, after all, would be violating that culture's right to a cultural identity. Hence, there is something deeply conservative about the politics of difference.[40]

These recent Critical analyses of legal discourse depart from early CLS work in all sorts of directions. It is difficult to find even the outlines of a new program in this eclectic development of inconclusive points of view. It is not impossible that Brown and Halley are right, of course, and that this will eventually converge on a new synthesis. Yet Kennedy's analysis seems the more plausible account of recent developments. The critical acid of Post-structuralism has not just corroded mainstream legal thought but has also eaten into CLS theory itself, and especially those parts of the theory that offer political alternatives.

CONCLUSION

What all the CLS perspectives discussed in this chapter have in common, despite the many differences, is an extraordinarily hermetic view of language. We are caged in by our linguistic conventions, which can be interpreted and manipulated, but which can no longer be evaluated as tools to come to grips with reality in any meaningful way. We have lost the world, because anything we could ever mean when we invoke the word *world* is what our linguistic conventions make that *world* appear to be. This is a good deal more radical than anything the Realists ever proposed. Indeed, it has eventually destabilized CLS as a coherent approach and led to the confusing array of viewpoints that now characterizes Critical analysis of law. This is often claimed to result inescapably from the profound new understanding of the fundamental importance of language. Yet, despite the conviction with which CLS theorists have spelled out the consequences of recent insights into the nature of language, their conclusions need not be accepted as inescapable. There are good reasons to be skeptical of their solipsistic understanding of language.

The application of Wittgenstein's insights into language, to begin with, seems incongruous with the general drift of his philosophy. For instance, Tushnet's claims about rule-following, discussed above, seem to proceed from a misunderstanding of Wittgenstein. Tushnet suggests it is the politics of the interpreters, rather than the rules, that determines meaning. The problem with this interpretation of Wittgenstein is that it proceeds from the conception that rules somehow precede or stand apart from social practices. Thus Tushnet in his example of the intelligence test does not show that the test questions reflect the political preconceptions of the testing authorities, but rather that looked at acontextually a given set of symbols can tell us very little. Only when we situate a set of symbols in the practice it belongs to, and understand the point and purpose of its use, does it become meaningful. This does not mean that rules are fundamentally indeterminate, but that rules can be understood only in their context of use, as part of the practice that gives them meaning. Tushnet, however, pries language and social practice apart and treats a rule as something that awaits later interpretation within a given practice. Yet the social context is not something apart and independent from rules, but something that is implicated in their very meaning right from the start. This suggests that the introduction into a language game cannot be equated with interpreting a set of rules, but that it involves initiation into the practice the language game belongs to. This includes understanding the purpose of that practice, knowing which problems and questions it is concerned with, and grasping the conventions, assumptions, and understandings implicit in it. In other words, it is a process that is more accurately described as acquiring experience and know-how than as interpreting the rules.[41]

Moreover, a lesson that Tushnet chose not to learn from Wittgenstein is that there is no way to step outside of one's language and conceive of the world in a completely novel way—not even for lawyers. As a result, there is no infinite interpretive freedom to provide legal rules with idiosyncratic meanings. If the judiciary diverges too far from the conventional understanding of words, it will be thought to provide interpretations of the rules that are off-the-wall, absurd, and unfair. Tushnet's suggestion that the Constitution could be interpreted as a text calling for socialism, even though the interpretive community of judges precludes such an interpretation, illustrates the problem. The issue here is not that judges are selected in a way that keeps them from thinking that an interpretation of the Constitution as a text calling for socialism makes sense, but that judges have to work within the framework of a larger linguistic community that would find such a reading of constitutional language bizarre and unacceptable. As Ronald Dworkin working from within the selfsame Wittgensteinian framework, has observed: "Judges think about law . . . within society, not apart from it; the general intellectual environment, as well as the common language that reflects and protects that environment, exercises practical constraints on idiosyncrasy and conceptual constraints on imagination."[42]

Boyle's application of Wittgensteinian insights fails, in turn, because it proves too much. Perhaps Boyle's example of the word *woman* can illuminate the problem with his approach. Applied to the word *woman*, Boyle's views on language suggest a number of conflicting conclusions. The reification argument presented by Boyle, to begin with, leads to the insight that the word *woman* contains sexist notions, which predispose language users to hold a lowly opinion of women. The accepted meaning of the word *woman*, the argument goes, is not neutral but embodies prejudices about women which are reified as characteristics of what women are truly like. At the same time, however, Boyle makes the argument that words cannot be thought of as having plain meanings. With regard to the word *woman,* this suggests that the term does not have a definite and settled meaning but should be thought of as an empty container which language users fill with their own preconceptions about what women are like. In that case, the accepted meaning of the word *woman* no longer determines the politics of the language users, but the language users' politics, instead, determines the meaning of the word *woman.* Finally, Boyle argues that we should give up not only the claim that words have essences but also that there can be a preconceptual understanding of what real-world phenomena are like. Hence, neither the word *woman* nor the notion of what a woman is can have a firm and stable significance. This, in turn, undermines Boyle's critique that the word *woman* contains sexist assumptions. If nobody can gain an understanding of what women are like, then there is no longer any basis, or standard, that Boyle can appeal to, to criticize the politically biased meaning contained in the word *woman.* As a result, Boyle cannot discount the possibility of forming warranted notions about the social world without undermining his own argument that legal discourse is politics.

Boyle is not unaware of these contradictions in CLS theory. CLS, he admits, wants to have it both ways: the idea of reification, of language shaping people's thought through the politically biased conceptions that are contained in it, as well as the idea that language is a pliant tool of communication that can be twisted at will to express some politically biased point of view. Boyle contends, however, that these two contradictory views of language can be reconciled through a mediating strategy. He invites us to hold the different accounts together "by faith long enough to have the experience of total critique."[43] This is a "leap of faith," to be sure, but without it, Boyle claims, we will never be able to experience the liberating insights of total critique.

The trouble does not stop with the application of Wittgenstein. Equally problematic is the CLS attempt to revitalise Realist insights on language with the use of Postmodern theory. As we saw earlier, Peller treats the CLS critique of legal discourse explicitly as a continuation of the Legal Realist critique of concepts. Indeed, Peller praises the Legal Realists for applying a mode of analysis very close to deconstruction, long before Derrida provided that procedure with its name. Yet he also criticizes them for their recourse to empirical analysis to provide legal concepts with a more accurate meaning. The Realists, he argues, claimed to have unmediated access to the facts of social life. They conceived of society "as a natural organism with determinate and universal functions which could be observed and measured simply according to some neutral calculus of sense impressions."[44] Thus, in Peller's view, the Realists believed that they could step outside of their discourse, their conceptual paradigm, and look at empirical phenomena without the help of the conceptual distinctions embedded in language. In their search for scientific objectivity, they deluded themselves into thinking that the distortions of concepts could be avoided in empirical research.

Peller's critique, however, seems to proceed from a misunderstanding of what the Realists set out to do. Notably, Peller does not consider the possibility that the Realists were advocating a Pragmatic approach to the problem of language. The Realists, as we saw in Chapter 6, were fully aware that observation, including observation by empirical social scientists, always implied the use of concepts and categories that organized the sense data in arbitrary ways. Unlike Peller, however, the Realists did not lose their enthusiasm for social science as a result. To them, strict neutrality of research terms simply was not a necessary precondition for the kind of social science they proposed. The reason for this was that from their Pragmatic point of view, the problem was not whether law was based on a view of society that could be shown to be true, but whether it was based on a view of society that informed law in a helpful way and brought about desired results, where "desired" was understood in terms of the conceptual framework employed. Peller assumes that the Realists were seeking absolute truth, that they were seeking to redefine legal concepts on the basis of a scientifically true account of the social world. The Realists, however, were aiming for something much less ambitious. They were looking for warranted hypotheses rather than absolute truth, desirable consequences rather than objective knowledge, and workable concepts rather than the one true language of the universe. No matter that they were caught in a conceptual framework that could never be proved to reflect the world truthfully and indubitably slanted their observation; they could still evaluate the results that could be achieved with it and see whether they conformed to the consequences that had been projected. Long before CLS appeared on the scene, Dewey had already taught the Realists that a quest for certainty would inevitably fail. But he also taught them that in a contingent world there was no reason to give up the effort to deal with social developments intelligently and to develop conceptual tools fitted to that end.

Peller, moreover, still proceeds from the assumption that deconstruction is a tool that can be put to constructive use. Yet it is unclear how it could ever help Peller's project. He seems to think that it can clear the ground for a redefinition of rape and that it can help bring about more substantial equality for blacks. Yet the usefulness of deconstruction is extremely doubtful for those objectives. Derrida developed deconstruction to undermine "logocentric" philosophy and to subvert the search for, and belief in, a direct, untainted, and unmediated avenue to objective truth. Consequently, his linguistic theory is aimed at exposing the fundamental ambiguity of language, at demonstrating that thought can never move beyond the conditions of its own production in discourse, and at explaining how any text is a self-contained jumble of words, an elusive collection of unstable signifiers, that frustrate any reference to objective reality and efface all traces of authorial intent. This seems to be an excellent technique for someone who wants to prove that it is impossible ever to get to the heart of the matter of rape, or who wants to poke fun at attempts to pin down the problem of racial equality. Yet, Peller does not want to show that no convincing conception of rape or racial equality can ever be provided, but that the present legal conception of rape and racial equality is wrong. For this, Peller needs to show that his inclusive view of rape and his alternative understanding of racial equality are somehow more accurate, just, convincing, fair, representative, or beneficial than the ones presently enforced by law. There will never be support for any of these claims within a deconstructive framework. Deconstruction simply leaves Peller no ground to stand on to forward alternatives for the legal rules he would like to change.

This problem is more widespread. Many of the Post-structuralist arguments in the Critical tool kit are inappropriate for the development of a coherent leftist alternative and tend to facilitate the anarchic free-for-all characteristic of present Critical analysis. Dalton's narrative approach in a way presaged the later fragmentation of CLS. She no longer formulates a solution for the totalitarian rigidity of law, but simply opts for the creation of a rich fund of narrative to draw from in order to soften and enrich the artificial reason of legal discourse. Law is more than a platform for the discussion of how people should live together in society. Law is also an institution that has to provide finality when disagreements over the terms of social cooperation do not get resolved and threaten to spiral out of control. After all, disputes do not always stay civil: disputes can go sour, they can fail to reach completion, they can spill over into other areas and draw in more people, and they can lead to violence and mayhem. To keep any of these things from happening and maintain social peace is one of the primary tasks of law. Hence, it might not always be advisable for law to encourage the continual reassessment and accommodation between the parties to a conflict, which Dalton calls for, or for law to get involved in conflicts in the participants' own terms. If the artificial reason of law often does little justice to the complexities and ambiguities of social life, then at least it has the benefit of artificially putting a stop to conflicts that threaten to get bogged down in those very same complexities and ambiguities.

All in all, the Pragmatic program of the Realists seems to have more going for it than does CLS Post-structuralism in dealing with the contingency of language. As a critical tool, the Post-structuralist understanding of language adopted by CLS scholars seems very hard to contain, even by their own admission. As long as deconstruction remains the preserve of Critical scholars and is employed only to criticize mainstream legal thought, it may be a powerful weapon that can be used to destroy legal illusions. Yet what happens when deconstruction is applied against CLS arguments? There is nothing in deconstruction that precludes it from being used for that purpose. Critical scholars also use words and concepts, which must also depend on differentiation for their meaning. Hence, with regard to their critique of the public/private distinction, one could argue that CLS depends on, for instance, a nature/social-construction dichotomy. Critical scholarship in that case would proceed from a rhetorical distinction between an empirical, natural sphere that is unknowable and inaccessible and a privileged discursive sphere that metaphorically creates our world for us. One could then go on to show that the two sides of this conceptual pair make sense only in terms of each other, that there are consequently traces of the natural in the socially constructed and vice versa, and finally that these traces can be extended to destabilize the concept of the socially constructed and undermine its privileged status. Somebody else could then go on to deconstruct the concepts used in this deconstruction of CLS deconstruction, and so on, and so forth. An infinite regress of critique upon critique would be the result.

This scenario might not be all that fanciful. Indeed, from the latest work that has emanated from Critical scholars one could conclude that this is in fact what has been happening to legal scholars that currently carry the CLS torch. Not only mainstream legal thought but also the consensus that existed within the CLS movement up to the early 1990s are now a hegemonic discourse that needs to be exposed and deconstructed. Thus Ford, as we saw earlier, wonders whether the "politics of difference" has not become a new orthodoxy which is just as intolerant and just as total as the integrationist discourse that preceded it. And thus Brown and Halley showed how feminist theory had turned against the erstwhile rejection of pornography. This rejection, they realized, had simply derived from "the sexual shame" which emanated from their "gender construction." Even if this is only an intervening period which will lead to the formulation of a new, leftist alternative, as Brown and Halley claim, this style of critique seems rather inward-looking and self-indulgent. It is a mode of critique which is extraordinarily preoccupied with itself, and it is hard to see how it could lead to anything else than the political quietism that Kennedy believed Left/MPM would result in.

CHAPTER EIGHT

Realizing Realism:
Reconstruction in Legal Theory

A feeling forward, or a being aware.
I reach, out, on: beyond the elm-topped rise
There is, not yet but forming now, a there
To be completed by the opened eyes.
—Thom Gunn[1]

But the point remains, nevertheless, that what measure
of utopia we are destined for—and it is probably a very
modest measure—must be of our own contrivance.
We are no longer headed for heaven in a perambulator
labeled evolution, laissez faire, or any other uncom-
prehended force. If we get there, it will be on our own
power.
—Edward S. Corwin[2]

So far we have compared Legal Realist ideas on history, social science, and
language with the insights they inspired in the Critical Legal Studies (CLS)
movement. This comparison has shown that CLS thought is not so much
an extension of Legal Realism as a departure from its basic insights. Where
the Realists adopted a moderate historicism in which legal development
could be explained as a series of functional adaptations to changing circumstances, CLS embraces a radical historicism in which the legal system is
portrayed as an autonomous, self-moving, ideological edifice, structuring
the social world rather than being structured by it. Where the Realists were
enthusiastic champions of empirical research in law, Critical scholars see
social science as both a conservative and a deterministic methodology tilted
toward the legitimization of the status quo. And where the Realists were
suspicious of the hypnotic power of words, which suggested the reality of
all sorts of nonexistent entities, Critical scholars claim that there is nothing beyond discourse, which forms the very limit and substance of all our
knowledge.

The most fruitful way to understand the basic assumptions of the Legal Realist movement, the one that renders the strongest version of Legal

Realism, is as a traditional Pragmatist approach to law. The Pragmatism of Charles Sanders Peirce, William James, and John Dewey, as Richard Posner put it, "gave legal realism such intellectual shape and content as it had."[3] This traditional Pragmatist approach which informed the Realist movement involved what legal Pragmatist Thomas Grey has described as a mix of, on the one hand, eighteenth-century empiricism inspired by the natural sciences, and on the other nineteenth-century historicism, Romanticism, and evolutionary biology. The Realists, in other words, much like the Pragmatist philosophers of their day, tried to fuse the method of science with the sensibility that all human endeavors, including science itself, were a product of the contingent historical context. This blend of intellectual traditions, as Grey notes, marks Pragmatism "off from even the sophisticated contemporary forms of scientific empiricist philosophy" and lends "a scope to pragmatism that no philosophy drawing inspiration entirely from the natural sciences can have."[4]

CLS scholars, however, have not taken Legal Realism seriously as a Pragmatic approach. Instead, they have treated Realism as a movement which started off with a wholesome contextual understanding of law—the perspective deriving from nineteenth-century Romanticism and historicism—but which was then seized, unfortunately, by the idea of empirical social science—the perspective deriving from eighteenth-century empiricism. For CLS scholars, these two strands seem so irreconcilable that even the possibility that they could be synthesized into a single approach is not seriously considered. As a result, CLS adherents tend to depict Realism as a confused and self-contradictory movement, divided against itself, with a positivist, scientific dimension that they reject and a critical, contextualist dimension that they seek to salvage.

The Realists, according to this argument, simply did not have a proper understanding of the issues they were grappling with. They did not have the benefit of, for instance, Wittgenstein's probing insights into language or Kuhn's corrosive conception of the incommensurability of scientific paradigms. These could have shown them that they were trying to combine things that could not be combined and that their excursions into science were wrongheaded. CLS scholars, on the other hand, have had to come to terms with these more recent intellectual developments and now are in a much better position to judge the Realist project. Hence, looking back from their more enlightened vantage point, they can contend that the Realist embrace of social science was a misguided effort to ground legal theory in empirical fact, whereas their recourse to contextualism was an early and visionary attempt to come to terms with the cultural and historical contingency of legal thought.[5]

Yet the question is whether Realism is really in need of any reconstruction by CLS scholars. Realism would be flawed if the synthesis of empiricism and contextualism that Grey sees as the hallmark of Pragmatism never came off the ground, if the two elements remained separate configurations within Realist theory. In that case, Realist social science would be unchastened by the realization that there are no pristine empirical facts, no neutral data untainted by one's frame of reference to judge scientific theories by, and it would be open to many of the criticisms of Critical scholars. Moreover, the Realist approach would truly be contradictory, consisting of two unreconciled, antithetical elements pulling in opposite directions and seriously undermining its coherence.

However, when Realism is duly understood as applied Pragmatism in the field of law, rather than an unsuccessful combination of positivist science and contextualist understanding, the presumed contradictions in its basic assumptions disappear. As was argued in Chapter 3, from a Pragmatist point of view there is no problem with the idea that scientific truth is relative to the conceptual framework within which it is generated. Indeed, that is one of the central claims of Pragmatism. The Pragmatist notion of science simply does not depend on unmediated access to the empirical world. It only requires a community of scholars working within a shared conceptual framework, freely and openly testing and criticizing each other's work and trying to achieve intersubjective agreement on which theory works best. Scientific truth, in other words, is primarily defined in terms of agreement among scholars, not in terms of correspondence to a preconceptual and objective realm of fact (although Pragmatism does assume that open scholarly debate in the long run will result in a consensus that conforms to what reality is like). The Pragmatic conception of science, moreover, is not in any basic conflict with historicist, or hermeneutic, or contextual sensibilities. Rather, these sensibilities are an integral part of that conception.

Another way to make this same point is to note that on the level of basic theoretical assumptions there is much agreement between Pragmatists and Legal Realists on the one hand, and Critical scholars on the other. Neither believes that there can be such a thing as objective, ahistorical knowledge, that is, knowledge that is not the product of the conceptual vocabulary of a certain culture in a certain stage of its history. Neither believes that there are any lasting certainties to be uncovered about human nature, human behavior, or society. And neither believes that the traditional Enlightenment conceptions of objectivity and truth are still tenable. However, where the Pragmatists developed these assumptions into a new conception of science, Critical scholars have developed them into a fundamental critique of science. This goes a long way in explaining why the CLS critique should have so little grip on the Pragmatist and Legal Realist notion of scientific research. The ingredients that make up that critique, by and large, are the same ingredients that went into the Pragmatist reconstruction of the notion of science. In other words, many of the objections that CLS has leveled against the Realist adoption of social science in legal research had long before been incorporated and reworked into the Pragmatist understanding of science that the Realists built on. Legal Realist social science, in a way, was already made resistant to the CLS objections to it.

If the CLS critique of Legal Realist social science falters and Legal Realism, duly understood as a Pragmatic legal theory, persists as a viable approach, then the question remains: What can we still learn from this faded, early twentieth-century movement at the beginning of the twenty-first century? The answer to this question, it will be argued in the remainder of this final chapter, is that Realism can provide us with a view of what legal scholarship can still be in an age in which the foundations of our knowledge seem to be crumbling and philosophical and scientific certainties have become suspect. What Legal Realism shows us is that we can do without a firm ground, that we can do without such tattered foundational concepts as rationality, objectivity, and human nature and still keep faith in the project of understanding and improving law through intelligent inquiry and empirical research.

THE REVIVAL OF PRAGMATISM

To be sure, this appeal to Pragmatism to provide an answer to the problems of Postmodernity is not a very original idea. If anything, Pragmatism was somewhat of an intellectual fad for a brief period. Some years ago Pragmatism underwent a revival not just in law but also in many other academic disciplines. What Legal Realism can still mean today will be sketched in reference to some of the work this Pragmatist revival has produced. Two broad strands of Pragmatism stand out in that revival. David Luban, an outspoken critic of the Pragmatist renaissance in law, has defined these two strands as "philosophical" and "postphilosophical" Pragmatism, a distinction that will be adopted below.

"Philosophical" Pragmatism, according to Luban, "advances recognizably philosophical theses, supported by recognizably philosophical arguments, and fits comfortably within the ambit of academic philosophy." These philosophical theses and arguments stay close to the Pragmatism first developed by Peirce, James, and Dewey. Canonical elements of this philosophical Pragmatism include, among other things, the definition of knowledge in terms of warranted assertability rather than truth, the recognition of the theory-ladenness of observation statements, and the embrace of epistemological holism against foundationalism.[6] These, of course, are the basic assumptions that have been associated with the Realist conception of science in this book. The Legal Realists were squarely within the tradition of old-style Pragmatism. Hence, it is with this philosophical strand of Pragmatism in the current revival that their thought has most affinity.

Postphilosophical Pragmatism, according to Luban, embraces the antiphilosophical idea that "all the standard 'isms'" represent a holdover, or perhaps a hangover, from a worldview that has outlived its usefulness." Postphilosophical Pragmatism, of which Richard Rorty is the most famous expositor, is a view that embraces "Wittgenstein's understanding of philosophical problems as candidates for therapy rather than solution."[7] Where philosophical Pragmatism seeks to frame a solution to the problems of Postmodernity, postphilosophical Pragmatism more or less aligns itself with Postmodernism and provides more ammunition for the claim that any attempts in philosophy, science, or law to achieve a semblance of objective knowledge is vain and misguided. Hence, Rorty has little patience with old Pragmatism's enthusiasm for science. Thus, in a recent essay he claims that the new Pragmatists have "become suspicious of the term 'scientific method'" and wish that people like Dewey "had not insisted on using this term as a catchphrase, since we are unable to provide anything distinctive for it to denote."[8]

In a way, postphilosophical Pragmatism stands to old Pragmatism as CLS stands to Legal Realism: it is highly interested in the cognitive relativism of the older movement but rejects its faith in science. As a result, the present significance of Legal Realist views on the topics discussed in this book—that is, law and history, law and social science, and law and language—will mainly be outlined in relation to the thought of philosophical Pragmatists who share a belief in the canonical, Pragmatic theses that the Realists adopted in their approach.

PRAGMATISM AND HISTORY

In Chapter 2 the Realist view of history was related to the nineteenth-century vogue of evolutionary theory and its spin-off functionalism. Much like the Pragmatists, the Legal Realists thought social institutions like law could be fruitfully interpreted in an evolutionary framework, as the product of a process of functional adaptation to problems thrown up by the ever-changing social environment and informed by the given cultural context. Consequently, history was important for the Realists, even though their posture was mainly forward-looking and reformist. History not only provided understanding of how the law had developed into what it was, but also provided a vantage point for critique, for showing that a legal rule which had once made sense no longer performed a useful function under present social or economic conditions.

This view of the role of history as a useful tool for the pursuits of legal scholars is still alive among contemporary Legal Pragmatists. Historical tours are practical, Thomas Grey argues: "intellectual genealogy is of more than 'merely historical' (antiquarian) interest. Living intellectual movements are not constituted wholly out of the present and its anticipations of the future. They also carry with them the marks of their context of origin."[9] Similarly, the leader of the Law and Economics movement and self-styled Legal Pragmatist, Richard Posner, has recently revived the Realist idea of history as a method to get rid of "survivals" in the law that have outlasted their relevance. "The backward-looking, tradition and precedent-ridden cast of legal thinking . . . is to be regretted," he claims; the "only worthwhile use of history in law is to debunk outmoded doctrines by showing them to be vestigial"[10] (which is not to deny, according to Posner, that old rules and opinions might be valuable repositories of legal wisdom and knowledge). And, again, in a more recent work he argues that "a certain kind of looking backward, a skeptical, debunking looking backward, can liberate us from thralldom to tradition and thus clear the decks for a forward-looking approach."[11]

These uses of history recommend the moderate historicism that the Realists practiced in many of their doctrinal articles rather than the radical historicism of CLS. The conviction that history can show us how a certain idea was shaped by its "context of origin" or how a legal doctrine has become "outmoded" implies that some historical context can be retrieved that can explain how that idea, or outmoded doctrine, took shape. This, in turn, implies that that particular idea or doctrine somehow fit with, or was a function of, a given set of historical circumstances. Differently put, it implies that it was once reasonable, under the circumstances, to believe that idea or develop that doctrine, even though it might no longer be. This is, more or less, all that the moderate historicism of the Legal Realists entails.

Another way to characterize this moderate historicism is with John Dewey's notion of "objective relativism." This idea of objective relativism meant, in the words of Hilary Putnam, that "certain things are right—*objectively right*—in certain circumstances and wrong—*objectively wrong*—in others, and the culture and the environment constitute relevant circumstances."[12] "Objectivity" here should, of course, be understood in its Pragmatic sense, as again in the words of Putnam, "the objectivity of any judgment that is warranted in its actual existential setting."[13] For law this historicism suggests that even though a certain rule or doctrine looks silly or irrational to us now, it might once have been quite reasonable to adopt it, given the historical circumstances, the culture, the cognitive tools, and the best knowledge of the people who conceived of it.

This is still the position taken by Richard Posner. "Indignation about historical injustice," he argues, "often reflects ignorance of history—of the circumstances that explain and sometimes justify practices that in the modern state of society (comfortable, rich, scientifically advanced, push-buttony) would be arbitrary and unjust."[14] For instance, Posner argues, if equal opportunity for women in the workplace is now an undisputed norm in the Western world, it is a fallacy to judge the practices of earlier generations by that standard. In the past, life expectancy was considerably shorter than it is today, and women needed to bear more children to be assured that a reasonable number of them would survive into adulthood. Most jobs, moreover, involved arduous physical labor. Under such circumstances equal distribution of men and women over the different professions might simply not have been an available alternative. Hence, what we regard as sexist arrangements now might in large measure have resulted from the exigencies of life in a society much less technologically developed and secure than our own. To assume that people in the past always could have, and should have, adopted the norms we cherish now, Posner argues, is to assume "an implausible plasticity of social arrangements."[15] This is an inverted version of the historicist argument of the Realists, of course. The typical Realist argument moved from past to present and would have been something like this: Even though inequality in job opportunities between men and women might once have been understandable, it no longer is, because most jobs no longer demand physical strength and improved health care has ended the need for large families.

It is important to note that this approach is very different from the more radical historicism advanced by CLS. Critical scholars' excursions into the past are not meant to show that things that seem unreasonable to us now might once have been quite reasonable to believe. The purpose of their historicism is, rather, to make the point that things people once firmly believed inevitably turned out to be flawed and prejudiced and that, therefore, our present, firmly held beliefs and convictions are also likely to be flawed and prejudiced. As a result, the idea that we possess dependable knowledge about what kind of legal regulation our situation requires is probably an illusion. To repeat the words of Mark Kelman quoted in Chapter 3: "Critical scholars often use a certain style of historicist inquiry to remind us how unlikely it is that things we may take for granted will always be so, because we can so readily see that things once taken for granted have hardly proven indispensable."[16] The aim of CLS historicism, in other words, is not to show there is more reason in past law than might at first glance appear, but that there is less reason in all law, both past and present.

This outlook is closely related to the view that law cannot be explained as a functional adaptation to a given historical context, because it is the concepts and categories of law which determine how that historical context is perceived in the first place. The aim of CLS scholars is to undermine the contention that there is anything necessary about the way the law is, in order to establish that law can be conceived of very differently if we so desired. If law to an important degree is the way it is because the social and economic circumstances demand it, then there would be little point in arguing for the kind of radical reform Critical scholars favor. Hence, they are at pains to demonstrate that the relation between law and its social context is largely fortuitous. Their main argument to establish this is to claim that the metaphors and concepts of which law consists are not a function of the given circumstances, but the given circumstances, as we perceive them, are a function of our contingent metaphors and concepts. First comes the word, and the world is reified in its image. As a result, there is much more scope for reimagining the way law organizes social life than we realize. We have only to appreciate that there is nothing imperative about the manner in which law orders society and realize that law is little more than an incidental set of concepts and metaphors organizing our understanding of social relations to embrace the possibility of radical change.

From a historical point of view this is all quite problematic. As was argued in Chapter 3, CLS historicism makes it very difficult to explain legal change, because it rejects social, economic, and political developments as plausible causes for legal development. This turns legal history into a sequence of detached conceptual paradigms and law into a self-moving ideo-logical structure hovering over the world of human affairs and changing for no identifiable reason. There is a second theoretical reason why this radical historicism of CLS should be rejected, however. If Realist historicism embraced a form of "objective relativism"—that is, the belief that there can be no absolute objectivity transcending historical circumstances, but that there can be an objective right or wrong on certain issues in specific existential settings—then the more radical CLS historicism endorses relativism plain and pure, that is, the idea that objectivity does not even exist relative to a given existential setting and that knowledge and values should primarily be seen as matters of ungrounded preference. If this seems more rigorous, it is also self-defeating. It falls victim to the standard philosophical rebuke against relativism, namely, that if everything is relative, also the claim that everything is relative is relative.

The moderate historicism of the Realists also commends itself for more pedestrian reasons, though. Realist legal history, which perhaps reached its peak in Llewellyn's doctrinal studies of sales law and warranty of quality, described the historical development of law as the product of a complex interplay between such factors as social and economic conditions, public opinion, legal doctrine, and the idiosyncratic character of individual judges. Momentous socioeconomic developments such as the change from an agricultural to an industrial society were often presented as a dominant force shaping law, but Realist history did not revert to a shallow economic determinism. For the Realists, the influence of socioeconomic developments on law was by no means a straightforward matter, and they were keenly aware of the influence of myriad cultural, intellectual, and personal factors on the evolution of law. It is important to remember that the idea of "functional adaptation," which lay at the basis of Pragmatist and Legal Realist notions of history, did not signify passive accommodation to the way things unfolded, but referred to the development of creative responses to changing life circumstances. In the words of Hans Joas, the concept of "adaptation" in Pragmatic thought "never meant routine and loss of subjectivity but practical innovation, *creative* solutions to real problems."[17] Hence, in Legal Realism history was not reduced to a mechanical process in which changes in the socioeconomic substructure automatically registered changes in the legal superstructure. Human intelligence and creativity were crucially involved in the development of law and had to be accounted for in historical explanation.

This Realist approach to historical analysis, at its best, was quite accomplished for a movement containing no historians and shows much affinity with the later work of a real historian: the grandfather of modern American legal history, James Willard Hurst. This affinity is not surprising; Hurst's approach was equally indebted to Pragmatism as Legal Realism and drew heavily on the thought of John Dewey. Pragmatic theory formed the very framework for much of his historical work.[18] Much like the Realists, Hurst sought to understand the development of law not as the result of a purely doctrinal dynamic, but as the result of a complex interaction with the wider society. In his work *The Growth of American Law,* Hurst started his analysis with a short description of his perspective on the historical development of law. American legal history, he claimed, taught "that apart from the toughness of institutional structure, law has been more the creature than the creator of events."[19] Hurst distinguished three main areas of influence: the physical, the technological, and the social setting of law. The physical setting—"not often a prime mover"—in the United States mainly involved the presence of a vast land area and a wealth of natural resources. These set the problems that American law had to deal with and helped shape the direction of law.[20] More important was the technological setting. New inventions and their application—steamboats, railways, factories, automobiles, mass media—created novel problems that law had to respond to. Technology was a force largely independent of law, Hurst claimed; "in almost every case, the scientist or inventor took the initiative, and the lawman came in only as complaints mounted that the new knowledge, or more likely its use, was too costly, might even, in fact, destroy life or security."[21]

Most important of all for the understanding of legal development, however, was the social setting. This social setting, for Hurst, consisted of both beliefs and patterns of habitual behavior:

> The most creative, driving, and powerful pressures upon our law emerged from the social setting. Social environment has two aspects. First, it is what men think: how they size up the universe and their place in it; what things they value and how much; what they believe to be the relations between cause and effect, and the way these ideas affect their notions of how to go about getting the things that they value. Second, it is what men do: their habits, their institutions. Ideas and institutions obviously are inseparable aspects of men's history. We do not have to try to decide which, if either, is the more powerful.[22]

Law was not an autonomous, self-contained body of rules, but moved with "the main currents of American thought." When law protected a certain interest, it was usually backing an activity that people had come to value, or to consider as beneficial to society. If in the nineteenth century people had believed in localism, self-reliance, and getting ahead, the law reflected this attitude. If in the early twentieth century they had become more aware of their interdependence and their "helplessness against impersonal social currents," the law changed to accommodate these sentiments.[23] Hurst put it concisely: "Because society, and law as a tool of society, are made by men, for men, they cannot help having the nature of men in them."[24] In this, Hurst, like the Realists, was not innocent of the notion that what people thought was shaped by what we would now call a paradigm. "Of course," he claimed, "men cannot think themselves beyond all limits of time, place, or habit, in forming their life in society. But we are concerned with what makes change rather than with the inert conditions that fix the frame within which its movements must take place."[25] In the spirit of old-style Pragmatism, Hurst acknowledged the existence of a paradigm but denied it much importance for the purposes of study.

If this understanding seems traditional compared to the Postmodern conception of history current in CLS, it is still quite innovative compared to the type of doctrinal legal history still widely practiced. One wonders whether CLS history, for all its theoretical sophistication, is really much of an improvement on the approach that Hurst and the Realists pioneered. Does a single-minded focus on law as an autonomous ideological structure really deliver better understanding, than a consideration of such profound social developments as the Industrial Revolution, the rise of the welfare state, or the revolution in information and communication technology? Is the difference between, for instance, nineteenth-century and present legal understanding really only about autonomous conceptual change within law, or does it matter that people no longer ride horses but drive cars, that they no longer buy goods from people they know but brands they trust from anonymous retail stores, that they no longer send letters but e-mails, and that they no longer read and discuss Herbert Spencer but Anthony Giddens, or Niall Ferguson, or Amitai Etzioni? Moreover, does it really make sense to claim that law primarily shapes what people think, as CLS would have it? Or does it make more sense to stick to the notion that what people think primarily shapes law, as the Realists and Hurst claimed? Most people are blissfully unaware of the law and its content, whereas most lawyers fully participate in social life. On the face of it, the idea that lawyers are affected by the values, beliefs, and concerns of the wider society would seem far more plausible than the idea that people are conditioned by legal concepts and categories of which they are largely ignorant.

Obviously, the type of legal history championed by the Realists and

James Willard Hurst is more in tune with the Pragmatic temperament than CLS historicism. Pragmatism treats law as an instrument in the service of human purpose. Thus, it tries to locate legal concerns within a wider social context and understand how law contributes, or fails to contribute, to the welfare of society. CLS history, however, seems premised on the assumption that the relationship between law and the supposed social functions it has to perform is largely vacuous. It pays little attention to the social context of law and reverts to pure doctrinal analysis of a critical, deconstructivist bend. Whatever the merits of this type of analysis, it will not provide an answer to the most central concerns of the Pragmatic legal scholar, namely, for what social purpose has a certain legal rule or doctrine been adopted? That is, what policy considerations informed it? How well has it functioned? And does it still serve a purpose? These questions cannot be solved through pure doctrinal analysis, however critical, but can be answered only by studying what a legal rule has brought about in real life. It demands an empirical approach, in other words, which will be the topic of the next section.

PRAGMATISM AND SOCIAL SCIENCE

Hans Joas has argued that a central feature of classical Pragmatism was the realization that only if the naive nineteenth-century belief in mechanistic and teleological scientific progress was given up "can we move forward to understanding the openness of the historical future, the risk- and responsibility-laden nature of present action."[26] Thus, scientific method was not conceived of by the Pragmatists as a routine that would automatically deliver social improvement, but rather as a "tool which, provided that it could be comprehensively institutionalized and applied to the problems of social reform under democratic conditions, would render further progress possible."[27] For the Pragmatists there was no predetermined ideal state of society that science would help uncover. Humans made their own future, and scientific method was there only to help them make it sensibly and deliberately. The point was that the method of science could not be a substitute for human creativity and imagination in dealing with social questions, but could only help to test, improve, and discipline creative intuition. Science was not a self-executing program, but a helpful procedure to be used in creatively shaping a desirable future. Hence, for the Pragmatists science did not efface human intentionality, but greatly improved and extended the potential of human beings to remake their world.

Yet, if the classic Pragmatist philosophers went to great lengths to distance themselves from the view that science would ensure progress toward a fixed ideal, then these efforts have largely been lost on CLS. Critical scholars, as we saw in Chapter 5, do not associate the application of scientific method to frame solutions to social problems as a form of creative action, but as a dissolution of creativity. Social science to them signals determinism and slavery to the principles of rationality and functionality. Creativity is a term Critical scholars tend to reserve for the capacity of human beings to symbolically and conceptually reimagine the world they inhabit, not for what they see as routine applications of scientific method aimed at conforming law to a presumed functional optimum. This misunderstanding of Pragmatism with regard to creativity lies at the heart of CLS hostility to social science in general and its embrace by the Legal Realists in particular. There is no reason, however, to accept this CLS critique of social science as valid. The Pragmatic embrace of social science cannot fairly be interpreted as a move to replace human initiative in social affairs with precepts drawn from scientific research. On the contrary, Pragmatism's enthusiasm for social science should be understood as an admonition for people to take social matters into their own hands, but to do it intelligently and responsibly, that is, with the use of the time-tested procedures of science.

The present-day meaning of this Pragmatic conception of social science can be highlighted with two recent examples from the revival of Pragmatism. The first is a study by Brian Tamanaha who has advocated a Pragmatic sociology of law. His contribution is mainly concerned with Pragmatism as a philosophy that can save social science from Postmodern critique. For this purpose, as we shall see, he could manage with a fairly bare conception of Pragmatism, a conception that steered clear of most substantive concerns. For Tamanaha, Pragmatism mainly needed to provide reassurance that social science would still make sense, even when it could no longer be provided with firm foundations. This narrow understanding, more or less, reduced Pragmatism to a single-issue movement. Consequently, Tamanaha has since moved on from his embrace of Pragmatism. Thus, in one of his latest works he notes that "the popularity of pragmatism was short-lived, for it was not evident what insight, if any, pragmatism offered to law. Pragmatic philosophy was primarily a negative critique of absolutist theories of truth." [28] This rejection should not distract from the fact that he made some apt observations about social science in a Pragmatic framework and that his comments will prove useful for our discussion.

The second example is Richard Posner and his defense of Pragmatism in a Law and Economics framework. Unlike Tamanaha, Posner is a convinced and committed Pragmatist. Moreover, unlike Tamanaha, Posner does not treat Pragmatism merely as an esoteric Philosophical theory that experienced a brief revival. He believes Pragmatism reflects a sensibility that is grounded in American society and expressed in American law. Indeed, Posner argues that Pragmatism in its everyday variety "has long been and remains the untheorized outlook of most Americans, one rooted in the usages and attitudes of a brash, fast-moving, competitive, forward-looking, commercial, materialistic, philistine society, with its emphasis on working hard and getting ahead."[29]

These two scholars, and the currents in legal theory they represent, are polar opposites in terms of jurisprudential politics—the first belonging to the liberal left and the second to the neoconservative right. The discussion that follows is not meant to deny these differences, nor to build a bridge, nor to stake out a middle ground, between them. Rather, the discussion will remain largely indifferent to the political inclinations of the two authors and will aim to be unabashedly parasitic on any and all of their ideas that can help to chart what sort of concerns, assumptions, and considerations Legal Realism can still give rise to today.

The work of both of these scholars can be related to the Realist legacy. Brian Tamanaha, to begin with, explicitly connects his proposals for sociological study of the law with the Pragmatic approach pioneered by the Realists. In his book *Realistic Socio-Legal Theory*, he candidly affirms that he "attempts to carry out the social scientific approach to law promoted by the Legal Realists," albeit with the incorporation of "insights about science which were not fully appreciated at the time they wrote."[30] Richard Posner is not as keen to acknowledge the Realists as his intellectual forebears. His Pragmatic embrace of social science is clearly reminiscent of the Realist project, but Posner—with different degrees of vehemence—has repeatedly denied any affinity with Legal Realism. He has chided the Realists for both their left-wing bias and their intemperate views. Legal Realism displayed a "naive enthusiasm for government," Posner believes, which marked it as a "liberal" movement. This left-wing slant, he claims, has become "part of the legacy of legal realism to today's neo-pragmatism, which is so dominated by persons of liberal or radical persuasion as to make the movement itself seem, not least in their own eyes, a school of left-wing thought."[31]

However, this left-wing bias for the most part covers the extent of Posner's objections to the Legal Realists. When it comes to their embrace of social science, Posner expresses a qualified support. It was mainly lack of method, he believes, that explains the shortcomings of their ventures into social science research:

> The Realists knew what to do—think things not words, trace the actual consequences of legal doctrines, balance competing policies—but not how to do any of those good things. It was not their fault. The tools of economics, statistics, and other pertinent sciences were insufficiently developed to enable a social-engineering approach to be taken to law. What *was* their fault . . . was a penchant for irresponsibility that the critical legal studies movement, which likes to think of itself as descended from legal realism, has inherited.[32]

If we take this remark by Posner as a reluctant admission that there is some common ground between Legal Realism and his own view of law, at least with regard to social science, we can include him in the analysis of what an empirical approach inspired by Legal Realism could still entail today.

Value-Free or Purposive Social Science

One of the things that makes Pragmatism attractive for empirically oriented legal scholars is its epistemology, which seems resistant to the Postmodern critique of science. That certainly holds true for Tamanaha. His sketch of a Pragmatic epistemological framework for sociolegal study is largely in keeping with the argument presented in this book so far. The notion that all perception and understanding is mediated by our contingent and biased conceptual paradigms and, therefore, not true in any absolute sense, from the Pragmatic point of view, does not make much of a difference for the practice of science. We simply cannot perceive the world except from within a perspective, Tamanaha argues. Hence, the practice of science is necessarily informed by the conceptual distinctions arising out of our sociocultural setting. To deny the validity of scientific knowledge on this ground is to be a disappointed absolutist, he claims, "lashing out in disappointment at our inability to rise above the conditions of our existence."[33] Pragmatists, instead, simply accept that absolutes are not attainable and proceed with the concepts, standards, and values that are part of their given existential setting. If these are partial and limited, they still suffice to produce scientific knowledge which is both reliable and valid for the circumstances at hand (and which is the only kind of knowledge situated and finite human beings can hope to generate, anyway). As a result, according to Tamanaha, Pragmatism mainly leaves things as it finds them. By and large, it reassures scientists that even without firm foundations they can keep on doing what they have always done, only now without the illusion that they are uncovering any ultimate truths about the world around them.

This broad support for all manner of empirical research leads Tamanaha to claim that Pragmatism is a substantively thin philosophy. Although Pragmatism is useful in bracing empirical sociolegal research per se, it is markedly less useful for the advancement of any particular substantive theory of law. This is so, according to Tamanaha, because Pragmatism principally involves a methodology of inquiry and a theory of truth and does not itself "say what the good is, how to live, what economic or political system to develop, or anything else of that nature."[34] Other than a rejection of legal formalism and a renunciation of absolutist notions of truth, Pragmatism provides the legal scholar with very few recommendations about what would be desirable in law.

Consequently, Tamanaha argues that recent attempts by legal theorists to derive substantive directions from Pragmatism have all been signal failures. As examples he cites arguments for more attention to "context," emanating from the Pragmatic stress on the social and cultural context; arguments for taking the "middle way," arising from the Pragmatic dislike for dualisms and dichotomies; and arguments for more "traditionalism," deriving from the Pragmatic notion that we can change existing institutions and practices only gradually and not all at once. These substantive arguments based on Pragmatic theory, Tamanaha comments, hardly give us any definite directions. Specifically, they do not tell us what the relevant context is that we should pay more attention to, what the—albeit desirable—middle way is that we should embrace, nor what the pertinent elements are in the legal tradition that we should salvage.[35] Hence, Pragmatism fails to provide anything cogent when it comes to the formulation of substantive theories of law.

As a result, Tamanaha argues that substantive questions are best left out of a realistic sociolegal approach altogether. Pragmatism, to him, suggests a "descriptive, non-normative approach."[36] In plain, commonsense terms, this means, according to Tamanaha, "carefully watching what people do, figuring out why they are doing it, and trying to grasp how it all comes together."[37] A pragmatically inspired approach to legal study would at most provide a testing ground for normative legal theories provided by others, he asserts, but would itself be careful to stay out of the politically contentious world of substantive theory. In other words, a Pragmatic approach means going back to the "scientific basics," to "impartial and disinterested investigation," and giving up "the impotent politics and the debunking anti-law attitude," characteristic, especially, of much CLS scholarship. It means a renewed focus on the "accumulation of knowledge," Tamanaha believes, which is "a valuable project that stands on its own merit."[38]

By and large Tamanaha is right to suggest that Pragmatism does not entail any full-fledged substantive theory. Hence, such ideologically divergent legal scholars as Posner and Tamanaha can both rightfully claim the title "Pragmatist." Yet from the observation that Pragmatism does not "say what the good is," it does not logically follow that Pragmatism understood as a methodology of inquiry must therefore not be interested in the good. Even if Pragmatism itself does not provide a particular view of the good, it can nonetheless demand that social science research be directed at *a* view of the good. And, indeed, that is exactly what Pragmatism does demand. Pragmatism entails what could be called a *commitment to commitment,* a dedication to scientific research that is not aloof, neutral, and descriptive but aimed at the achievement of a substantive end. This makes Tamanaha's insistence that his Pragmatic sociolegal theory should be "a descriptive, non-normative approach" highly problematic.

Fundamental to the Pragmatic conception of social science is the idea that inquiry is furthered by acting on the world, by consciously trying to bring about a socially desired state of affairs. Only by actively trying to achieve a certain result do we learn anything about how it can be achieved. Hence, the Pragmatic stance is not to collect a great deal of information on social phenomena in the hope that this will decide for us what we should want to achieve. (In that case the CLS equation of social science with determinism would be entirely valid.) Rather, the Pragmatic approach is first to decide what we want to achieve and then to learn from the efforts to bring it about. Differently put, Pragmatist epistemology revolves around the idea of social science as a purposive practice, as a practice aimed at making a difference. Dewey, indeed, fiercely rejected the notion that pure description of social phenomena would amount to a social science:

> Observing, collecting, recording and filing tomes of social phenomena without deliberately trying to do something to bring a desired state of society into existence only encourages a conflict of opinion and dogma in their interpretation. If the social situation is itself confused and chaotic because it expresses socially unregulated purpose and haphazard private intent, the facts themselves will be confused, and we shall add only intellectual confusion to practical disorder. When we deliberately employ whatever skill we possess in order to serve the ends which we desire, we shall begin to attain a measure of at least intellectual order and understanding.[39]

This does not mean that Pragmatism suggests that social scientists can embrace any possible grand design of society they like as a basis for social experimentation. Ideals, goals, and desired ends in Pragmatism are understood as imaginative extensions of the values and purposes already inherent in existing social practices.[40] Hence, Pragmatism demands that social science is informed by substantive goals and expects that these substantive goals will be continuous with the values inherent in the social practice in question.

This purposive aspect of the Pragmatic notion of social science is not some optional accessory that can simply be discarded and replaced with something like nonnormative description. The Pragmatic conception of social science as a purposive practice seems intimately connected to its epistemology. Why should social scientists acquiesce in the given, historically contingent conceptual framework of their cultural group, after all, unless they see themselves as sharing in its project and trying to edge it on to a new stage of development? Tamanaha's promotion of descriptive and nonnormative social research, in contrast, seems more in keeping with positivist or critical rationalist notions of social science aimed at making contributions to the body of knowledge that are independent of the biases of time and place. Indeed, there would be little sense in talking about the "accumulation of knowledge," to use Tamanaha's words, if social science knowledge was tied to contingent historical conditions and had only a limited shelf life, as Pragmatism seems to suggest. The positivist and critical rationalist approaches, in turn, presuppose notions of transhistorical and transcultural objectivity that are open to exactly the kind of antifoundationalist critique that led Tamanaha to embrace Pragmatism in the first place.

That Tamanaha does not stress the purposive aspect of the Pragmatist conception of social science is not surprising. It would involve embracing a value theory which he is at pains to avoid. Moreover, the notion of social engineering, which is central to Pragmatic social science, has fallen on hard times. Critics from the right have identified social engineering with the optimistic policies of the welfare state and have criticized it for not providing any successful solutions to the woes of society. Critics from the left have associated social engineering with the administered state, with unhinged and domineering technocrats orchestrating social life. Neither of these associations necessarily follow from Pragmatism, though. Since Pragmatism does not claim to possess the blueprint of the ideal society, it does not say what particular policies should be embraced or discarded. It merely tells us to draw on existing social arrangements and the values inhering in them to frame socially desired ends and to be self-conscious, deliberate, and empirically informed about the way we try to achieve them. Technocratic control, in turn, is at odds with the democratic spirit of Pragmatism. The choice for, and assessment of, government policy was not envisaged to be the prerogative of a small set of policy experts, but was always meant to involve public debate and the democratic decision-making process. Indeed, it animated Dewey's extensive work in the field of education and his stress on instilling a critical, scientific attitude in the popular mind. Not technocracy, but elevated and informed democracy was the object of Pragmatism.

This brings us to a second reason why Tamanaha's claim that Pragmatism is substantively empty is too sweeping. The Pragmatic definition of *truth* as a proposition that scholars will end up agreeing to after a process of free and open debate implies the adherence to a discourse ethics. Brute force could decide scholarly debates, but then the outcome could hardly be accepted by anyone as the best possible knowledge on the subject. Hence, only if the debate satisfies some basic prerequisites—were all the arguments heard, could everybody speak freely, were the standards of evaluation open to challenge, could rival theories be introduced—can the end result be accepted as "true" in the Pragmatic sense. This discourse ethics is broadly democratic and antiauthoritarian and constitutes a rudimentary substantive theory of democratic institutions. Indeed, Dewey himself and also philosophers like Jürgen Habermas and Hilary Putnam have developed a scientific discourse ethics along these lines. At the very least, adherence to a Pragmatic epistemology would seem to presuppose acceptance of such a discourse ethics.

A final problem with Tamanaha's renunciation of substantive issues involves his interpretation of what Pragmatic truth, understood as a consensus among scholars, amounts to. Tamanaha seems very wary of substantive issues because they are contentious and move away from the consensus that scholars should seek to achieve. In contrast to the Realists, whose posture was nearly always argumentative and polemical, Tamanaha's first impulse seems to be to reconcile rival theories, to mediate opposing viewpoints, and to ease disagreements. Yet that the Pragmatic idea of truth depends on an eventual consensus among scholars about which theory functions best does not imply that, as a matter of course, the final consensus should represent and reconcile all antecedent opinion. For a Pragmatist there should be nothing pathological about intellectual disagreement and strife; it is the way ideas are tested and people make up their minds.

This penchant for mediation seems to be more in line with the postphilosophical strand of neo-Pragmatism than the philosophical strand that Ta-manaha identifies with. For postphilosophical Pragmatists, there can be no rational resolution of contentious issues on the basis of evidence, or facts, or argument. Rival theories, to them, primarily signify different vocabular-ies, different ways of talking about the world. Hence, when one theory gains support among scholars, for postphilosophical Pragmatists that does not mean it is being corroborated by the evidence to the satisfaction of more and more people, but that one vocabulary is gaining ascendancy at the cost of another, reflecting a shift in power in favor of the social group that employs the triumphant vocabulary. When the resolution of intel-lectual disagreements is seen in this light, their settlement in favor of one theory, rather than another, no longer seems such an attractive proposition, for it basically means that one social group has become hegemonic and has imposed its vocabulary on others. As a result, from the postphilosophi-cal perspective, mediation between opposing points of view seems to be a fairer way to resolve issues because it respects the perspectives of all.

This preference for mediation, however, makes most sense for those who have lost faith in the ability of scholars to resolve issues through rea-sonable debate and who see accepted scientific knowledge as little more than the end result of academic power plays. Yet the philosophical Pragma-tists that Tamanaha builds on have not given up on the competence of the community of scholars to eventually arrive at the best solution to the scien-tific questions at hand on the basis of open and reasoned discussion. This best solution might result from mediation between different standpoints, but it need not and should not be preferred out of principle. A philosophi-cal Pragmatist might even argue that mediation and compromise can pre-maturely cut the debate short and thereby undermine the process through which scholars determine what is most warranted to believe under the cir-cumstances.

Posner has also provided an outline of the kind of Pragmatism that he would like the legal community to embrace. In this outline many of the epistemological presuppositions of Pragmatism are highlighted. It will, therefore, provide a good starting point for the discussion of Posner's ideas on social science:

> Pragmatism in the sense that I find congenial means looking at problems con-cretely, experimentally, without illusions, with full awareness of the limitations of human reason, with a sense of the "localness" of human knowledge, the difficulty of translations between cultures, the unattainability of "truth," the consequent im-

portance of keeping diverse paths of inquiry open, the dependence of inquiry on culture and social institutions, and above all the insistence that social thought and action be evaluated as instruments to valued human goals rather than as ends in themselves. These dispositions, which are more characteristic of scientists than of lawyers (and in an important sense pragmatism is the ethics of scientific inquiry), have no political valence. They can, I believe, point the way to a clearer understanding of law. Law as currently conceived in the academy and the judiciary has too theocratic a cast. There is too much emphasis on authority, certitude, rhetoric, and tradition, too little on consequences and on social-scientific techniques for measuring consequences. There is too much confidence, too little curiosity, and insufficient regard for the contributions of other disciplines.[41]

Posner's "pragmatist manifesto" shares many of the elements that have been associated with Legal Realism in this book. It openly recognizes the myriad influences of time and place on the construction of knowledge but nevertheless keeps faith with science as the single best method for determining what is most warranted to believe. It proposes an instrumentalist perspective which focuses primarily on the practical consequences of legal rules, rather than on their doctrinal logic and propriety. Yet Posner places different emphases on these familiar Pragmatic elements than does Tamanaha, as we shall see.

In *The Problematics of Moral and Legal Theory*, Posner has tied this interest in Pragmatism and social science to the aim of fostering a process of "professionalization" in law. Posner perceives a universal trend toward professionalization in Western society, a development which was first glimpsed by Weber and consists of "the bringing of more and more activities under the governance of rationality." Posner agrees with Weber that this growth of rational methods has irrevocably led to "the disenchantment of the world," to the loss of mystique attached to traditional professions like law as they become progressively more rational and transparent.[42] Posner believes this is largely a beneficial development. Hence law, which he considers one of the last vestiges of "enchantment" in modern society, should embrace the inevitable trend toward rationalization. Legal scholars should reject what he calls a "mystifying professionalism" and work toward the achievement of a true professionalism. The purpose of the professional mystique of law, the appearance of law as an inscrutable and exalted occupation that requires the mastery of highly esoteric knowledge and refined skills, is mainly to create a monopoly for the legal guild and conceal its shortage of useful and practical knowledge. This professional mystique is of little use to anyone, Posner believes, and the failure to provide counsel based on sound empirical knowledge in the end will only undermine the legal profession. The way out is Pragmatism. Pragmatism, he maintains, can redirect lawyers toward a true professionalism. It can lead toward "a disposition to ground policy judgments on facts and consequences rather than on conceptualisms and generalities."[43]

Thus, Posner takes the Pragmatic counsel that legal rules should be evaluated on the basis of their consequences quite seriously. Although he embraces all of the social sciences to achieve this aspiration, his main interest is in economic analysis of law, in assessing law against the standard of the maximization of wealth, in weighing the costs and benefits of particular legal arrangements. This endeavor would seem to serve a substantive goal, as will be argued below, but Posner prefers to cling to the idea of value-neutral science. Posner seems to agree with Tamanaha that Pragmatism has "no inherent political valence." The "uncritical devotion to the pieties of the Left" by many neo-Pragmatists, he claims, only betrays that they are not "genuine pragmatists," but "dogmatists in pragmatists' clothing."[44] Unlike Tamanaha, however, this does not lead Posner to conclude that social scientific study of the law in the Pragmatic mold should therefore be descriptive. This is probably so because Posner stresses the Pragmatic conception of law as an instrument to valued human goals to a far greater extent than does Tamanaha. If the focus of social science is on how well law serves the welfare of society, it would be inconsistent to argue for a strictly descriptive social science. For an instrumentalist the point of social science is not to describe law, but to evaluate it, to analyze how law contributes to the achievement of desired goals.

For Posner, this does not mean that empirically oriented legal scholars should themselves choose the substantive ends their research is directed at. The resort to social science to determine which legal option is most conducive to social welfare, Posner argues, works best when there is a degree of consensus on what would be a desirable state of affairs for society. Social scientists, he argues, "can criticize moral codes by showing lack of functionality, of instrumental efficiency or rationality," but such types of criticism are more properly styled "value clarification" than "value argument."[45] Social scientists, in other words, can show that certain ends are ill conceived because they do not fit existing social and economic circumstances very well or do not have a realistic chance of succeeding. Yet they cannot tell society which ends it should prefer:

> The point is that the expert, the scholar, does not choose the goal, but is confined to studying the paths to the goal and so avoids moral issues. If, as is sometimes the case, the goals of society are contested—some people want prosperity

while others would sacrifice prosperity to equality—then all the expert can do is show how particular policies advance or retard each goal. He cannot arbitrate between the goals unless they are intermediate goals—way stations to a goal that commands a consensus.[46]

Hence, social science can provide law with clear guidance only when there is political agreement on where society wants to go. When such agreement is lacking, social science is of only limited use. Since interminable political and moral disagreement is now, and will most likely remain, a characteristic feature of law, this enduring political and moral controversy within the legal community will continue to put limits on the use of social science.[47]

In order to elucidate the kind of values implicit in legal practice, Posner does not argue for the expansion of moral and political philosophy in law. Moral and political philosophy are incapable of resolving contentious issues. Hence, he strongly opposes their use in law. Although he admits that there is development in the moral and political beliefs of society, which subsequently have an influence on law, he rejects the notion that these developments have any connection to the thought of what he calls "academic moralists." Changes in the moral code of society can emanate from the development of new scientific insights that contradict factual assertions implicit in the old moral code; they can emerge from changes in the material conditions of society that enable changes in the existing social order to occur; or they can originate from the influence of a "charismatic moral leader" who, "perceiving a mismatch between existing morality and a changing society, uses nonrational methods of persuasion to alter moral feeling."[48] Academic moralists are not such charismatic leaders, however, but professional scholars who mainly write for their own set: like-minded academic moralists.

This forceful rejection of moral and political philosophy seems more in keeping with the attitude of the positivist social scientists of yesteryear, however, than with the Pragmatic temperament.[49] Criticism such as this was once quite common among social scientists and was based on the confident belief that social science could uncover the objective "Is" about social behavior, while substantive theories of justice, morality, and politics could never pass beyond the level of personal preferences, however nicely dressed up in academic language and presented as objective "Ought." Yet claims of objectivity have been scaled down considerably in the social sciences since then, and values have emerged as a legitimate consideration in the study of social practices. Indeed, the revival of Pragmatism is one of the manifestations of this trend and suggests that moral and political values should be considered as part of the cultural and intellectual framework within which empirical research proceeds. That Posner should repeat such a quaint rebuke is therefore fairly odd and contradicts his own renunciation of positivist notions of truth and objectivity and his recognition of "the dependence of inquiry on culture and social institutions."

This is even more so because Posner's own approach is so clearly geared toward a substantive vision. In his work Posner leaves little doubt about his preference for a conservative, neoliberal, free-market order. This is not meant as criticism. There might be something wrong with the content of Posner's substantive view, but from a Pragmatic perspective there is nothing wrong with his commitment to *a* vision. It lends coherence and purpose to his Law and Economics approach. There is a *point* to Posner's varied research projects (something which is sorely lacking in Tamanaha's approach). In this, Posner resembles the Realists, who also had a substantive view of the direction in which law should be moving, although one diametrically opposed to Posner's—that is, toward the development of the very administrative welfare state that Posner seeks to scale down. Cardozo's famous maxim for adjudication, that "there can be no wisdom in the choice of a path unless we know where it will lead," seems to be heeded by the Realists and Posner not just in law but also in their own research projects.

In this, both differ markedly from CLS. CLS has chosen the path of fundamental, all-out critique of the liberal-legalist system, but with the exception of Roberto Unger, it seems largely uninterested in where that path should lead. And even in the case of Unger, one could argue that there is an element of prevarication. His visions are remarkably open-ended and forever preoccupied with the creation of institutional conditions that are not oppressive, with "the freeing of individuals from the grip of . . . background structures," and with the provision of space to transform and remake themselves into . . . whatever.[50] It would be far too oppressive to define what people should strive for any more precisely than that. Defining roles is what such oppressive ideologies as liberal legalism and technocratic rationalism do. CLS adherents do not believe in working within those frameworks and refuse to be co-opted into the system by trying to get laws passed and policies adopted that would bring us closer to the world they desire. Instead they spend their energies in exposing these very practices as forms of oppressive discursive politics. With this mode of critique CLS seems to foreclose even the possibility of proposing any constructive program of its own. In this respect the criticism that Rorty has recently leveled against the academic "cultural Left" is pertinent to CLS. To such neoliberal theories as Posner's touting the free market, Rorty argues, the cultural Left "has little to say in reply." For, like the cultural Left generally, CLS "prefers not to talk about money." Its principal worry "is a mindset rather than a set of economic arrangements."[51] Posner is happy to agree with Rorty on this count. A CLS adherent like Duncan Kennedy, who openly acknowledges that his mode of aggressive "viral" critique undermines even his own leftist program, to Posner seems to embrace "a formula for political quietism," which, he adds sardonically, is fine by him.[52]

Behaviorism Versus Interpretivism

The type of social science that Tamanaha seeks to apply in the study of law is a synthesis of behaviorism and interpretivism. As was discussed in Chapter 3, social science has been deeply divided in the second half of the twentieth century over these two basic methods—the first arguing for a social science on the model of the natural sciences, which mainly focuses on quantitative patterns in the observable behavior of people, and the second touting an interpretive stance, which primarily focuses on meaning, on what people think and on how their concepts and metaphors inform their social practices. This split between behaviorism and interpretivism largely postdated the Realist movement. The Realists, as we saw, were not troubled by the supposed incompatibility of these two perspectives and often fused them without hesitation.

This is clearly something Tamanaha wants to go back to. He regrets the highly politicized opposition between behaviorism and interpretivism, because neither approach does a very good job at explaining human behavior standing alone. Both approaches contain serious blind spots. Behaviorism in its single-minded focus on causal relationships between observable behavior patterns presents a valuable, grand-scale overview of what people do, independent of what they say they are doing (which, after all, could be nothing more than self-interested or self-serving rationalization). Yet to achieve this detached panoramic view, behaviorism is dependent on measurable categorizations of behavior that severely deform the complexity of social life and present a reductionist picture of what in the end are richly textured and meaningful social actions. Interpretivism, in turn, does do justice to the complex self-understanding of social actors, but it has trouble accounting for the influence of material power and self-interest in what people do and say they do. Furthermore, interpretive studies are notoriously subjective and necessarily microscopic in scope, which makes it difficult to translate their significance to the macro level.[53] Tamanaha suggests, therefore, that we bury the antagonism between behaviorism and interpretivism: "Since behavior and meaning are inseparable aspects of human interaction, it would seem obvious that social science must pay attention to both."[54] While interpretivism is a necessary correction to behaviorism, Tamanaha argues, it is also dependent on that approach: "Interpretivism is actually parasitic upon behaviorism, for it is only through observing behaviour that meaning can be discerned, as the pragmatists recognized. And disputes over meaning (over the proper interpretation) can only be settled through continued observations about behaviour, over longer periods of time or broader in scope, or through comparing behavior in different contexts."[55]

To facilitate the proposed reintegration of interpretivism and behaviorism, Tamanaha suggests the use of a "symbolic interactionist" framework for the understanding of law. This suggestion draws on the work of Herbert Mead, a social theorist within the Pragmatic tradition. Symbolic interactionism can provide a bridge between empirical sociolegal scholarship, on the one hand, and the work of lawyers and doctrinal legal theorists, on the other. Interactionism straddles the divide between those who take an external view of law—social scientists studying law as a social institution—and those who take an internal or participant view of law—legal scholars and theorists who see themselves as developing and refining law as a coherent system of rules. Since symbolic interactionism embraces the notion that law is "what the legal actors say law is, as determined by their shared meaning system," sociological study of law within an interactionist framework becomes continuous with the self-understanding of legal actors and its development in doctrinal legal scholarship.[56]

On the whole, this integrated approach defended by Tamanaha fits with the kind of legal scholarship that Legal Realism could still suggest today. Tamanaha's appreciation of the need to focus on both meaning and behavior in the study of social behavior is a continuation of what seems most worthwhile in the Realist legacy. Yet it would have made more sense within the framework of a purposive social science approach aimed at engaging with what legal actors say they are up to than it does in the descriptive approach that Tamanaha wants us to adopt.

The differences in Posner's Pragmatic outlook, in turn, also lead to differences in his social scientific approach. Posner's heavy stress on consequences implies a social scientific program that is more interested in policy evaluation, in measuring the success with which legal arrangements bring about their declared objectives, in comparing the effects of alternative legal solutions and weighing their respective social costs and benefits. This focus on consequences principally suggests the use of economics, but Posner claims that there is also an important role to play for the other social sciences with respect to the evaluation of the social effects of law. Thus, he claims that he assigns "large roles, in a mature legal professionalism having a social science orientation, to other disciplines, including sociology—a traditional rival of economics."[57] Even though sociology has become marginalized in the legal academy as a result of its "association with discredited ideas"—such as the abandoned notion that crime is largely the result of social deprivation—Posner believes it would be a big mistake to write it off, because "sociologists of law have made incontestably valuable and important contributions."[58] Neither does he want to restrict social science to only hard quantitative analysis. Soft qualitative research—case studies and the like—is equally worthwhile.[59] Taken as a whole, what appeals to Posner in the sociology of law "is its empirical cast and its refusal to take for granted that legal doctrines track legal practices," which comprises a perspective that is "sorely lacking both in conventional legal analysis and in highfalutin constitutional and jurisprudential theorizing."[60]

This last remark—that sociologists refuse to take for granted that legal doctrine tracks legal practice—points to an important difference between Posner's and Tamanaha's approach. Posner is markedly less interested in interpretivism, in understanding law as a meaningful social practice. Where Tamanaha believes the self-understanding of legal actors and the way it gives shape to law as a social institution should always be the point of departure for social science research and should always be given charitable treatment, Posner seems to believe it is one of the major advantages of social science that it does not have to do any such thing, that in social science research the reasons that legal actors provide for what they are doing can be met with open skepticism and be subjected to critical scrutiny. Indeed, prominent among the attributes of sociology that Posner lists as valuable contributions is its "skepticism about the knowledge claims of professions and intellectual disciplines" and "the penetrating analyses of professional behavior that this skepticism has encouraged."[61] This is the type of sociology which his critique of the "professional mystique" of law builds on, of course, and which takes the decidedly uncharitable view of the self-understanding of legal actors as self-interested and self-serving. That Posner should diverge from Tamanaha on this issue is not surprising. His background is in Law and Economics, after all, which seeks to account for legal behavior through an explanatory model largely foreign to law. In other words, Posner tries to gain insight into law by explaining what lawyers do not in terms of their own legal vocabulary, but in terms of the conceptual vocabulary of economics—which is a vocabulary that rests heavily on the companion notions of self-interest and rational choice to boot. Hence, for Posner to privilege the vocabulary that legal actors themselves use as the most appropriate one for understanding law would be to undermine the validity of his own economic approach.

Even though Posner's work clearly exudes a respect for formalistic reasoning and a respect for precedent, he does not make a principled choice for legal discourse as the most proper vocabulary to understand law. Naturally the vocabulary of economics is very important for him in explaining legal behavior. This is not necessarily at odds with Pragmatism. Rorty has argued that from a Pragmatic standpoint there is no reason to accord epistemic privilege to the vocabulary with which social actors explain their own actions. Hermeneutical social scientists who do accord such privilege harbor "the mistaken assumption that somebody's *own* vocabulary is always the best vocabulary for understanding what he is doing, that his own explanation of what's going on is the one we want." This, according to Rorty, is "a special case of the confused notion that science tries to learn the vocabulary which the universe uses to explain itself to itself." If that is the case, he argues, "we are thinking of our explanandum as if it were our epistemic equal or superior." Yet this is not always prudent, since there obviously are "cases in which the person's, or culture's, explanation of what it's up to is so primitive, or so nutty, that we brush it aside." Hence, in Rorty's view, "the only general hermeneutical rule is that it's always wise to ask what the subject *thinks* it's up to before formulating our own hypotheses," because the subject might come up with a satisfactory vocabulary for explaining its own behavior. But this is no more than "an effort at saving time, not a search for the 'true meaning' of the behavior."[62] Posner's use of an observation language provides him with a tool to circumvent one of the problems with hermeneutical or interpretive analysis, namely, that it is committed to taking people's explanations of their own actions at face value. For a pure hermeneutical approach, there is little recourse to other modes of explanation that can be used to question, or critically appraise, what people say they are doing. For Posner, economics and the sociology of knowledge can provide such alternative modes of explanation.

PRAGMATISM AND LANGUAGE

Intellectual historian John Diggins argues that while Dewey considered language to be a benign and socially integrative tool, Postmodern, or Poststructuralist philosophy presents it as a treacherous, divisive, and oppressive medium: "Where Dewey saw in language the power of social cohesion, the poststructuralist sees in it the pleasures of linguistic disruption. To Foucault, language confines, restricts, excludes, incarcerates; to Derrida, it reverses meanings, contradicts syntax, betrays purposes; to Dewey, it stabilizes meanings and synthesizes ends and methods."[63] This basic difference in outlook with regard to language is repeated in Legal Realism and CLS, which build on these respective philosophies. The Realists were skeptical of the power of words. They were concerned that words misled people and hardened thought around its accepted conceptions. Yet the Realists never doubted the advantages of language as a tool for social cooperation and advancement. For CLS, however, language is no longer an instrument for concerted effort but a battleground in which the power struggles of society are fought. It is through language that hegemonic groups within society can impose their understanding of the world on minority groups and exert influence on how problems and disputes are resolved. Hence, language is tainted by the power relations in society and is deeply political. It is not an innocent tool that can be used unconditionally by lawyers and scholars, but a biased medium that prejudges the outcome of both scholarly research and legal disputes. As a result, CLS theory is focused on language and discourse to a far greater extent than is Legal Realism. It has become every bit as linguicentric as contemporary philosophy and has centered on legal discourse as the single most important variable in questions of law. CLS adherents have argued that the Legal Realists have not grasped the far-ranging consequences of their word-skepticism and have stuck to an untenable and naive trust in empirical research to resolve conceptual issues.

Yet Chapter 6 demonstrated that, except for their referential linguistics, the Legal Realist view of language is by no means incoherent or indefensible. Rather, serious questions arise about CLS adherents' various radicalizations of Realist word-skepticism and anticonceptualism. In these radicalizations three assumptions seem to play a key role: (1) the idea that language games, or paradigms, or discourses are self-executing programs that lead language users to arrive at certain given conclusions; (2) the idea that language games are fundamentally incommensurable; and (3) the idea

that interpretation is a ubiquitous and all-encompassing activity. These assumptions are by no means confined to CLS but are current in many types
of contemporary scholarship. Consequently, several of the neo-Pragmatist
philosophers and theorists have formulated arguments against them. A discussion of these responses will highlight the topicality and continued relevance of a Pragmatic theory of language.

Paradigms

The idea that language games, or paradigms, or discourses are self-executing programs, to begin with, is central to the CLS idea that a hegemonic discourse like "liberal legalism" can predetermine the outcome of legal
disputes. Paradigms in CLS scholarship seem to be understood as fixed
grooves that lead the mind along the same route to the same predictable
conclusions. Thus, what is crucially at stake in law for CLS is the choice
for one conceptual vocabulary rather than another, for these conceptual
vocabularies determine what makes legal sense and what does not, and
thus, ultimately, what the outcome of a legal dispute will be. If a discourse
left room for a wide range of disagreement, the CLS argument would lose
much of its force. If lawyers caught up in the liberal legalist paradigm, for
instance, could still develop a wide range of opinion with the use of exactly
the same set of liberal concepts and criteria, the conceptual paradigm could
no longer be considered to predetermine legal outcomes.

Philosophical Pragmatists tend to reject the idea that discourses should
be understood as such fixed routines or programs. Thus, Hilary Putnam
has argued that the idea of language games as "automatic performances"
is "a caricature of our lives with our language," because "people speaking
what is in every sense *one* language, not adopting a 'new vocabulary' or
anything like that, very, very often are unable to come into agreement using
the 'criteria' they know."[64] That this assertion is warranted is borne out by
the plurality of views that can be observed all around us in almost any cultural or ideological group. Pragmatism itself is a case in point. Even though
Pragmatists are committed to a certain philosophical framework and work
from certain shared concepts—"consequences," "action," "warranted assertability," "experience"—they have nonetheless managed to develop a bewil-
dering array of views on the basis of these concepts. Pragmatism has been
wedded to both welfare-state and free-market liberalism, to conservatism,
to Marxism, and even to fascism. These different applications of Pragmatic
thought are not all equally defensible, of course, but the central Pragmatic

concepts by themselves cannot tell us what the relative worth of these views is. What can decide between these competing versions of Pragmatism is reasoned argument and empirical investigation, which is precisely the point that Putnam wants to make. Language games, or conceptual vocabularies, or discourses do not do our thinking for us, but provide us with a tool kit, a set of concepts and criteria to reason and examine with. What we subsequently do with that conceptual tool kit—that is, the theories and proposals we construct with it—is entirely subject to the discipline of human intelligence and the censure of empirical reality.

That is not to say that the choice for a particular conceptual framework cannot load the dice in favor of one substantive view rather than another. Obviously, if only the concepts of free-market economics were available, it would be far more difficult to develop the idea of a centrally planned economy, and if only the theological concepts of Roman Catholicism were available, it would be far more difficult to develop a secular understanding of the human condition. The basic concepts we use do matter. Hence, Realist skepticism of accepted legal categories and concepts was an entirely sensible strategy. Yet to reduce people's opinions and beliefs largely to the reigning discourse is to fall victim to a form of linguistic idealism. Language users are not automata that simply plug in the program of their conceptual paradigm to arrive at foregone conclusions. Language users can, and do, use their concepts reflexively and creatively to arrive at unpredictable results. Our understanding of the world would remain static if this was not possible. Nor could diversions from mainstream understanding like CLS be explained if our shared conceptions would leave no room for maneuver.

Dewey was not innocent of the insight that our understanding was shaped by the concepts we used. "[E]xperience is already overlaid and saturated with the products of reflection of past generations and by-gone ages," he claimed. "It is filled with interpretations, classifications, due to sophisticated thought, which have become incorporated into what seems to be fresh, naive empirical material." Yet Dewey did not believe that there was no escaping the influence of the concepts and categories we inherit when we adopt the going understanding of our cultural group. Pragmatism, indeed, was all about holding parts of this inherited conceptual apparatus up to scrutiny:

> An empirical philosophy is in any case a kind of intellectual disrobing. We cannot permanently divest ourselves of the intellectual habits we take on and wear when we assimilate the culture of our own time and place. But intelligent furthering of culture demands that we take some of them off, that we inspect them

critically to see what they are made of and what wearing them does to us. We cannot achieve recovery of primitive naïveté. But there is possible a cultivated naïveté of eye, ear and thought, one that can be acquired only through the discipline of severe thought.[65]

For Dewey, language did not circumscribe the limits of our world quite as definitively as it seems to do for CLS. People could be self-conscious about the concepts and categories current in their group and withstand the understandings implicit in them. A fresh, naive understanding of social phenomena independent of the distinctions implicit in the concepts we inherited was possible.

Hence, although a conceptual vocabulary can certainly be thought of as pushing understanding in a certain direction and favoring certain conclusions over others, it would be a mistake to think that language users have no influence over where they are pushed and that they cannot confront their concepts with the consequences that follow from them or with the way they experience the world around them. If like CLS adherents we understand legal discourse as a kind of Orwellian Newspeak, it is good to remember that in *1984* not even Newspeak could quell the critical imagination of protagonist Winston Smith and make him accept the ideology of Ingsoc; only physical torture could achieve that. Llewellyn's remark about the adequacy of the conceptual tools of law captures this looser understanding of the relation between language users and their conceptual vocabulary quite well. "*Unless* the *stock* intellectual equipment is apt," he claimed, "it takes extra art or intuition to get proper results with it. Whereas *if* the stock intellectual equipment is apt, it takes extra ineptitude to get sad results with it."[66] That a screwdriver is a tool specifically designed for tightening screws does not mean it cannot be used to drive in nails. It just takes extra time, effort, and resourcefulness to hammer in a nail with a screwdriver. Similarly, that a concept fits with a certain view of the world does not mean that in light of experience it can never be applied to develop an alternative understanding. It just takes more time and effort.

Incommensurability

A second assumption about language that is central to the CLS radicalization of Legal Realism is the idea that language games, or conceptual paradigms, are incommensurable. This Kuhnian notion is quite familiar in present-day scholarship and boils down to something like this: we always understand the world from within a paradigm; that is, we make sense of things with the concepts, standards, and criteria current in our social group. Thus, evaluating an alternative paradigm belonging to a different social group unavoidably involves the application of our partial standards to a paradigm informed by quite different standards. There is no Archimedean point, no neutral position outside of any paradigm, from which the relative value of these different paradigms can be evaluated. Consequently, we can never say that one way of understanding the world is more accurate, more valuable, or more rational than another. Different ways of talking about the world should, instead, be thought of as fundamentally incomparable. The aim of this argument within CLS theory is mainly to cast doubt on the pretense of mainstream legal thought that it already orders society in a most rational and reasonable fashion and that it cannot be greatly improved upon by alternative views. This confident belief that present legal understanding conforms to objective standards of rationality and reasonableness, according to CLS, is in fact completely indefensible; it is nothing more than a rhetorical strategy to privilege the reigning legal paradigm over possible alternatives.

This incommensurability argument also seems inimical to Pragmatist notions of language. As we saw in Chapter 6, the Realists believed that concepts could outlive their relevance and that the conceptual machinery of law needed to be constantly kept up to date with changing conditions. This implies that certain conceptual vocabularies are to be preferred over others and that judgments can be made about their relative value. Although CLS adherents have been skeptical of this Realist view, it is not necessarily in conflict with Kuhn's notion of incommensurability. To be sure, for Kuhn it is impossible to judge whether one paradigm is better than another, in the sense of more true to reality than another. Yet he does not doubt that certain paradigms can be considered better for Pragmatic reasons, that is, relative to a particular human concern or interest. Hence, whether astrology or astronomy gives a truer account of the nature of the universe from a Kuhnian perspective is an unresolvable question. Yet whether astronomy will provide a better paradigm than astrology for planning a manned expedition to Mars is not. Past experience with astronomy has shown that, as far as space travel is concerned, it is a paradigm much to be preferred to astrology. Hence, at least for the purpose of shooting rockets to Mars, astronomy can safely be considered a better conceptual paradigm than astrology.

These two senses in which concepts and conceptual vocabularies can be understood to relate to reality are both present in the Pragmatic theory of language. The referential linguistics discussed in Chapter 6, which sought to define meaning in terms of the real objects words referred to, builds on the notion of meaning as true representation of reality, whereas what was termed functional linguistics in Chapter 6, the approach which related meaning to the functions concepts performed in a given context of use, builds on the idea of meaning as true in relation to a certain human concern or interest. In his description of the Pragmatic theory of language, Nicholas Rescher refers to roughly these same two elements as "*semantics*" and "*pragmatics.*" *Pragmatics*, he contends, is concerned with "functional issues of usage and effective communicative procedure," while *semantics* deals with "informative issues of linguistic meaning and truth."[67] One of Rescher's examples might further clarify these terms. *Pragmatics* is involved in the conventions of everyday language use. If you see a box of apples at the grocery store with the label "Fresh Apples" and then conclude that these objects are indeed apples, you do not conclude this because you have watertight proof that they really are apples and not wax replicas but because you know that in the context of grocery shopping—with everything this involves from common trade practices to advertising regulations—it is warranted to believe that objects labeled "apples" at the grocery store are in fact the edible fruit commonly referred to as apples. *Semantics*, on the other hand, is not concerned with the conditions that make the statement "these are apples" *warrantedly assertable*, but with the conditions that make that statement *true*. This involves a great deal more than just the standards and criteria of conventional language use in an established social practice. To prove that the statement "these are apples" is true, you have to confirm the presence of a potentially infinite list of properties that apples have to possess to be branded authentic apples: do they have apple cores and not just sand in the middle, did they grow on apple trees or were they synthesized in a replicator, are they not simply deformed pears of some sort, do they have apple DNA, the right shape and flavor?[68] Although these truth conditions play a part in the Pragmatic theory of language, according to Rescher, it is mainly *pragmatics,* or use conditions, that the Pragmatic notion of language is focused on.[69] Pragmatism, in other words, is mainly interested in understanding meaning in reference to a social context informed by certain human concerns and needs, like purchasing apples for nutrition.

With regard to the incommensurability thesis, this means that from a Pragmatic perspective some language games, or paradigms, or discourses, can still be regarded as better than others, because they have proved to do a better job at fulfilling the human concerns that they are applied in the service of. According to Rescher, this move is made not so much on utilitarian grounds, but "because the matter of truth as such often retreats into the background." Truth conditions are simply impossible to meet and would lead to a breakdown of communication. So, as a matter of "communicative policy," we rely on use conditions instead, "a pragmatic resort validated by a track record of effectiveness in the service of our practical objectives."[70]

Putnam has even argued that the very notion of describing things "as they really are" is confused, for roughly the same reasons that led Rorty to reject hermeneutics as the one true mode for understanding social behavior in the earlier discussion of social science:

> Kant was himself subject to a confusion. The confusion was to suppose that a description which is shaped by our conceptual choices is somehow, for that very reason, not a description of its object "as it really is." As soon as we make *that* mistake, we open the door to the question, "Well, if our descriptions are only *our* descriptions, descriptions shaped by our interests and nature, then what is the description of the things as they are *in themselves*?" But this "in themselves" is quite empty—to ask how things are "in themselves" is, in effect, to ask how the world is to be described in the world's own language, and there is no such thing as the world's own language, there are only the languages that we language users invent for our various purposes.[71]

Hence, the one sense in which Kuhn thought paradigms could still be considered better or worse, namely, in reference to a particular human purpose, is also the sense in which Pragmatism understands the notion of meaning. And the sense in which Kuhn believed paradigms could not be considered better or worse, namely, as true accounts of reality, is the sense that Pragmatists have downplayed, or even discarded as confused, in their discussions of language.

Interpretation

The final notion that is common to the CLS extension of the Realist ideas on language is the notion that interpretation is ubiquitous and necessary for any instance of language use. For CLS it is not the utterance, the text, or the legal rule that determines meaning, but the community of listeners, readers, or lawyers that decide what meaning should be attached to a statement. Since the language of law is fundamentally open-ended, this means that in principle a great many interpretations could be given to what a legal rule requires. Hence, that a legal rule is applied in a relatively uniform fashion in everyday practice means that the interpretive community of lawyers has chosen to attach only a certain meaning to that legal rule and to discard other possible interpretations. In other words, a decision has been made that a rule should be understood as A and not as B or C, even though A, B, and C are all possible and plausible interpretations of the rule. Since the way a legal rule is understood and interpreted will have an effect, sometimes even a profound effect, on how society is ordered and on how legal disputes get settled, this determination of meaning, this decision to privilege interpretation A over B and C, is a political act.

What is problematic in this understanding, from a Pragmatic point of view, is the failure to see that language use does not necessarily involve interpretation, but can also be understood as mastery of a technique, or as a type of know-how. The Wittgensteinian idea that language is part of a "form of life" is also present in the Pragmatic conception of language. For the Pragmatists, language was a social creation. "Habits of speech," Dewey claimed, "including syntax and vocabulary, and modes of interpretation have been formed in the face of inclusive and defining situations of context." Because language was intimately interwoven with the practices of social life, people tended not to notice their importance, Dewey contended: "We are not explicitly aware of the role of context just because our every utterance is so saturated with it that it forms the significance of what we say and hear."[72] Language, in other words, did not somehow miraculously appear on the social scene from an outside source to be subsequently given meaning by its users, but grew up with the social conventions it described and facilitated and was, therefore, thoroughly implicated and involved in the way people structured their lives. Hence, to learn a language, especially one's native tongue, is not an interpretive process aimed at finding out what the symbols and sounds of that language mean, but an initiation into a way of life and a grasping of its point. For lawyers this initiation consists of their professional training and apprenticeship, a process in which they are acquainted with legal materials and problems, with the way those materials and problems are handled in legal practice, with the implicit standards and values current in that practice and with the way lawyers think and behave. This tacit knowledge of the going practice of law makes it possible for the trainee to naturally understand what meaning a rule or concept should have in the legal context. This is not an interpretation in the sense of deciding between different readings of the rule, but rather an understanding of the legal "form of life" and the way the rule fits into it. "To be a judge," Stanley Fish has said, "is not to be able to consult the rules (or, alternatively, to be able to disregard them) but to have become an extension of the know-how that gives the rules (if there happen to be any) the meaning they will immediately and obviously have."[73]

This makes interpretation both a notion that does not fully capture what lawyers do when they apply rules and a notion that suggests a much greater degree of plasticity than an understanding of the interdependency of language and social practice would warrant. If language games are part of a form of life, then understanding language can no longer be presented as a preference for a certain interpretation in a range of possible interpretations. Understanding language then becomes indistinguishable from understanding the social practice that gave rise to the discourse and all the standards, conventions, and values implicit in that practice. Moreover, the CLS notion of interpretation creates the impression that by awarding a different meaning to a word, by choosing to interpret it differently, understanding and practices would somehow change accordingly. Yet if one ties language to a form of life, accepted meaning would seem to be more tenacious than that. Different interpretations of a concept or a rule can be thought up easily enough, of course, but a way of life is not a suit that you can simply take off and replace with another. We can certainly hold some parts of our garment up for scrutiny, as Dewey suggested, but even that is not easy.

CONCLUSION

Pragmatism, we saw in this last chapter, still possesses a remarkable vitality, and there has been a great deal of interest in the movement in recent years. The CLS project on the other hand is in a process of disintegration. With their total critique CLS theorists have maneuvered themselves into a cul-de-sac. The only real conclusion that seems to follow from CLS is resigned condemnation of the world. This resigned condemnation has been reiterated in many shapes and forms ever since the movement got started, but it is simply too unsatisfactory a purpose to keep an intellectual movement going. Moreover, for a movement that wants to set our imaginations free and that wants to open up the law for new ways of understanding, CLS has become rather formulaic and repetitive. All this is tragic. Yet it would be even more tragic if Realism were to be tarred with the same brush, if its involuntary association with CLS were to cause it to suffer the same fate. The Legal Realists did not ask to be enlisted into the CLS project. We should not simply take the CLS scholars' word for it that the Realists belong in their ranks, that they are the avant-garde of the CLS movement.

The Realists had a project of their own. This project may seem to run parallel to the CLS venture from the vantage point of the Critical scholar. This study, however, suggests that the Realist movement has struck out on a very different course. It is a course toward intelligent reform within a broadly democratic framework and it is a course still worth pursuing.

Reference Matter

Notes

CHAPTER ONE

1. Gunn 1994, p. 39.
2. Joas 1993, p. 2.
3. C. K. Allen, cited in Twining 1973, p. 69.
4. Duxbury 1995, p. 65.
5. White 1973, p. 67.
6. Hofstadter 1955, p. 196.
7. Hofstadter 1955, p. 198.
8. For an interesting contemporary account of Legal Realism as a movement framed against the cultural background of literary Realism, see Hopkins 1983, pp. 29–60.
9. Langdell 1871, p. viii.
10. Langdell 1888, p. 123.
11. See Gilmore 1977, p. 70; Duxbury 1995, p. 6.
12. White 1997, p. 16.
13. H. L. A. Hart attacked predictivism in his essay "Definition and Theory in Jurisprudence" (1953). Rights should not be treated as a description, or prediction, of real behavior, he argued, but as a move in a language game. See Hart 1983, pp. 31–35.
14. Leiter 2001, pp. 288–90.
15. Pound 1910, p. 36.
16. Pound 1909, p. 464.
17. Llewellyn 1930, n. 3, p. 435.
18. Hutchinson 1989, p. 3.
19. See Horwitz 1992, pp. 270–71; Hutchinson 1989, pp. 2–7; Livingston 1982, pp. 1669–90; Schlegel 1979, pp. 459–63; Tushnet 1980, pp. 20–32; and Tushnet 1981, pp. 1205–37.
20. Tushnet 1991, p. 1524.
21. Tushnet 1991, p. 1524.

22. Tushnet 1991, p. 1525.
23. Tushnet 1991, pp. 1527–28.
24. Gordon 1983, pp. 286–87.
25. Gordon 1983, p. 287.
26. Gordon 1983, p. 289.
27. Gordon 1983, p. 289.
28. Dewey (1910) 1997, p. 15.
29. Joas 1993, p. 1.
30. Kelman 1987, p. 213.
31. Kelman 1987, p. 214.
32. Gordon 1984, p. 70.
33. Gordon 1984, p. 103.
34. Gordon 1984, p. 109.
35. Gordon 1984, p. 71.
36. For a discussion of the misconceptions about Pragmatism among members of the Frankfurt School, see Joas 1993, pp. 79–91.
37. Joas 1996, p. 133.
38. Duxbury 1995, p. 97.
39. Horwitz 1992, pp. 180–81.
40. Horwitz 1992, p. 271.
41. Leiter 2005, pp. 50–51.
42. Dewey 1924, p. 17.
43. Llewellyn 1930, p. 28.
44. Haack 2003, p. 124.
45. Bentham (1776) 1988, p. 8.
46. Twining 2000, pp. 94–102.
47. Leiter 2001, p. 280 and Dagan 2007.
48. Schlegel 1995, p. 260.
49. Twining 1973, pp. 82–83.
50. Hull 1997, p. 15.
51. Dennett (1995) 1996, p. 82.
52. Twining 1973, p. 54.
53. Rorty 1998, p. 28.

CHAPTER TWO

1. Whitman (1891–91) 1975, p. 428.
2. Marx, "The Eighteenth Brumaire of Louis Bonaparte," (1852), in: McLellan 1977, p. 300.
3. Hobsbawm 2005.
4. Structuralism and Postmodernism (or post-Structuralism) are at odds, of course. This study does not try to suggest otherwise. Yet, CLS claims to unite these two strands in its legal theory and draws on both. Consequently, as far as the representation of CLS is concerned, Structuralism and Postmodernism are described as complementary rather than contradictory.
5. Kalman 1986, pp. 37–42.

6. Llewellyn 1930 (1960), p. 44.
7. See, for instance, Gordon 1981, p. 1030.
8. Gould and Lewontin 1979, pp. 581–98.
9. Llewellyn 1930, p. 454.
10. Holmes 1881, p. 1.
11. In his biography of Oliver Wendell Holmes, G. Edward White has shown that this famous passage from *The Common Law* was a slight modification of a similar passage in a book notice on Langdell's *Selection of Cases on the Law of Contracts*. The original passage in the book notice was more explicitly critical of the Langdellian "logical" approach to legal understanding. It seems apparent that the reference to "logic" is directed at Langdell. White 1993, pp. 150–51.
12. Holmes 1897, p. 468.
13. Diggins 1994, p. 357.
14. Holmes 1897, p. 469.
15. Holmes 1913, pp. 67–68.
16. Holmes (1920) 1952, p. 225.
17. Holmes 1897, p. 469.
18. Holmes 1897, p. 474.
19. Holmes 1897, pp. 468–69.
20. Holmes 1992, p. 122.
21. Holmes 1992, p. 141.
22. Quoted in Hofstadter 1944, p. 19.
23. Gould 1996, p. 142.
24. Burrow 1968, pp. 45–46.
25. Burrow 1992, p. 29.
26. Spencer (1892) 1966, p. 34.
27. Spencer (1892) 1966, p. 31.
28. Spencer (1892) 1966, p. 203.
29. Spencer (1892) 1966, p. 26.
30. Holmes (1920) 1952, p. 281.
31. Holmes (1920) 1952, p. 305.
32. Holmes 1992, p. 140.
33. Holmes 1992, p. 122.
34. Holmes (1920) 1952, p. 305. The observation is false, of course. It assumes that there is a fixed quantum of wealth to go around. Holmes does not take into consideration the possibility that the total amount of wealth may shrink or expand as a result of the economic policy or redistributive regime chosen.
35. Lester Ward's first sociological treatise, *Dynamic Sociology*, was published in 1883. Holmes was at least aware of Ward's introduction of human intelligence in the Darwinist framework; see Holmes (1920) 1952, pp. 289–90.
36. Purcell 1973, p. 10.
37. In Hofstadter 1944, p. 111.
38. Dewey (1910) 1997, p. 68.
39. Dewey (1910) 1997, p. 72.
40. Purcell 1973, p. 9.
41. Menand 2001, p. 370.

42. Menand 2001, p. 369.
43. Dennett 2006, pp. 186, 268.
44. Dennett (1995) 1996, p. 362.
45. Dennett (1995) 1996, p. 349.
46. Lerner 1933, p. 687.
47. Nelles 1934a, p. 862.
48. Nelles 1934b, p. 1050.
49. Nelles 1934b, p. 1073.
50. Powell 1918, p. 647.
51. Lerner 1933, pp. 698–99.
52. Hamilton 1931b, p. 1169.
53. Hamilton 1931b, p. 1186.
54. Hamilton 1931b, p. 1156.
55. Llewellyn 1936, p. 699n.
56. Llewellyn 1936, pp. 713–15.
57. Compare Llewellyn's sketch with one of the opening statements of Turner's frontier thesis: "Behind institutions, behind constitutional forms and modifications, lie the vital forces that call these organs into life and shape them to meet changing conditions. The peculiarity of American institutions is, the fact that they have been compelled to adapt themselves to the changes of an expanding people— to the changes involved in crossing a continent, in winning a wilderness, and in developing at each area of this progress out of the primitive economic and political conditions of the frontier into the complexity of city life" (Turner 1893, p. 199).
58. Llewellyn 1936, p. 732.
59. Llewellyn 1936, p. 733.
60. Llewellyn 1937, p. 353.
61. Llewellyn 1937, p. 373.
62. Llewellyn 1939a, p. 725.
63. Llewellyn 1939a, p. 726.
64. Llewellyn 1939b, p. 877.
65. Llewellyn 1939b, p. 876.
66. Richards 2000, p. 1.
67. The person who originally coined the phrase is Seymour Papert (Dennett [1995] 1996, pp. 122–23).

CHAPTER THREE

1. Tennyson (1850) 1965, p. 230.
2. Vonnegut (1985) 1990, p. 22.
3. Novick 1988, p. 628.
4. Novick 1988, pp. 556–57.
5. Ankersmit 2005, p. 39.
6. Ankersmit 2005, p. 40.
7. Ankersmit 2005, p. 44.
8. See Bailyn 1967; Wood (1969) 1972; and Pocock 1975.
9. Diggins 1984, p. 355.

10. Kelman 1987, p. 214.
11. Horwitz 1992, p. 271.
12. Gordon 1981, p. 1017.
13. Rorty 1999, p. 269.
14. Horwitz 1973, p. 275.
15. Horwitz 1973, p. 276.
16. Horwitz 1973, p. 281.
17. Horwitz 1973, p. 281.
18. Diggins 1984, p. 359.
19. Horwitz 1977, p. xi.
20. Horwitz 1977, p. xiii.
21. Horwitz 1992, p. viii.
22. Kennedy 1980, p. 4.
23. Kennedy 1980, pp. 22–23.
24. Kennedy 1997, p. 41.
25. Gordon 1981, pp. 1018–19.
26. Gordon 1981, p. 1017.
27. Unger 1987b, p. 1.
28. Tushnet 1989, p. 157.
29. Tushnet 1989, p. 157.
30. Tushnet 1989, p. 165.
31. Tushnet 1989, p. 166.
32. Tushnet 1989, p. 166.
33. Gordon 1981, p. 1026.
34. Gordon 1981, p. 1026.
35. Gordon 1981, p. 1028.
36. Gordon 1981, p. 1029.
37. Gordon 1981, p. 1032.
38. Gordon 1981, p. 1033.
39. Gordon 1981, p. 1034.
40. Gordon 1981, p. 1035.
41. Gordon 1984, p. 70.
42. Gordon 1984, p. 71. Gordon's interpretation of Gould is not entirely fair. Gould does not claim that cultural variety in human responses to their environment makes adaptation a useless concept. In fact, he claims in the very same section that Gordon refers to that evolutionary biology can provide fruitful analogies for the explanation of human behavior. "Much of human behavior is surely adaptive," he argues, "if it weren't we wouldn't be around anymore." Furthermore, he claims that "even when an adaptive behavior is nongenetic, biological analogy may be useful in interpreting its meaning. Adaptive constraints are often strong, and some functions may have to proceed in a certain way whether their underlying impetus be learning or genetic programming" (Gould 1996, p. 357). Gordon's mistaken use of Gould might not be a coincidence, but invited by the gist of Gould's work (see Dennett [1995] 1996, pp. 262–312).
43. Gordon 1984, p. 71.
44. Gordon 1984, pp. 117–19.

45. Gordon 1984, p. 119.
46. Gordon 1984, p. 123.
47. Unger 1987a, p. 24.
48. Unger 1987a, p. 25.
49. Unger 1987a, p. 198.
50. Unger 1987a, p. 198.
51. Unger 1987a, p. 189.
52. Unger 2005, p. 15.
53. Tushnet 1977, p. 105.
54. Tushnet 1977, p. 94.
55. Tushnet 1977, p. 100.
56. Livingston 1982, p. 1679.
57. Gordon 1984, p. 109.
58. Gordon 1984, p. 117.
59. Holmes 1913, pp. 67–68.

CHAPTER FOUR

1. James (1907) 1992, p. 110.
2. Bacon (1620) 1962, pp. 92–93. Also see Gould (2003) 2004 on the widespread misconceptions about Bacon, p. 109.
3. Fuller 1934, pp. 429–62; Hart 1983, pp. 24, 131.
4. Rumble 1968, pp. 178–80; Ingersoll 1966, pp. 253–66; Schubert 1964, pp. 2–13.
5. Twining 1973, pp. 54–55.
6. Purcell 1973, p. 78.
7. Kalman 1986, p. 3; Duxbury 1995, p. 97; Schlegel 1995.
8. Llewellyn 1931a, p. 1236.
9. Horwitz 1992, p. 172.
10. Horwitz 1992, p. 182.
11. Purcell 1973, pp. 117–58.
12. Gunnell 1988, p. 77.
13. Joas 1993, pp. 94–116.
14. "A Realistic Jurisprudence—The Next Step" was solely Llewellyn's work. "Some Realism About Realism—Responding to Dean Pound," a response to Roscoe Pound's critique of the first article, however, was written in conjunction with Jerome Frank. Yet Frank refused to sign his name to the article.
15. Twining 1973, p. 71.
16. Llewellyn 1930, p. 443.
17. Llewellyn 1930, p. 444.
18. Llewellyn 1930, p. 444.
19. Llewellyn 1930, pp. 452–53.
20. Llewellyn 1930, pp. 446–47, n. 12.
21. Llewellyn 1930, p. 458.
22. Llewellyn 1930, p. 454.
23. Pound 1931.

24. Llewellyn 1931a, pp. 1229–30.
25. Llewellyn 1931a, p. 1232.
26. Llewellyn 1931a, pp. 1232–33.
27. Llewellyn 1931a, p. 1237.
28. Llewellyn 1931a, p. 1236.
29. Frank (1930) 1970, p. 263.
30. Dewey 1924, pp. 17–27.
31. Llewellyn 1931a, pp. 1236–37.
32. Llewellyn 1931a, p. 1236.
33. Llewellyn 1962, p. 96.
34. Frank (1930) 1970, p. 307.
35. Frank (1930) 1970, p. 308.
36. Frank (1930) 1970, p. 310.
37. Frank (1930) 1970, p. 105.
38. Douglas 1929, p. 681.
39. Moore 1941, pp. 210–11.
40. Cook 1927, p. 306.
41. Cook 1927, p. 307.
42. Cook 1927, p. 309.
43. Purcell 1973, pp. 50–51.
44. Frank 1932a, p. 576.
45. Frank 1932a, p. 578.
46. Schlegel 1995, pp. 24–25, 57–61, 69.
47. Douglas 1929, p. 674.
48. Douglas 1929, p. 675.
49. Douglas 1929, p. 682.
50. Cohen 1935, p. 821.
51. Arnold (1937) 1968, p. 136.
52. Arnold (1937) 1968, p. 378.
53. Llewellyn 1940, p. 1360.
54. Llewellyn 1941, p. 290.
55. Llewellyn 1941, p. 293.
56. Twining 2000, pp. 79, 80.
57. Llewellyn 1962, p. 194.
58. Dawkins (1996) 1997.
59. Cook 1927, p. 308.
60. Frank 1932b, p. 657.
61. Cohen 1935, p. 846.
62. Hart 1983, p. 27.
63. Twining 2000, pp. 119–21.
64. Dagan 2007, p. 617.
65. Llewellyn 1931a, p. 1236.
66. Llewellyn 1931a, p. 1249.
67. Cook 1927, p. 308.
68. Cook 1927, pp. 308–9.
69. Keyserling 1933, pp. 437–38.

70. Laski 1917, pp. 134–35.
71. Llewellyn 1940, p. 1365.
72. Llewellyn 1940, p. 1387.
73. Llewellyn 1940, pp. 1390–91.
74. Horwitz 1992, p. 211.
75. Wiseman 1987, pp. 520–24.
76. Quoted in Wiseman 1987, pp. 523–24.
77. Twining 1973, p. 314.
78. Twining 1973, p. 320.
79. Twining 1973, p. 316.
80. Putnam 1995, p. 21.

CHAPTER FIVE

1. Winters 2003, p. 126.
2. *The Big Lebowski,* produced by Ethan Coen, directed by Joel Coen, 1998.
3. Carroll (1865, 1871) 1983, chap. 5.
4. Gordon 1983, pp. 282–83.
5. Gordon 1983, pp. 282–83.
6. See p. 76 of this volume.
7. Horwitz 1992, p. 182.
8. Trubek 1984, p. 586.
9. Trubek 1984, p. 589.
10. Trubek 1984, p. 592.
11. Tushnet 1981, p. 1207.
12. Tushnet 1980, p. 21.
13. Tushnet 1980, pp. 22–23.
14. Boyle 1985, p. 697.
15. Kelman 1987, p. 13.
16. Hutchinson 1989, p. 5.
17. Fitzpatrick and Hunt 1987, p. 7.
18. Fitzpatrick and Hunt 1987, p. 8.
19. Boyle 1985, pp. 707–8.
20. Boyle 1985, p. 720.
21. Unger 1975, p. 33.
22. Unger 1975, p. 33.
23. Hutchinson 1989, pp. 5–6.
24. Freeman 1981, p. 1229.
25. Boyle 1985, pp. 700–701.
26. Unger 1987a, pp. 131–32.
27. Unger 1987a, p. 2.
28. Peller 1985, p. 1274.
29. Peller 1985, p. 1276.
30. Peller 1985, pp. 1274–75.
31. Kelman 1987, p. 253.
32. Kelman 1987, pp. 249–50.

33. Gordon 1984, pp. 102–3.
34. Gordon 1984, p. 109.
35. Rorty 1982, p. 206.
36. Rorty 1982, p. 204.
37. Rorty 1982, p. 206.
38. Putnam 1995, pp. 74–75.
39. Dewey (1929) 1997, p. 351.
40. Ewald 1988, p. 699.
41. See pp. 46–47 of this volume.
42. Haack 2003, p. 163.

CHAPTER SIX

1. Beck 2002.
2. Dickinson 1994, p. 19.
3. Cohen 1935, p. 809.
4. Holmes (1920) 1952, p. 238.
5. For the relationship between O. W. Holmes and Benthamite linguistic theory, see Pohlman 1984, pp. 106–43.
6. *Towne v. Eisner,* 245 U.S. 418 (1919).
7. *Gompers v. United States,* 233 U.S. 604 (1914).
8. Purcell 1973, p. 47.
9. Ogden and Richards (1923) 1972, pp. 10–12.
10. Ogden and Richards (1923) 1972, p. 14.
11. Ogden and Richards (1923) 1972, p. 96.
12. Ogden and Richards (1923) 1972, p. 125.
13. Ogden and Richards (1923) 1972, p. 47.
14. Ogden and Richards (1923) 1972, p. 31.
15. Ogden and Richards (1923) 1972, p. 33.
16. Ogden and Richards (1923) 1972, p. 29.
17. Ogden and Richards (1923) 1972, p. 29.
18. Ogden and Richards (1923) 1972, p. 122.
19. Ogden and Richards (1923) 1972, p. 122.
20. Ogden and Richards (1923) 1972, p. 123.
21. Ogden and Richards (1923) 1972, p. 47.
22. Ogden and Richards (1923) 1972, p. 309.
23. Ogden and Richards (1923) 1972, p. 26.
24. Ogden and Richards (1923) 1972, p. 328.
25. Dewey 1983, p. 223.
26. Dewey 1985, p. 4.
27. Dewey (1929) 1997, p. 170n.
28. Dewey (1929) 1997, pp. 138, 140.
29. See Wienpahl 1976, p. 272.
30. Dewey (1929) 1997, p. 153.
31. Dewey (1929) 1997, p. 155.
32. Dewey (1929) 1997, pp. 142–43.

33. Dewey (1929) 1997, p. 153.
34. Frank (1930) 1970, p. 97.
35. Frank (1930) 1970, p. 98.
36. Frank (1930) 1970, p. 91.
37. Frank (1930) 1970, pp. 98–99.
38. Clark 1933, p. 647.
39. Arnold (1937) 1968, p. 119.
40. Llewellyn (1930) 1960, p. 49.
41. Llewellyn 1962, p. 28.
42. Llewellyn 1962, p. 23.
43. Llewellyn 1962, p. 27.
44. Llewellyn 1962, p. 16.
45. Green 1928, pp. 1029–30.
46. Green 1928, p. 1031n.
47. Arnold (1937) 1968, p. 349.
48. Frank (1930) 1970, p. 72.
49. Llewellyn (1930) 1960, p. 72.
50. Llewellyn (1930) 1960, p. 72.
51. Llewellyn 1930, p. 457.
52. Llewellyn 1931a, p. 1237.
53. Arnold 1931a, pp. 57–58.
54. Arnold 1931b, p. 803.
55. Arnold 1931b, p. 814.
56. Arnold 1931b, p. 822.
57. Llewellyn 1962, p. 78.
58. Llewellyn 1962, pp. 80–81.
59. Llewellyn 1962, p. 13.
60. Clark and Sturges 1928, p. 714.
61. Frank (1930) 1970, p. 263.
62. Cohen 1935, p. 833.
63. Cohen 1935, p. 838.
64. Cohen 1935, p. 823.
65. Cohen 1935, p. 838.
66. Arnold (1937) 1968, p. 121.
67. Arnold (1937) 1968, p. 148.
68. Llewellyn (1930) 1960, p. 41.
69. Llewellyn 1941, p. 184.
70. Llewellyn 1941, p. 196.

CHAPTER SEVEN

1. Carroll (1865, 1871) 1983, chap. 6.
2. Rorty 1982, pp. 3–18.
3. Unger 1975, p. 31.
4. Unger 1975, p. 32.
5. Unger 1975, pp. 32–33.

6. Unger 1975, p. 34.

7. Singer 1984, p. 35.

8. Tushnet 1981, p. 1217.

9. The relevant paragraphs are 198 and 201: 198. "'But how can a rule shew me what I have to do at *this* point? Whatever I do is, on some interpretation, in accord with the rule.'" 201. "'This was our paradox: no course of action could be determined by a rule, because every course of action can be made to accord with the rule. The answer was: if everything can be made out to accord with the rule, then it can also be made out to conflict with it. And so there would be neither accord nor conflict here" (Wittgenstein [1953] 1967, pp. 80–81e). Wittgenstein talks about this paradox in reference to language as a rule-governed practice, or language game, and argues that the application of rules in novel circumstances is never a straightforward matter, but always demands an act of judgment. Rules can always be interpreted to produce a number of different results. Hence, the rules that govern a language game by themselves cannot tell us what to do, and insofar as the routines of language application are stable, this stability must derive from a source other than rules. Critical scholars have taken this to mean that language is inherently pliable, that rules cannot compel the conclusions that follow from them. Thus Wittgenstein's understanding of rule-following is used to support a strong skepticism about the determinacy of legal rules, which denies the very possibility that rules can guide judges.

10. Tushnet 1988, p. 55; and 1989, pp. 174–75.

11. Tushnet 1988, p. 56.

12. Tushnet 1988, p. 56.

13. Tushnet 1988, pp. 56–57n.

14. Boyle 1985, pp. 708–9.

15. Boyle 1985, p. 709n.

16. Boyle 1985, p. 713.

17. Boyle 1985, p. 720.

18. Peller 1985, p. 1155.

19. Peller 1985, p. 1155.

20. Peller 1985, p. 1164.

21. Cohen 1935, p. 815; Peller 1985, pp. 1229–30.

22. Peller 1985, pp. 1237–38.

23. Peller 1985, pp. 1261–62.

24. Peller 1985, p. 1262.

25. Peller 1985, p. 1190.

26. Peller 1995, pp. 74–75.

27. Dalton 1985, p. 1007.

28. Dalton 1985, p. 999.

29. Dalton 1985, pp. 999–1000.

30. Dalton 1985, pp. 1000–1001.

31. Dalton 1985, p. 1095.

32. Kennedy 1997, p. 11.

33. Brown and Halley 2002, pp. 26–27.

34. Brown and Halley 2002, p. 21.

35. Brown and Halley 2002, p. 21.

36. Brown and Halley 2002, p. 27.
37. Ford in Brown and Halley 2002, p. 75.
38. Ford in Brown and Halley 2002, p. 42.
39. Ford in Brown and Halley 2002, p. 43.
40. Ford in Brown and Halley 2002, pp. 65–66.
41. Frank Michelman, for instance, argues that Tushnet only grasped part of the idea that Wittgenstein tried to convey. Michelman agrees with Tushnet that "from Wittgenstein we learned that a set of instructions can never finish explaining how itself is to be read." Yet, he maintains, the Wittgensteinian lesson does not stop there, but "goes on to insist that judgments of error, mistake, and incompetency in the use of rules are nonetheless possible within a practice, a language-game, or a form of life" (Michelman 1981, p. 1227). The fact that rules by themselves do not tell us what consequences should follow from them, does not mean that we can interpret them any way we like in the context of their use.

Wittgenstein, in paragraph 201 of *Philosophical Investigations,* contends that "there is a way of grasping a rule which is *not* an *interpretation*, but which is exhibited in what we call 'obeying the rule' and 'going against it' in actual cases." What Wittgenstein wants to draw attention to is that following a rule does not necessarily imply an act of interpretation. Rule-following can also be understood as mastery of a technique, as acquired know-how. When people speak in their native language, they follow rules of grammar and definition to correctly form sentences, but it would be odd to think of them as interpreting those rules when they talk. They simply apply the rules unthinkingly and probably cannnot articulate exactly what rules they are applying.

42. Dworkin 1986, p. 88.
43. Boyle 1985, pp. 758–59.
44. Peller 1985, p. 1258.

CHAPTER EIGHT

1. Gunn 1994, p. 212.
2. Corwin 1988, p. 80.
3. Posner 1991, p. 29.
4. Grey 1991, p. 11.
5. There is considerable irony in this position. CLS is opposed to the positivist notion that science is something that is cumulative, something in which there is progress. CLS instead sides with Kuhn and can see the development of knowledge only as a succession of incommensurable paradigms, one no better than the other. Yet the CLS view of its own position in relation to Legal Realism seems to imply a belief in exactly the kind of intellectual progress Critical scholars deny; it presents a story of how the flawed approach of Legal Realism could be improved upon with the use of subsequent developments in scholarship and eventually culminate in CLS theory.
6. Luban 1996, p. 46.
7. Luban 1996, pp. 46–47.
8. Rorty 1991, p. 91. This quotation should not be taken to mean that Rorty is

hostile to social science. He is not. He is only hostile to the idea that social science knowledge can have any privileged epistemological status, that it is treated as anything more than just a useful vocabulary to talk about society.

9. Grey 1991, p. 11.

10. Posner 1999, p. 208.

11. Posner 2001, p. 181.

12. Putnam 1981, p. 162.

13. Putnam 1981, p. 167.

14. Posner 1999, p. 166.

15. Posner 1999, p. 26.

16. Kelman 1987, p. 214.

17. Joas 1993, p. 83.

18. For a discussion of the Pragmatic underpinnings of Hurst's work, see Gordon 1975, pp. 44–55.

19. Hurst 1950, p. 6.

20. Hurst 1950, p. 7.

21. Hurst 1950, pp. 10–11.

22. Hurst 1950, p. 11.

23. Hurst 1950, p. 13.

24. Hurst 1950, p. 15.

25. Hurst 1950, p. 12.

26. Joas 1996, p. 250.

27. Joas 1996, p. 249.

28. Tamanaha 2006, p. 48.

29. Posner 2003, p. 50.

30. Tamanaha 1997, p. xi.

31. Posner 1995, p. 393.

32. Posner 1995, p. 393.

33. Tamanaha 1997, p. 30.

34. Tamanaha 1997, p. 34.

35. Tamanaha 1997, pp. 38–43.

36. Tamanaha 1997, p. 253.

37. Tamanaha 1997, p. 57.

38. Tamanaha 1997, pp. 254–55.

39. Dewey (1931) 1998, p. 371.

40. For the Pragmatic conception of ideals, see Taekema 2003, pp. 28–31.

41. Posner 1990, p. 465.

42. Posner 1999, p. 201.

43. Posner 1999, p. 227.

44. Posner 1995, p. 393.

45. Posner 1999, p. 45.

46. Posner 1999, p. 46.

47. Posner 1999, p. 211.

48. Posner 1999, p. 85.

49. Posner seems to echo the claims of such an old judicial behavioralist as Glendon Schubert, who thought that it would be as inappropriate to include "the meta-

physical lore of traditional jurisprudence" in a book on judicial behavior as it would be "to include a chapter on alchemy in a text on metallurgy, or to include a set of horoscopes in a book on astrophysics" (Schubert 1964, p. 9).

50. Unger 1998, p. 9.
51. Rorty 1998, p. 79.
52. Posner 1999, p. 271.
53. Tamanaha 1997, pp. 59–89.
54. Tamanaha 1997, p. 90.
55. Tamanaha 1997, p. 70.
56. Tamanaha 1997, p. 152.
57. Posner 1999, p. 211.
58. Posner 1999, pp. 212–13.
59. Posner 1999, p. 226.
60. Posner 1999, p. 215.
61. Posner 1999, p. 211.
62. Rorty 1982, p. 200.
63. Diggins 1994, p. 461.
64. Putnam 1995, p. 34.
65. Dewey (1929) 1997, pp. 34–35.
66. Llewellyn 1939b, p. 876.
67. Rescher 2000, p. 150.
68. Rescher 2000, pp. 151–52.
69. Rescher 2000, p. 161n5.
70. Rescher 2000, p. 163.
71. Putnam 1995, p. 29.
72. Dewey 1985, p. 4.
73. Fish 1989, p. 128.

Bibliography

Ankersmit 2005
  Frank Ankersmit, *Sublime Historical Experience*, Stanford, CA: Stanford University Press 2005.
Arnold (1937) 1968
  Thurman Arnold, *The Folklore of Capitalism*, New Haven, CT, and London: Yale University Press 1968.
Arnold 1931a
  Thurman Arnold, "Criminal Attempts—The Rise and Fall of an Abstraction," *Yale Law Journal* 40 (1930), pp. 53–76.
Arnold 1931b
  Thurman Arnold, "The Restatement of the Law of Trusts," *Columbia Law Review* 31 (1931), pp. 800–823.
Bacon (1620) 1857–74
  Francis Bacon *Novum Organum*, in: Spedding, Ellis, and Heath, *The Works of Francis Bacon* Vol. 4, London 1857–74, pp. 39–248.
Bailyn 1967
  Bernard Bailyn, *The Ideological Origins of the American Revolution*, Cambridge, MA: Harvard University Press 1967.
Bechtler 1978
  Thomas W. Bechtler, "The Background of Legal Realism," in: Thomas W. Bechtler (ed.), *Law in a Social Context: Liber Amicorum Honouring Professor Lon L. Fuller*, Deventer: Kluwer 1978, pp. 7–48.
Beck 2002
  Ulrich Beck, "The Silence of Words and Political Dynamics in the World Risk Society," http://logosonline.home.igc.org/beck.htm, 2002.
Bentham (1776) 1988
  Jeremy Bentham, *A Fragment on Government*, Cambridge: Cambridge University Press 1978.

Blackmore 1999
    Susan Blackmore, *The Meme Machine*, Oxford: Oxford University Press 1999.
Boyle 1985
    James Boyle, "The Politics of Reason: Critical Legal Theory and Local Social Thought," *University of Pennsylvania Law Review* 133 (1985), pp. 685–780.
Brown and Halley 2002
    Wendy Brown and Janet Halley (eds.), *Left Legalism/Left Critique*, Durham, NC, and London: Duke University Press 2002.
Burrow 1992
    J. W. Burrow, "Holmes in His Intellectual Milieu," in: Robert W. Gordon (ed.), *The Legacy of Oliver Wendell Holmes, Jr.*, Stanford, CA: Stanford University Press 1992, pp. 17–30.
Burrow 1968
    J. W. Burrow, "Editor's Introduction," in: Charles Darwin, *The Origin of Species*, London: Penguin 1968, pp. 11–48.
Cairns 1931
    Huntington Cairns, "Law and Anthropology," *Columbia Law Review* 31 (1931), pp. 32–55.
Carroll (1865, 1871) 1983
    Lewis Carroll, *Alice's Adventures in Wonderland & Through the Looking Glass and What Alice Found There*, Mahwah, NJ: Watermill Press 1983.
Clark 1933
    Charles E. Clark, "The Restatement of the Law of Contracts," *Yale Law Journal* 42 (1933), pp. 643–67.
Clark and Sturges 1928
    Samuel O. Clark and Wesley A. Sturges, "Legal Theory and Real Property Mortgages," *Yale Law Journal* 37 (1928), pp. 691–715.
Cohen 1935
    Felix S. Cohen, "Transcendental Nonsense and the Functional Approach," *Columbia Law Review* (1935), pp. 809–49.
Cohen 1931
    Felix S. Cohen, "The Ethical Basis of Legal Criticism," *Yale Law Journal* 41 (1931), pp. 201–20.
Cohen 1927
    Morris Cohen, "Property and Sovereignty," *Cornell Law Quarterly* 13 (1927), pp. 8–30.
Cook 1927
    Walter Wheeler Cook, "Scientific Method and the Law," *American Bar Association Journal* 13 (1927), pp. 303–9.
Corwin 1988
    Edward S. Corwin, *Corwin on the Constitution: On Liberty against Government*, Vol. 3, Ithaca, NY, and London: Cornell University Press 1988.
Dagan 2007
    Hanoch Dagan, "The Realist Conception of Law," *University of Toronto Law Journal* 57 (2007), pp. 607–60.

Dalton 1985
Clare Dalton, "An Essay in the Deconstruction of Contract Doctrine," *Yale Law Journal* 94 (1985), pp. 997–1114.

Danielsen and Engle 1995
Dan Danielsen and Karen Engle (eds.), *After Identity: A Reader in Law and Culture*, New York and London: Routledge 1995.

Dawkins (1996) 1997
Richard Dawkins, *Climbing Mount Improbable*, London: Penguin Books 1997.

Dawkins (1986) 1991
Richard Dawkins, *The Blind Watchmaker*, London: Penguin Books, 1991.

Dawkins (1976) 1999
Richard Dawkins, *The Selfish Gene*, Oxford and New York: Oxford University Press 1999.

Dennett 2006
Daniel Dennett, *Breaking the Spell: Religion as a Natural Phenomenon*, London: Penguin 2006.

Dennett 2003
Daniel C. Dennett, *Freedom Evolves*, New York: Viking 2003.

Dennett (1995) 1996
Daniel C. Dennett, *Darwin's Dangerous Idea: Evolution and the Meanings of Life*, New York: Touchstone 1996.

Dewey (1931) 1998
John Dewey, "Social Science and Social Control," in: Larry A. Hickman and Thomas M. Alexander (eds.), *The Essential Dewey:Pragmatism, Education, Democracy*, Bloomington IN: Indiana University Press 1998, pp. 369–71.

Dewey (1929) 1997
John Dewey, *Experience & Nature*, 2nd edition, Chicago: Open Court 1997.

Dewey (1910) 1997
John Dewey, *The Influence of Darwin on Philosophy and Other Essays*, Amherst, NY: Prometheus 1997.

Dewey 1985
John Dewey, "Context and Thought," in: Jo Ann Boydston (ed.), *John Dewey: Later Works, 1925–1953*, Vol. 6, Carbondale and Edwardsville: Southern Illinois University Press 1985, pp. 3–21.

Dewey 1983
John Dewey, "Review: The Meaning of Meaning: A Study of the Influence of Language upon Thought and of the Science of Symbolism," in: Jo Ann Boydston (ed.), *John Dewey: The Middle Works, 1899–1924*, Vol. 15, Carbondale and Edwardsville: Southern Illinois University Press 1983, pp. 223–25.

Dewey 1924
John Dewey, "Logical Method and Law," *Cornell Law Quarterly* 10 (1924), pp. 17–27.

Dickinson 1994
Emily Dickinson, *The Selected Poems of Emily Dickinson*, Ware, UK: Wordsworth 1994.

Diggins 1994
John P. Diggins, *The Promise of Pragmatism: Modernism and the Crisis of Knowledge and Authority*, Chicago and London: University of Chicago Press 1994.

Diggins 1992
John P. Diggins, *The Rise and Fall of the American Left*, New York and London: Norton 1992.

Diggins 1984
John P. Diggins, *The Lost Soul of American Politics: Virtue, Self-Interest, and the Foundations of Liberalism*, New York: Basic Books 1984.

Douglas 1929
William O. Douglas, "A Functional Approach to the Law of Business Associations," *Illinois Law Review* 23 (1929), pp. 673–82.

Duxbury 1995
Neil Duxbury, *Patterns of American Jurisprudence*, Oxford: Clarendon Press 1995.

Dworkin 1986
Ronald Dworkin, *Law's Empire*, London: Fontana Press 1986.

Ewald 1988
William Ewald, "Unger's Philosophy: A Critical Legal Study," *Yale Law Journal* 97 (1988), pp. 665–775.

Fish 1989
Stanley Fish, *Doing What Comes Naturally: Change, Rhetoric, and the Practice of Theory in Literary and Legal Studies*, Durham and London: Duke University Press 1989.

Fitzpatrick and Hunt 1987
Peter Fitzpatrick and Alan Hunt, *Critical Legal Studies*, Oxford: Basil Blackwell 1987.

Frank 1932a
Jerome Frank, "Mr. Justice Holmes and Non-Euclidean Legal Thinking," *Cornell Law Quarterly* 17 (1932), pp. 568–603.

Frank 1932b
Jerome Frank, "What the Courts Do in Fact," *Illinois Law Review* 26 (1932), pp. 645–66.

Frank (1930) 1970
Jerome Frank, *Law and the Modern Mind*, Gloucester, UK: Peter Smith 1970.

Freeman 1981
Alan D. Freeman, "Truth and Mystification in Legal Scholarship," *Yale Law Journal* 90 (1981), pp. 1229–37.

Fuller 1934
Lon Fuller, "American Legal Realism," *University of Pennsylvania Law Review* 82 (1934), pp. 429–62.

Gabel and Kennedy 1984
Peter Gabel and Duncan Kennedy, "Roll Over Beethoven," *Stanford Law Review* 36 (1984), pp. 1–55.

Gilmore 1977
Grant Gilmore, *The Ages of American Law*, New Haven, CT, & London: Yale University Press 1977.

Gilmore 1961
Grant Gilmore, "Legal Realism: Its Cause and Cure," *Yale Law Journal* 70 (1961), pp. 1037–48.

Gordon 1984
Robert W. Gordon, "Critical Legal Histories," *Stanford Law Review* 36 (1984), pp. 57–125.

Gordon 1983
Robert W. Gordon, "New Developments in Legal Theory," in: D. Kairys (ed.), *The Politics of Law*, New York: Pantheon Books1983, pp. 281–93.

Gordon 1981
Robert W. Gordon, "Historicism in Legal Scholarship," *Yale Law Journal* 90 (1981), pp. 1017–62.

Gordon 1975
Robert W. Gordon, "Introduction: J. Willard Hurst and the Common Law Tradition in American Legal Historiography," *Law & Society* (1975), pp. 9–55.

Gould (2003) 2004
Stephen Jay Gould, *The Hedgehog, the Fox and the Magister's Pox: Mending and Minding the Misconceived Gap Between Science and the Humanities*, London: Vintage 2004.

Gould 1996
Stephen Jay Gould, *The Mismeasure of Man*, London: Penguin 1996.

Gould and Lewontin 1979
Stephen Jay Gould and R. Lewontin, 'The Spandrels of San Marco and the Panglossian Paradigm: A Critique of the Adaptationist Programme,' *Proceedings of the Royal Society*, Vol. B205, 1979, pp. 581–98.

Grey 1991
Thomas Grey, "What Good Is Legal Pragmatism," in: Michael Brint and William Weaver (eds.), *Pragmatism in Law and Society*, Boulder, CO: Westview Press 1991, pp. 9–28.

Green 1928
Leon Green, "The Negligence Issue," *Yale Law Journal* 37 (1928), pp. 1029–47.

Gunn 1994
Thom Gunn, *Collected Poems*, New York: Farrar, Straus & Giroux 1994.

Gunnell 1988
John G. Gunnell, "American Political Science, Liberalism, and the Invention of Political Theory," *American Political Science Review* 82 (1988), pp. 71–87.

Haack 2003
Susan Haack, *Defending Science—Within Reason: Between Scientism and Cynicism*, Amherst, MA: Prometheus Books 2003.

Haack 1998
Susan Haack, *Manifesto of a Passionate Moderate: Unfashionable Essays*, Chicago and London: University of Chicago Press 1998.

Hamilton 1932
  Walton Hamilton, "Property According to Locke," *Yale Law Journal* 42 (1932), pp. 864–80.
Hamilton 1931a
  Walton Hamilton, "The Jurist's Art," *Columbia Law Review* 31 (1931), pp. 1073–93.
Hamilton 1931b
  Walton Hamilton, "The Ancient Maxim Caveat Emptor," *Yale Law Journal* 40 (1931), pp. 1132–87.
Hart 1983
  H. L. A. Hart, *Essays in Jurisprudence and Philosophy*, Oxford: Clarendon Press 1983.
Hobsbawm 2005
  Eric Hobsbawm, "In Defence of History," *Guardian* January 15, 2005.
Hofstadter 1955
  Richard Hofstadter, *The Age of Reform: From Bryan to F.D.R.*, New York: Alfred A. Knopf 1955.
Hofstadter 1944
  Richard Hofstadter, *Social Darwinism in American Thought: 1860–1915*, Philadelphia: University of Pennsylvania Press 1944.
Holmes 1992
  Oliver Wendell Holmes, *The Essential Holmes: Selections from the Letters, Speeches, Judicial Opinions, and Other Writings of Oliver Wendell Holmes, Jr.*, ed. Richard A. Posner, Chicago and London: University of Chicago Press 1992.
Holmes (1920) 1952
  Oliver Wendell Holmes, *Collected Legal Papers*, New York: Peter Smith 1952.
Holmes 1913
  Oliver Wendell Holmes, *Speeches by Oliver Wendell Holmes*, Boston: Little, Brown and Company 1913.
Holmes 1897
  Oliver Wendell Holmes, "The Path of the Law," *Harvard Law Review* 10 (1897), pp. 457–78.
Holmes 1881
  Oliver Wendell Holmes, *The Common Law*, Boston: Little, Brown and Company 1881.
Hopkins 1983
  James D. Hopkins, "The Development of Realism in Law and Literature During the Period 1883–1933: The Cultural Resemblance," *Pace Law Review* 4 (1983), pp. 29–60.
Horwitz 1992
  Morton J. Horwitz, *The Transformation of American Law: 1870–1960*, New York and Oxford: Oxford University Press 1992.
Horwitz 1977
  Morton J. Horwitz, *The Transformation of American Law 1780–1860*, Cambridge and London: Harvard University Press 1977.

Horwitz 1973
    Morton J. Horwitz, "The Conservative Tradition in the Writing of American
    Legal History," *American Journal of Legal History* 17 (1973), pp. 275–94.
Hull 1997
    N. E. H. Hull, *Roscoe Pound & Karl Llewellyn: Searching for an American Jurispru-
    dence*, Chicago and London: University of Chicago Press 1997.
Hurst 1950
    James Willard Hurst, *The Growth of American Law: The Law Makers*, Boston:
    Little, Brown and Company 1950.
Hutchinson 1989
    Alan C. Hutchinson, *Critical Legal Studies*, Totowa, NJ: Rowman & Littlefield
    1989.
Ingersoll 1966
    David E. Ingersoll, "Karl Llewellyn, American Legal Realism, and Contempo-
    rary Legal Behavioralism," *Ethics* 76 (1966), pp. 253–66.
James (1907) 1992
    William James, "Pragmatism: A New Name for Some Old Ways of Thinking,"
    in: Doris Olin (ed.), *William James Pragmatism: In Focus*, London and New
    York: Routledge 1992.
Joas 1996
    Hans Joas, *The Creativity of Action*, Chicago: University of Chicago Press 1996.
Joas 1993
    Hans Joas, *Pragmatism and Social Theory*, Chicago and London: University of
    Chicago Press 1993.
Kalman 1986
    Laura Kalman, *Legal Realism at Yale, 1927–1960*, Chapel Hill and London: Uni-
    versity of North Carolina Press 1986.
Kelman 1987
    Mark Kelman, *A Guide to Critical Legal Studies*, Cambridge, MA, and London:
    Harvard University Press 1987.
Kennedy 1997
    Duncan Kennedy, *A Critique of Adjudication (fin de siècle)*, Cambridge, MA, and
    London: Harvard University Press 1997.
Kennedy 1980
    Duncan Kennedy, "Toward an Historical Understanding of Legal Conscious-
    ness: The Case of Classical Legal Thought in America, 1850–1940," *Research in
    Law and Sociology* 3 (1980), pp. 2–24.
Kennedy 1979
    Duncan Kennedy, "The Structure of Blackstone's Commentaries," *Buffalo Law
    Review* 28 (1979), pp. 209–21.
Keyserling 1933
    Leon H. Keyserling, "Social Objectives in Legal Education," *Columbia Law Re-
    view* 33 (1933), pp. 437–61.
Langdell 1888
    Christopher Columbus Langdell, "Teaching Law as a Science," *American Law
    Review* (1888), pp. 123–25.

Langdell 1871
   Christopher Columbus Langdell, *A Selection of Cases on the Law of Contracts*, Boston: Little, Brown 1871.
Laski 1917
   Harold Laski, "The Basis of Vicarious Liability," *Yale Law Journal* 26 (1917), pp. 105–35.
Leiter 2005
   Brian Leiter, "American Legal Realism," in: Martin P. Golding and William A. Edmundson (eds.), *The Blackwell Guide to the Philosophy of Law and Legal Theory*, Malden, Oxford, and Carlton: Blackwell Publishing 2005, pp. 50–66.
Leiter 2001
   Brian Leiter, "Legal Realism and Legal Positivism Reconsidered," *Ethics* 111 (2001), pp. 278–301.
Lerner 1933
   Max Lerner, "The Supreme Court and American Capitalism," *Yale Law Journal* 42 (1933), pp. 668–701.
Livingston 1982
   Debra Livingston, "Round and 'Round the Bramble Bush': From Legal Realism to Critical Legal Scholarship," *Harvard Law Review* 95 (1982), pp. 1669–90.
Llewellyn 1962
   Karl N. Llewellyn, *Jurisprudence: Realism in Theory and Practice*, Chicago and London: University of Chicago Press 1962.
Llewellyn (1960) 1976
   Karl N. Llewellyn, *The Common Law Tradition: Deciding Appeals*, Boston and Toronto: Little, Brown & Company 1976.
Llewellyn 1941
   Karl N. Llewellyn, "My Philosophy of Law," in: *My Philosophy of Law: Credos of Sixteen American Scholars*, Boston: Boston Law Book 1941, pp. 181–97.
Llewellyn 1940
   Karl N. Llewellyn, "The Normative, the Legal, and the Law-Jobs: The Problem of Juristic Method," *Yale Law Journal* 49 (1940), pp. 1355–1400.
Llewellyn 1939a
   Karl N. Llewellyn, "Across Sales on Horseback," *Harvard Law Review* 52 (1939), pp. 725–46.
Llewellyn 1939b
   Karl N. Llewellyn, "The First Struggle to Unhorse Sales," *Harvard Law Review* 52 (1939), pp. 873–904.
Llewellyn 1937
   Karl N. Llewellyn, "On Warranty of Quality, and Society: II," *Columbia Law Review* 37 (1937), pp. 341–409.
Llewellyn 1936
   Karl N. Llewellyn, "On Warranty of Quality, and Society," *Columbia Law Review* 36 (1936), pp. 699–744.
Llewellyn 1931a
   Karl N. Llewellyn, "Some Realism About Realism: Responding to Dean Pound," *Harvard Law Review* 44 (1931), pp. 1222–64.

Llewellyn 1931b
Karl N. Llewellyn, "What Price Contract? An Essay in Perspective," *Yale Law Journal* 40 (1931), pp. 704–51.

Llewellyn (1930) 1960
Karl N. Llewellyn, *The Bramble Bush: On Our Law and Its Study*, Dobbs Ferry, NY: Oceana Publications 1960.

Llewellyn 1930
Karl N. Llewellyn, "A Realistic Jurisprudence: The Next Step," *Columbia Law Review* 30 (1930), pp. 431–65.

Llewellyn and Hoebel 1941
Karl N. Llewellyn and E. Adamson Hoebel, *The Cheyenne Way: Conflict and Case Law in Primitive Jurisprudence*, Norman: University of Oklahoma Press 1941.

Luban 1996
David Luban, "What's Pragmatic About Legal Pragmatism?" *Cardozo Law Review* 18 (1996), pp. 43–73.

McLellan 1977
David McLellan (ed.), *Karl Marx: Selected Writings*, Oxford: Oxford University Press 1977.

Moore 1941
Underhill Moore, "My Philosophy of Law," in: *My Philosophy of Law: Credos of Sixteen American Scholars*, Boston: Boston Law Book 1941, pp. 203–25.

Menand 2001
Louis Menand, *The Metaphysical Club: A Story of Ideas in America*, London: Flamingo 2001.

Michelman 1981
Frank I. Michelman, "Politics as Medicine: On Misdiagnosing Legal Scholarship," *Yale Law Journal* 90 (1981), pp. 1224–28.

Nelles 1934a
Walter Nelles, "Toward Legal Understanding: I," *Columbia Law Review* 34 (1934), pp. 862–89.

Nelles 1934b
Walter Nelles, "Toward Legal Understanding: II," *Columbia Law Review* 34 (1934), pp. 1041–75.

Nelles 1932
Walter Nelles, "Commonwealth v. Hunt," *Columbia Law Review* 32 (1932), pp. 1128–69.

Nonet and Selznick 1978
Philippe Nonet and Philip Selznick, *Law and Society in Transition: Toward Responsive Law*, New York: Harper & Row 1978.

Novick 1988
Peter Novick, *That Noble Dream: The "Objectivity Question" and the American Historical Profession*, Cambridge: Cambridge University Press 1988.

Ogden and Richards (1923) 1972
C. K. Ogden and I. A. Richards, *The Meaning of Meaning: A Study of the Influence of Language upon Thought and of the Science of Symbolism*, London: Routledge 1972.

Oliphant 1928
Herman Oliphant, "A Return to Stare Decisis," *American Bar Association Journal* 4 (1928), pp. 159–61.

Peller 1995
Gary Peller, "Race Consciousness," in: Dan Danielsen and Karen Engle (eds.), *After Identity: A Reader in Law and Culture*, New York and London: Routledge 1995, pp. 67–82.

Peller 1985
Gary Peller, "The Metaphysics of American Law," *California Law Review* 73 (1985), pp. 1151–290.

Pocock 1975
J. G. A. Pocock, *The Machiavellian Moment: Florentine Political Thought and the Atlantic Republican Tradition*, Princeton, NJ, and London: Princeton University Press.

Pohlman 1984
H. L. Pohlman, *Justice Oliver Wendell Holmes & Utilitarian Jurisprudence*, Cambridge and London: Harvard University Press 1984.

Posner 2003
Richard A. Posner, *Law Pragmatism and Democracy*, Cambridge: Harvard University Press 2003.

Posner 2001
Richard A. Posner, *The Frontiers of Legal Theory*, Cambridge: Harvard University Press 2001.

Posner 1999
Richard A. Posner, *The Problematics of Moral and Legal Theory*, Cambridge and London: Belknap Press 1999.

Posner 1995
Richard A. Posner, *Overcoming Law*, Cambridge and London: Harvard University Press 1995.

Posner 1991
Richard A. Posner, "What Has Pragmatism to Offer Law?" in Michael Brint and William Weaver (eds.), *Pragmatism in Law and Society*, Boulder, San Francisco and Oxford: Westview Press 1995, pp. 29–46.

Posner 1990
Richard A. Posner, *The Problems of Jurisprudence*, Cambridge and London: Harvard University Press 1990.

Pound 1931
Roscoe Pound, "The Call for a Realist Jurisprudence," *Harvard Law Review* 44 (1931), pp. 697–711.

Pound 1910
Roscoe Pound, "Law in the Books and Law in Action," *American Law Review* 44 (1910), p. 12.

Pound 1909
Roscoe Pound, "Liberty of Contract," *Yale Law Journal* 18 (1909), pp. 454–87.

Powell 1918
Thomas Reed Powell, "The Logic and Rhetoric of Constitutional Law," *Journal of Philosophy* 15 (1918), pp. 645–58.

Purcell 1973
Edward A. Purcell Jr., *The Crisis of Democratic Theory: Scientific Naturalism & the Problem of Value*, Lexington: University Press of Kentucky 1973.

Putnam 1995
Hilary Putnam, *Pragmatism: An Open Question*, Oxford: Blackwell 1995.

Putnam 1981
Hilary Putnam, *Reason, Truth and History*, Cambridge and New York: Cambridge University Press 1981.

Rescher 2000
Nicholas Rescher, *Realistic Pragmatism: An Introduction to Pragmatic Philosophy*, Albany, NY: SUNY Press 2000.

Richards 2000
Janet Radcliffe Richards, *Human Nature after Darwin: A Philosophical Introduction*, London and New York: Routledge 2000.

Rodell (1939) 1957
Fred Rodell, *Woe Unto You, Lawyers!* New York: Pageant Press 1957.

Rodell 1936
Fred Rodell, *Fifty-Five Men: The Story of the American Constitution*, New York: Telegraph Press 1936.

Rorty 1999
Richard Rorty, *Philosophy and Social Hope*, London: Penguin Books 1999.

Rorty 1998
Richard Rorty, *Achieving Our Country: Leftist Thought in Twentieth-Century America*, Cambridge, MA: Harvard University Press 1998.

Rorty 1991
Richard Rorty, "The Banality of Pragmatism and the Poetry of Justice," in: Michael Brint and William Weaver (eds.), *Pragmatism in Law and Society*, Boulder, CO: Westview Press 1991, pp. 89–98.

Rorty 1982
Richard Rorty, *Consequences of Pragmatism*, Brighton, UK: Harvester Press 1982.

Rumble 1968
Wilfrid E. Rumble Jr., *American Legal Realism: Skepticism, Reform, and the Judicial Process*, Ithaca, NY: Cornell University Press 1968.

Schlegel 1995
John Henry Schlegel, *American Legal Realism & Empirical Social Science*, Chapel Hill and London: University of North Carolina Press 1995.

Schlegel 1979
John Henry Schlegel, "American Legal Realism and Empirical Social Science: From the Yale Experience," *Buffalo Law Review* 28 (1979), pp. 459–586.

Schubert 1964

Glendon Schubert (ed.), *Judicial Behavior: A Reader in Theory and Research*, Chicago: Rand McNally 1964.

Shennan 2002

Stephen Shennan, *Genes, Memes and Human History: Darwinian Archaeology and Cultural Evolution*, London: Thames & Hudson 2002.

Singer 1984

Joseph William Singer, "The Player and the Cards: Nihilism and Legal Theory," *Yale Law Journal* 94 (1984), pp. 1–70.

Spencer (1892) 1966

Herbert Spencer, *Social Statistics, Abridged and Revised; Together with The Man Versus the State*, Osnabrück, Germany: Proff & Co. 1966.

Taekema 2003

Sanne Taekema, *The Concept of Ideals in Legal Theory*, The Hague: Kluwer 2003.

Tamanaha 2006

Brian Z. Tamanaha, *The Perils of Pervasive Legal Instrumentalism*, Nijmegen: Wolf Legal Publishers 2006.

Tamanaha 1997

Brian Z. Tamanaha, *Realistic Socio-Legal Theory: Pragmatism and a Social Theory of Law*, Oxford: Clarendon Press 1997.

Tennyson (1850) 1965.

Alfred Tennyson, "In Memoriam A. H .H.," *Tennyson: Poems and Plays*, London: Oxford University Press 1965, pp. 230–66.

Trubek 1984

David M. Trubek, "Where the Action Is: Critical Legal Studies and Empiricism," *Stanford Law Review* 36 (1984), pp. 575–622.

Turner 1893

Frederick Jackson Turner, "The Significance of the Frontier in American History," *The Annual Report of the American Historical Association* (1893), pp. 199–227.

Tushnet 1991

Mark Tushnet, "Critical Legal Studies: A Political History," *Yale Law Journal* 100 (1991), pp. 1515–44.

Tushnet 1989

Mark Tushnet, "Following the Rules Laid Down: A Critique of Interpretivism and Neutral Principles," in: Allan C. Hutchinson (ed.), *Critical Legal Studies* Totowa, NJ: Rowman & Littlefield 1989, pp. 157–78.

Tushnet 1988

Mark Tushnet, *Red, White and Blue: A Critical Analysis of Constitutional Law*, Cambridge: Harvard University Press 1988.

Tushnet 1981

Mark Tushnet, "Legal Scholarship: Its Causes and Cure," *Yale Law Journal* 90 (1981), pp. 1205–37.

Tushnet 1980

Mark Tushnet, "Post-Realist Legal Scholarship," *Society of Public Teachers of Law* (1980), pp. 20–32.

Tushnet 1977
Mark Tushnet, "Perspectives on the Development of American Law: A Critical Review of Friedman's *A History of American Law*," *Wisconsin Law Review* (1977), pp. 81–109.

Twining 2000
William Twining, *Globalisation & Legal Theory*, London, Edinburgh, and Dublin: Butterworths 2000.

Twining 1973
William Twining, *Karl Llewellyn and the Realist Movement*, London: Weidenfeld and Nicolson 1973.

Unger 2005
Roberto Mangabeira Unger, *What Should the Left Propose?* London and New York: Verso 2005.

Unger 1998
Roberto Mangabeira Unger, *Democracy Realized: The Progressive Alternative*, London and New York: Verso 1998.

Unger 1987a
Roberto Mangabeira Unger, *Social Theory: Its Situation and Its Task: A Critical Introduction to Politics, a Work in Constructive Social Theory*, Cambridge, MA: Cambridge University Press, 1987.

Unger 1987b
Roberto Mangabeira Unger, *False Necessity: Anti-Necessitarian Social Theory in the Service of Radical Democracy*, Cambridge: Cambridge University Press 1987.

Unger 1975
Roberto Mangabeira Unger, *Knowledge and Politics*, New York: Free Press 1975.

Vonnegut (1985) 1990
Kurt Vonnegut, *Galápagos*, London: Paladin 1990.

White 1997
G. Edward White, "The American Law Institute and the Triumph of Modernist Jurisprudence," *Law and History Review* 15 (1997), pp. 1–47.

White 1993
G. Edward White, *Justice Oliver Wendell Holmes: Law and the Inner Self*, New York and Oxford: Oxford University Press, 1993.

White 1973
Morton White, *Pragmatism and the American Mind: Essays and Reviews in Philosophy and Intellectual History*, New York: Oxford University Press 1973.

Whitman (1891–2) 1975
Walt Whitman, *The Complete Poems*, Harmondsworth, UK: Penguin 1975.

Wienpahl 1976
Paul Wienpahl, "Dewey's Theory of Language and Meaning," in: Sidney Hook (ed.), *John Dewey: Philosopher of Science and Freedom*, Westport, CT: Greenwood Press 1976, pp. 271–88.

Wilson 1978
Edward O. Wilson, *On Human Nature*, Cambridge, MA: Harvard University Press 1978.

Winters 2003
   Yvor Winters, *Yvor Winters: Selected Poems*, New York: Library of America 2003.
Wiseman 1987
   Zipporah Batshaw Wiseman, "The Limits of Vision: Karl Llewellyn and the Merchant Rules," *Harvard Law Review* 100 (1987), pp. 465–545.
Wittgenstein (1953) 1967
   Ludwig Wittgenstein, *Philosophical Investigations*, trans. G. E. M. Anscombe, Oxford: Blackwell 1967.
Wood (1969) 1972
   Gordon S. Wood, *The Creation of the American Republic 1776 –1787*, New York and London: Norton 1972.

Index

Dawkins, Richard, 94
Deconstruction, 10, 114, 161–64, 172, 173–75
Democracy: behaviorism and, 78; Bentham
    and, 25; émigré scholars and, 78; Langdell
    and, 6; Legal Realism and, 2, 105;
    Pragmatism and, 1, 13, 15, 16, 29–30, 44,
    77, 123, 188, 195, 214
Dennett, Daniel, 27, 54, 221n42; meme
    theory, 46
Derrida, Jacques, 23, 160, 161, 162, 164, 172,
    174, 205
De Saussure, Ferdinand, 133, 161
Dewey, John, 21, 29–30, 78, 88–89, 122, 140,
    173, 178, 186; on language, 128–29, 135–38,
    146, 149–50, 205, 207–8, 212, 213; on law,
    22, 84; naturalism, 14, 44–45; objective
    relativism, 183; philosophical pragmatism,
    181; on science, 103–4, 124; on social
    science, 123, 193, 195
Dickinson, Emily, 128
Diggins, John, 36, 58, 61, 205
Douglas, William, 86, 90–91
Duxbury, Neil, 3, 19, 75
Dworkin, Ronald, 171

Emotivism, 132–33, 145
Eugenics movement, 45
Evolution, 31, 35, 36, 38, 39, 44–46,
    53–55, 177; CLS critique of, 17–19, 63,
    67, 69–70, 221n42; deterministic versus
    voluntaristic, 40–41, 42–43, 44, 47, 72;
    individualistic versus collectivistic, 40,
    42; Legal Realism and, 32, 34, 47, 86,
    182; Panglossianism, 34; Pragmatism
    and, 14–15, 18–19, 29, 44–45, 129, 136,
    178; Spencer and, 40–41, 42, 44; Oliver
    Wendell Holmes and, 36, 38, 40, 41–43.
    See also: Adaptationism; Functionalism;
    Meme theory; Social Darwinism
Ewald, William, 125

Fish, Stanley, 23, 212–13
Ford, Richard T., 169, 175
Formalism, 3, 6, 8–9, 115, 159, 192
Foucault, Michel, 23, 57, 122, 123, 160, 205
Frank, Jerome: on instrumentalism,
    98; on language, 138–39, 142, 143,
    146; Llewellyn-Pound exchange,
    82–86, 222n14; non-Euclideanism, 88;
    predictivism, 95; rule skepticism, 142; on
    science 86

Frankfurt School, 116
Freeman, Alan D., 116
Freud, Sigmund, 138–39
Frontier thesis, 51, 220n57
Fuller, Lon, 75
Functionalism, 15, 17–19, 47; CLS critique
    of, 67, 69, 71–72, 119–21, 125; Felix Cohen
    on, 91, 146; William Douglas on, 86,
    90–91; Jerome Frank on, 146; and Legal
    Realism, 32, 33–34, 35, 53–55; 75, 84, 89–
    94, 104–5, 182; Bronislaw Malinowski,
    134–5. *See also:* Adaptationism;
    Darwinism; Evolution; Meme theory
Functional linguistics, 128–29, 134–38, 210–11

Galileo, 114
Gordon, Robert, 12–13, 17, 59, 70, 110; on
    Cartesianism, 65–66; on functionalism,
    66–68, 71–72, 73 120–21, 221n42;
    historicism, 62; on policy analysis, 106–7;
    structuralism, 68
Gould, Stephen Jay, 34, 39, 67, 221n42,
    222n2
Gramsci, Antonio, 12
Green, Leon, 141
Grey, Thomas, 178, 179, 182
Gunn, Thom, ix, 1, 177
Gunnell, John, 77

Haack, Susan, 23–24, 125–26
Habermas, Jürgen, 116, 122, 195
Halley, Janet, 167–68, 169, 175–76
Hamilton, Walton, 49–50
Hart, H. L. A., 8, 75, 95–97, 217n13
Hegemony, 12, 169, 175, 196, 205, 206
History: CLS, 56–60; Oliver Wendell
    Holmes, 35–36, 46; Legal Realist, 17,
    31–35, 47–53; particularistic, 27; presentist,
    32
Historicism, 16–19, 33–34; Frank Ankersmit
    on, 57; of CLS, 57–60; of CLS and Legal
    Realism compared, 71–74, 177, 184–5; of
    Robert Gordon, 17, 62, 65–68; of Walton
    Hamilton, 49–50; of Oliver Wendell
    Holmes 36–38; of James Willard Hurst,
    186–8; of Mark Kelman, 17; of Karl
    Llewellyn, 50–53; of Walter Nelles, 47–48;
    of Richard Posner, 183; of Thomas Reed
    Powell, 48–49; Pragmatism and, 178,
    179, 182, 183; of Mark Tushnet 63–65; of
    Roberto Mangabeira Unger, 63, 69

Jurists: Profiles in Legal Theory

GENERAL EDITOR

William Twining

Allen D. Boyer, *Sir Edward Coke and the Elizabethan Age*
John Dinwiddy, edited by William Twining, *Jeremy Bentham*
Roger Cotterrell, *Emile Durkheim: Law in a Moral Domain*
Colin Imber, *Ebu's-su'ud and the Islamic Legal Tradition*
Edited by Robert W. Gordon, *The Legacy of Oliver Wendell Holmes, Jr.*
Robert S. Summers, *Lon L. Fuller*